ARCO

Everything you need to score high on

Praxis I PPST

4th Edition

ARCO EDITORIAL BOARD

MACMILLAN • USA

4th Edition

Macmillan General Reference
A Simon & Schuster Macmillan Company
1633 Broadway
New York NY 10019-6785

Macmillan Publishing books may be purchased for business
or sales promotional use. For information, please write:
Special Markets Department, Macmillan Publishing USA,
1633 Broadway, New York, NY 10019.

Library of Congress Number: 97-81108

ISBN: 0-02-862462-9

Manufactured in the United States of America

10 9 8 7 6 5 4 3 2 1

CONTENTS

THE PRAXIS SERIES: PROFESSIONAL ASSESSMENTS FOR BEGINNING TEACHERS

The Praxis Series consists of standardized examinations designed to measure the academic proficiencies of students entering or completing teacher preparation programs and individuals seeking professional certification. Developed and administered by the Educational Testing Service, the Praxis Series assesses knowledge and skills at three levels of proficiency.

- Praxis I: Academic Skills Assessments measures basic proficiency in reading mathematics and writing.
- Praxis II: Subject Assessments measures content area knowledge.
- Praxis III: Classroom Performance Assessment provides a training and evaluation framework for classroom performance.

PRAXIS I: ACADEMIC SKILLS ASSESSMENTS

Praxis I: Academic Skills Assessments measures basic proficiency in reading, mathematics, and writing by means of the Pre-Professional Skills Tests (PPST) or the Computer-Based Academic Skills Assessments (CBT). It may be used as an entrance exam for teacher-training programs or as a preliminary licensing exam.

The Pre-Professional Skills Tests (PPST)

The PPST is a traditional paper-and-pencil test containing standard multiple-choice questions and an essay question on a designated topic. It consists of three tests as follows:

Test 1: Reading. A 60-minute test consisting of 40 multiple-choice questions based on 100- to 200-word passages and shorter statements of a sentence or two. Questions fall into the following topic areas:

Literal Comprehension (approximately 55% of test questions)
- main idea questions
- supporting idea questions
- organization questions
- vocabulary questions

Critical and Inferential Comprehension (approximately 45% of test questions)
- argument evaluation questions
- inferential reasoning questions
- generalization questions

Test 2: Mathematics. A 60-minute test consisting of 40 multiple-choice questions divided among the following topic areas:

Conceptual Knowledge (approximately 15% of test questions)
- number sense
- operation sense

Procedural Knowledge (approximately 30% of test questions)
- computation
- estimation
- solving ratio, proportion, and percent problems
- solving equations and inequalities

Representations of Quantitative Information (approximately 30% of test questions)
- interpretation of graphs, charts, and tables
- identifying and recognizing patterns in data
- predicting trends and making inferences from data
- understanding relationships between values in a table or graph

Measurement and Informal Geometry (approximately 15% of test questions)
- U.S. and metric systems
- using geometric concepts to solve linear, area, and volume problems
- recognizing and using geometric properties and relationships

Formal Mathematical Reasoning
- interpreting logical connectives and quantifiers
- determining validity of arguments
- identifying generalizations

Test 3: Writing.   A 60-minute test divided into two 30-minute sections. One section consists of 45 multiple-choice questions and the other section consists of a single essay question on an assigned topic. The multiple-choice questions are divided among the following topic areas:

Usage (approximately 55% of multiple-choice questions)
- identifying errors in grammar
- identifying errors in word choice
- identifying errors in punctuation and capitalization

Sentence Correction (approximately 45% of multiple-choice questions)
- selecting the correct and most effective rephrasing of a sentence
- correcting errors of grammar, usage, and word choice

The Computer-Based Academic Skills Assessments (CBT)

The CBT is a computer-delivered test. The questions appear on the computer screen and examinees indicate their answers using the computer keyboard or a mouse. Questions may require examinees to select single or multiple responses, to highlight or reorder information, or to provide their own answers. For the Writing Test candidates can choose to handwrite or word process their essay.

The CBT is a computer-adaptive test. That means the test questions are computer selected based on an examinee's answers to previous questions. In a computer-adaptive test, the computer calculates a score after each question and uses this score to choose the next question.

Like the PPST, the CBT consists of three tests. Candidates may take one, two, or all three tests at one time. Following is a brief description of each computer-based test.

Test 1: Reading.   90-minute test consisting of 36 computer-generated test questions based on 200- to 400-word passages—some accompanied by graphs, charts, or diagrams—from the areas of social science, science and nature, humanities, and education. Questions may require test-takers to highlight information, to move information from one place to another, to choose one or more answers, or to check boxes in a table. Questions fall into the following topic areas:

Comprehension (approximately 60% of test questions)
- main idea and summary questions
- supporting idea and detail questions
- organization questions

Analysis and Application (approximately 40% of test questions)
- applying ideas presented to other situations
- recognizing arguments and their logic
- determining inferences and assumptions
- defining words in context
- distinguishing facts from opinions

Test 2: Mathematics.   A 55-minute test consisting of 29 computer-delivered questions that may require test-takers to highlight an answer choice, to move numbers or symbols from one place to another, to complete a graph or table, to mark a point on a scale, or to enter a numerical response. Questions are divided among the following topic areas:

Number Sense and Operation Sense (approximately 25% of test questions)
- understanding the order of numbers
- recognizing equivalent forms of a number
- performing computations in problem solving
- selecting a sequence of operations
- recognizing alternative ways to solve problems
- using a calculator in problem solving

Mathematical Relationships (approximately 20% of test questions)
- applying ratios, proportions, and percents
- determining probabilities
- formulating equations
- solving equations and inequalities

Data Interpretation (approximately 25% of test questions)
- reading and understanding data presented in various formats
- recognizing relationships in data
- constructing and completing tables, charts, and graphs
- determining average, range, median, or mode of a set of data

Geometry and Measurement (approximately 20% of test questions)
- determining length, perimeter, area, and volume of two- and three-dimensional figures
- using various systems of measurement and converting from one to another
- Reasoning (approximately 10% of test questions)
- interpreting sentences containing logical connectives and quantifiers
- drawing conclusions from given statements
- determining validity of conclusions

Test 3: Writing.   A 66-minute test presented in two sections: a 26-minute computer-adaptive section containing 35 multiple-choice questions and a 40-minute essay section consisting of a single essay. The writing test is divided among the following topic areas:

Error Recognition (50% of test score)
- recognizing errors in structure
- recognizing errors in word choice
- recognizing errors in punctuation and capitalization

Essay Writing (50% of test score)
- ability to formulate a thesis or state a position clearly
- ability to organize ideas logically and to support ideas with appropriate examples or details
- ability to vary sentence structure and to write clearly, correctly, and effectively

PRAXIS II: SUBJECT ASSESSMENTS

Praxis II: Subject Assessments measures knowledge of the subjects prospective teachers will teach. A college education and some education courses or teacher-training exposure are assumed as preparation for Praxis II.

Praxis II includes the NTE Core Battery Tests of Communication Skills, General Knowledge, and Professional Knowledge; the NTE Specialty Area tests; the Multiple Subjects Assessment for Teachers (MSAT); and the new Subject Assessments, including the Content Area Performance Assessment tests.

The NTE Core Battery

The NTE Core Battery consists of the following three tests:

Communication Skills. A two-hour test divided into four 30-minute sections testing a candidate's ability to listen, read, and write well. Questions are divided among the following content areas:

- Listening (36% of test score)–40 multiple-choice questions based on spoken material delivered via audiotape
- Reading (30% of test score)–30 multiple-choice questions based on reading passages varying in length from a single statement to 250 words
- Writing (17% of test score)—45 multiple-choice questions representing three question types—English Usage, Sentence Correction, and Composition Strategies
- Essay (17% of test score)—a 30-minute writing sample based on a single assigned topic

General Knowledge. A two-hour test divided into four separately timed 30-minute sections designed to measure knowledge from four important disciplines:

- Social Studies (26% of test score)—30 multiple-choice questions covering United States and world history; major political systems; major economic structures; great ideas in psychology, sociology, and anthropology; and essential features of world geography
- Mathematics (23% of test score)—25 multiple-choice questions assessing the knowledge students are expected to have acquired through elementary school up to and including at least one year of high school mathematics
- Literature and Fine Arts (26% of test score)—35 multiple-choice questions designed to assess the candidate's knowledge of fine arts and literature from a variety of cultures and time periods. Most questions are based on passages from literature or reproductions of art or architecture.
- Science (26% of test score)—30 multiple-choice questions evaluating a candidate's knowledge of earth science, biology, and physical sciences on the level that an elementary or junior high school teacher should know

Professional Knowledge. A two-hour test divided into four separately timed 30-minute sections of 35 questions each. Professional Knowledge questions are designed to measure knowledge of the four major functions of teaching and other factors that influence educational practice. Questions are divided among the following topic areas:

- Planning Instruction (9% of test questions)—13 multiple-choice questions concerning selecting objectives, designing instructional activities, and organizing resources to achieve instructional objectives
- Implementing Instruction (24% of test questions)—33 multiple-choice questions concerning selecting various instructional strategies and using various instructional techniques, materials, and resources

- Evaluating Instruction (14% of test questions)—20 multiple-choice questions concerning methods for gathering information about student progress and reporting student progress
- Managing the Instructional Environment (19% of test questions) —27 multiple-choice questions concerning providing a positive classroom climate and fostering appropriate student behavior
- Professional Foundations (24% of test questions)—33 multiple-choice questions concerning identifying influences of factors other than direct instruction on education and recognizing the social, economic, cultural, and psychological foundations of education
- Professional Functions (10% of test questions)—14 multiple-choice questions concerning understanding the roles and responsibilities of teachers in school and community and awareness of professional issues and research

Multiple Subjects Assessment for Teachers (MSAT)

The Multiple Subjects Assessment for Teachers (MSAT) is used primarily in California to test the knowledge and critical-thinking skills of prospective elementary school teachers. The MSAT consists of a multiple-choice test called the Content Knowledge Test and a short-answer test called Content Area Exercises.

The Content Knowlege Test is a two-hour test consisting of 120 multiple-choice questions divided among the following subject areas:

• Literature and Language Studies	24 questions
• Mathematics	24 questions
• Visual and Performing Arts	12 questions
• Physical Education	8 questions
• Human Development	8 questions
• History/Social Sciences	22 questions
• Science	22 questions

Content Area Exercises is a three-hour test consisting of 18 short essay questions divided among the following subject areas:

• Literature and Language Studies	3 questions
• Mathematics	3 questions
• Visual and Performing Arts	2 questions
• Physical Education	2 questions
• Human Development	2 questions
• History/Social Sciences	3 questions
• Science	3 questions

Note: Nonprogrammable calculators are allowed for the MSAT tests

Specialty Area Tests and New Subject Assessments

The chart on pages x to xiii indicates test times and number of multiple-choice or essay questions for the other specialty area tests and subject assessments that are part of Praxis II.

For Additional Information About the Praxis Series

Additional information about test dates and registration procedures can be found in the *Registration Bulletin* that is available at most college education offices or from Educational Testing Service at the following address:

> The Praxis Series
> Educational Testing Service
> P.O. Box 6051
> Princeton, NJ 08541-6051
> Phone: 609-771-7395

Specialty Area Tests and New Subject Assessments

SUBJECT AREA	TEST TIME	NUMBER OF MULTIPLE-CHOICE QUESTIONS	NUMBER OF ESSAY QUESTIONS
Arts			
Art Education	2 hrs	150	—
Art Making	1hr	—	2 + 2 exercises
Art: Content, Traditions, Criticism, and Aesthetics	1 hr	—	3
Art: Content Knowledge	2 hrs	120	—
Music Education	2 hrs	150	—
Music: Concepts and Processes	1 hr	—	2
Music: Analysis	1 hr	—	1 + 2 exercises
Music: Content Knowledge	2 hrs	135	—
Theatre	2 hrs	108	—
Biology and General Science			
Biology	2 hrs	150	—
Biology: Content Knowledge, Part 1	1 hr	75	—
Biology: Content Knowledge, Part 2	1 hr	75	—
Biology: Content Essays	1 hr	—	3
Biology: Pedagogy	1 hr	—	1
Biology and General Science	2 hrs	160	—
General Science	2 hrs	120	—
General Science: Content Knowledge, Part 1	1 hr	60	—
General Science: Content Knowledge, Part 2	1 hr	60	—
General Science: Content Essays	1 hr	—	3
Business and Technology			
Accounting (PA)	1 hr	80	—
Agriculture	2 hrs	140	—
Agriculture CA	2 hrs	148	—
Agriculture PA	2 hrs	140	—
Business Education	2 hrs	160	—
Computer Literacy/Data Processing	2 hrs	120	—
Cooperative Education	2 hrs	157	—
Data Processing (PA)	1 hr	87	—
Home Economics Education	2 hrs	150	—
Marketing (PA)	1 hr	80	—
Marketing Education	2 hrs	120	—
Office Technology	2 hrs	135	—
Office Technology (PA)	1 hr	86	—
Secretarial (PA)	1 hr	83	—
Technology Education	2 hrs	150	—
Vocational General Knowledge	2 hrs	110	—

SUBJECT AREA	TEST TIME	NUMBER OF MULTIPLE-CHOICE QUESTIONS	NUMBER OF ESSAY QUESTIONS
Business and Technology (*continued*)			
Business PA: Accounting	1 hr	80	—
Business PA: Data Processing	1 hr	87	—
Business PA: Marketing	1 hr	80	—
Business PA: Office Technology	1 hr	86	—
Business PA: Secretarial	1 hr	83	—
Education			
Early Childhoold Education	2 hrs	150	—
Education in the Elementary School	2 hrs	150	—
Elementary Education: Curriculum, Instruction, and Assessment	2 hrs	110	—
Elementary Education: Content Area Exercises	2 hrs	—	4
Health Education	2 hrs	120	—
Health and Physical Education	2 hrs	145	—
Physical Education	2 hrs	150	—
Physical Education: Content Knowledge	2 hrs	120	—
Physical Education: Movement Forms—Analysis and Design	1 hr	—	2
Physical Education: Movement Forms—Video Evaluation	1 hr	—	2
Physical Education: Pedagogy	1 hr	—	1
Pre-Kindergarten Education	2 hrs	103	—
Safety/Driver Education	2 hrs	125	—
Education of Students with Disabilities			
Education of Students with Mental Retardation	2 hrs	150	—
Special Education	2 hrs	150	—
Special Education: Application of Core Principles Across Categories of Disability	1 hr	50	—
Special Education: Knowledge-Based Core Principles	1 hr	60	—
Special Education: Teaching Students with Behavioral Disorders/Emotional Disturbance	1 hr	50	—
Special Education: Teaching Students with Learning Disabilities	1 hr	50	—
Special Education: Teaching Students with Mental Retardation	1 hr	50	—
Special Education: Preschool/Early Childhood	2 hrs	110	—
Teaching Deaf and Hard of Hearing Students	2 hrs	120	—
Teaching Speech to Students with Language Impairments	2 hrs	120	—
Teaching Students with Emotional Disturbance	2 hrs	120	—
Teaching Students with Learning Disabilities	2 hrs	120	—
Teaching Students with Orthopedic Impairments	2 hrs	130	—
Teaching Students with Physical and Mental Disabilities	2 hrs	120	—
Teaching Students with Visual Impairments	2 hrs	120	—

SUBJECT AREA	TEST TIME	NUMBER OF MULTIPLE-CHOICE QUESTIONS	NUMBER OF ESSAY QUESTIONS
English, Reading, and Communication			
Communication	2 hrs	150	—
English Language and Literature	2 hrs	150	—
English Language, Literature, and Composition: Content Knowledge	2 hrs	150	2
English Language, Literature, and Composition: Essays	2 hrs	—	2
English Language, Literature, and Composition: Pedagogy	1 hr	—	2
Introduction to the Teaching of Reading	2 hrs	135	—
Reading Specialist	2 hrs	145	—
Speech Communication	2 hrs	150	—
Teaching English as a Second Language	2 hrs	120	—
Guidance, Administration, and School Services			
Audiology	2 hrs	150	—
Educational Leadership: Administration and Supervision	2 hrs	145	—
Library Media Specialist	2 hrs	145	—
School Food Service Supervisor	2 hrs	120	—
School Guidance and Counseling	2 hrs	140	—
School Psychologist	2 hrs	135	—
School Social Worker	2 hrs	120	—
Speech-Language Pathology	2 hrs	150	—
Languages			
Foreign Language Pedagogy PA	1 hr	55	—
French	2 hrs	155-160	—
French: Productive Language Skills	1 hr	—	9 exercises
French: Linguistic, Literary, and Cultural Analysis	1 hr	—	3 exercises
French: Content Knowledge	2 hrs	140	
German	2 hrs	160	—
German: Content Knowledge	2 hrs	140	—
Italian	2 hrs	130	—
Japanese	100 min	130	—
Latin	2 hrs	130	—
Russian	100 min	102	—
Spanish	2 hrs	160	—
Spanish: Content Knowledge	2 hrs	140	—
Spanish: Productive Language Skills	1 hr	—	9 exercises
Spanish: Linguistic, Literary, and Cultural Analysis	1 hr	—	3 exercises
Spanish: Pedagogy	1 hr	—	3 exercises

SUBJECT AREA	TEST TIME	NUMBER OF MULTIPLE-CHOICE QUESTIONS	NUMBER OF ESSAY QUESTIONS
Mathematics			
Mathematics	2 hrs	110	—
Mathematics: Content Knowledge	2 hrs	50	—
Mathematics: Proofs, Models, and Problems, Part 1	1 hr	—	4 exercises
Mathematics: Proofs, Models, and Problems, Part 2	1 hr	—	3 exercises
Mathematics: Pedagogy	1 hr	—	3
Physical Science			
Chemistry	2 hrs	120	—
Chemistry: Content Knowledge	1 hr	50	—
Chemistry: Content Essays	1 hr	—	3
Chemistry, Physics, and General Science	2 hrs	140	—
Earth/Space Science	2 hrs	120	—
Earth Science: Content Knowledge	2 hrs	100	—
Physical Science: Content Knowledge	1 hr	60	—
Physical Science: Content Essays	1 hr	—	3
Physical Science: Pedagogy	1 hr	—	1
Physics	2 hrs	100	—
Physics: Content Knowledge	1 hr	50	—
Physics: Content Essays	1 hr	—	3
Principles of Learning and Teaching			
Principles of Learning and Teaching: Grades K-6	2 hrs	45	6
Principles of Learning and Teaching: Grades 7-12	2 hrs	45	6
Social Sciences			
Economics	2 hrs	105	—
Environmental Education	2 hrs	140	—
Geography	2 hrs	135	—
Government/Political Science	2 hrs	125	—
Psychology	2 hrs	120	—
Social Studies	2 hrs	150	—
Social Studies: Content Knowledge	2 hrs	130	—
Social Studies: Analytical Essays	1 hr	—	2
Social Studies: Interpretation of Materials	1 hr	—	5
Social Studies: Pedagogy	1 hr	—	2
Sociology	2 hrs	115	—
World and U.S. History	2 hrs	130	—

Part I
About the PPST

INTRODUCTION TO THE PPST

The Pre-Professional Skills Tests (PPST) consist of separate tests of proficiency in reading, mathematics, and writing. The tests may be taken individually or in combination and are used for a variety of purposes. Many people are required to take part or all of the PPST in order to be certified to teach in the public schools. The following states currently require or accept scores on the PPST as part of the certification process for teachers:

Arizona	Nevada
Delaware	North Carolina
District of Columbia	Oklahoma
Hawaii	Oregon
Kansas	Tennessee
Maine	West Virginia
Minnesota	Wisconsin
Nebraska	

Many people in other states are required to take the PPST in order to enter or to graduate from an educational program or to earn a specific job credential. Altogether, institutions and agencies in forty-five states use the PPST for admissions, placement, certification, or evaluation.

The PPST is given approximately eight times a year in test centers around the country. The tests are developed and administered by Educational Testing Service. You can get more information about PPST test registration and fees by writing to:

Praxis Series
Educational Testing Service
P.O. Box 6051
Princeton, NJ 08541-6051

The Reading Test consists of 40 multiple-choice questions, based on short passages, which must be answered in 60 minutes. The Mathematics Test also consists of 40 multiple-choice questions to be answered in 60 minutes. The Writing Test includes two distinct components: a section of 45 multiple-choice questions to be answered in 30 minutes, and an essay to be written by the test-taker in 30 minutes. Each test will be described in greater detail later in this chapter. If you take all three skills tests on the same day, you should plan on about four hours for the test administration. This includes time for filling out necessary forms, listening to test directions, and taking rest breaks.

Approximately six weeks after you take the PPST, you should receive your test scores. Each of the skills-area tests is scored separately, so you will receive a separate score for each test you take. For the Reading and Math tests, the number of right answers, or the "raw score," is converted to a score on a scale from 150 to 190. For the Writing Test, the number of right answers from the multiple-choice part is combined with the essay score to form a composite score; this new score is then converted to the 150–190 scale. Through a process called "equating," the different editions of each test are made comparable for the purposes of scoring. That means that even if you take a version of the Reading Test that is more difficult than another version, you should not be penalized. Your scaled score will reflect adjustments made to compensate for different levels of difficulty among test forms. Thus, scores from different editions of the Reading Test are comparable. You cannot, however, compare scores for the different PPST Skills tests; for example, a Reading Test score is not comparable to a Math Test score.

Each state or institution determines its own passing score, or "cut score." You can generally expect to make the cut score if you get two-thirds or more of the questions right, though this is not guaranteed.

Now, let's examine each of the tests more closely:

THE READING TEST

The reading questions of the PPST will be based on a number of different passages of varying length and difficulty. You'll have 60 minutes of testing time in which to read the passages and answer a total of forty questions. Some brief passages of only a few sentences or a short paragraph will have only one question attached; longer passages consisting of several paragraphs may be accompanied by up to five questions. The passages are taken from different kinds of writing and from different fields, such as science, economics, politics, art and literature, history, and philosophy. Your reaction may be, "I've studied some of these areas, but how can I answer a question on a topic I haven't studied?" Don't be daunted. The questions don't presuppose that you have studied any particular area: The passage contains everything you need to answer the questions.

The questions themselves are of different types and test a number of different reading and critical-thinking skills. About 50 percent of the questions are comprehension questions; they test your ability to understand information directly presented in written material. Such questions may ask about a passage's main idea or supporting ideas. About 30–40 percent of the questions require you to demonstrate your ability to analyze material by asking about inferences that can be made concerning an author's purpose, assumptions, or attitudes. A small number of questions will ask you to evaluate a passage's strengths or weaknesses, or to identify the techniques a passage uses to achieve specific effects.

The following sample passage and questions illustrate the format of the Reading Test.

During the past four decades the fishery scientists of the West have studied the dynamics of fish populations with the objective of determin-
Line ing the relation between the amount of fishing
(5) and the sustainable catch. They have developed a substantial body of theory that has been applied successfully to a large number of animal populations and has led to major improvement in the management of some of the major marine fisher-
(10) ies.

The theory has been developed for single-species populations with man as a predator. Much of it is based on the Darwinian concept of a constant overpopulation of young that is reduced
(15) by density-dependent mortality resulting from intraspecific competition. The unfished population tends toward a maximum equilibrium size with a relatively high proportion of large, old individuals. As fishing increases, both population size
(20) and proportions of large, old individuals are reduced, but growth is increased and natural mortality is reduced. Fishing mortality eventually takes the place of most natural mortality. If the amount of fishing is increased too much, the
(25) individuals will tend to be taken before realizing their potential growth, and total yield will be reduced. The maximum sustainable yields can be taken at an intermediate population size that in

some populations is about one-third to one-half
(30) the unfished population size.

G. V. Nikolskii, of Moscow State University, develops his theory from a different approach. He is a non-Darwinian and is (he says) a non-mathematician; rather he considers himself an
(35) ecologist and a morphologist. He argues that Darwin's concept of constant overpopulation has led to neglect of the problem of protecting spawners and young fish. He argues also that Darwin's concept of a variety as an incipient spe-
(40) cies has led to extensive mathematical analysis of racial characteristics without understanding of the adaptive significance of the characters. Nikolskii considers the main laws of population dynamics to be concerned with the succession of
(45) generations: their birth, growth, and death. The details are governed by the relative rates of adaptation and environmental change. The mass and age structure of a population are the result of adaptation to the food supply. The rate of growth
(50) of individuals, the time of sexual maturity, and the accumulation of reserves vary according to the food supply. These factors in turn influence the success of reproduction in ways that tend to bring the size of the population into balance with
(55) its food supply.

1. The main concern of the researchers discussed in this passage is

   (A) ecology as related to fishing
   (B) effects of pollution on fish
   (C) endangered species of fish
   (D) commercial fishing
   (E) development of fishing methods

(D) At first reading of this passage, one might get the impression that the researchers care about the fish. Careful reading of the first paragraph, especially ". . . the relation between the amount of fishing and the sustainable catch," reveals that the purpose of the research is commercial interest.

2. According to this passage, those theories based on Darwinian concepts assume fish population to be controlled mainly by the

   (A) life expectancy within the species
   (B) amount of fishing pressure on the species
   (C) amount of food available to the species
   (D) racial characteristics of the species
   (E) size of the fish caught within a species

(B) The Darwinian theory is that overpopulation is controlled by natural mortality. The Darwinian theorists substitute fishing mortality for natural mortality and so attempt to control and manipulate population by controlling fishing pressure.

3. According to this passage, Nikolskii's theory is based on a concept that assumed fish population to be controlled mainly by the

   (A) death rate within the species
   (B) amount of fishing pressure on the species

   (C) amount of food available to the species
   (D) racial characteristics of the species
   (E) size of the fish caught within a species

(C) Nikolskii feels that the food supply governs the success of reproduction, which he considers to be highly adaptive. See lines 51 to 54.

4. The author indicates that the main difference between the two theories is the

   (A) amount of fish that can be harvested
   (B) methods used to catch fish
   (C) potential growth rate of fish
   (D) cause of population variation in fish
   (E) effect of food supply on the size of the fish

(D) The *cause* of population variation is a *theoretical* difference; hence (D) is the correct answer to the question. The other differences are practical and procedural.

5. Which of the following is NOT mentioned as affecting fish population?

   (A) fishing pressure
   (B) fishing methods
   (C) food supply
   (D) quality of environment
   (E) management techniques

(B) The fishing method employed may well have an effect on the number of fish taken, but this article does not discuss fishing methods.

The "Reading Skills Review" chapter provides you with analyses of additional sample questions and a systematic method for approaching the test.

THE MATHEMATICS TEST

The PPST Mathematics Test measures mathematical skills that are commonly learned from the early grades through high school. You will have 60 minutes in which to answer the forty questions on the test. The questions cover topics in arithmetic, algebra, geometry, and other areas; however, trigonometry and calculus are typically not represented. Many of the questions will require you to apply interpretive rather than computational skills; that is, they will test your understanding of mathematical concepts and systems. For instance, you might be asked to compare different fractions to determine which is the least or the greatest, or you might have to convert a fraction to a decimal. In addition to understanding numbers, you should also be able to use the symbolic language of math, such as is frequently used in algebra. These questions test whether or not you know how a problem should be solved rather than what the solution is. Many of the questions also reflect real-life situations, so you might be asked to figure out discounts, compute rates of speed, read charts and graphs, and demonstrate familiarity with different units and systems of measurement, including the metric system. In order to do well on the exam, you will have to have knowledge of basic operations (multiplication, addition, etc.), on the properties governing operations (commutativity, associativity, etc.). It will also help to be familiar with some formulas from algebra and geometry.

Here are some sample questions to introduce you to the PPST Mathematics Test:

1. Which of the following is greater than $\frac{1}{3}$?

(A) .33

(B) $(\frac{1}{3})^2$

(C) $\frac{1}{4}$

(D) $\frac{1}{.3}$

(E) $\frac{.3}{2}$

(D) $\frac{1}{.3} = \frac{10}{3} = 3\frac{1}{3}$

2. If a discount of 20% off the marked price of a jacket saves a man $15, how much did he pay for the jacket?

(A) $35

(B) $60

(C) $75

(D) $150

(E) $300

(B) Let x = amount of marked price.

Then $\frac{1}{5}$x = 15

x = 75

75 − 15 = $60

3. A carpenter needs four boards, each 2 feet 9 inches long. If wood is sold only by the foot, how many feet must he buy?

(A) 9

(B) 10

(C) 11

(D) 12

(E) 13

(C) Four boards, each 2′9″ long, total 11 feet. The carpenter must buy 11 feet of wood.

4. If $\frac{a}{b} = \frac{3}{5}$, then $15a =$

(A) 3b

(B) 5b

(C) 6b

(D) 9b

(E) 15b

(D) $\frac{a}{b} = \frac{3}{5}$

$5a = 3b$

Multiply both sides by 3.

$15a = 9b$

5. If a train covers 14 miles in 10 minutes, then the rate of the train in miles per hour is

(A) 140

(B) 112

(C) 84

(D) 100

(E) 98

(C) 10 minutes $= \frac{1}{6}$ hour

In one hour, the train will cover 6(14), or 84 miles.

THE WRITING TEST

Section 1: Multiple Choice

Section 1 of the PPST Writing Test is designed to measure your knowledge of correct and effective written expression. Correct writing uses appropriate punctuation, diction, grammar, and sentence structure. Effective writing is not only correct but also clear and fluent, avoiding wordiness and awkwardness.

The 45 multiple-choice questions, which must be answered in 30 minutes, are of two types. Questions 1 through 25 are of the first type; they are essentially error-recognition questions. Each question presents a sentence in which four parts are underlined and lettered. You must decide whether or not one of the underlined parts contains an error. If so, your answer is the letter that corresponds to that underlined part. No sentence contains more than one error. The sentence may also be correct as presented; that is, it may contain no errors. In this case, your answer would be the fifth among the five answer choices, (E).

Here are two samples to illustrate the format of this type of question:

1. The emigration of large numbers of persons each
$\qquad$ A $\qquad\qquad$ B
year were gradually reducing the excess popula-
$\quad$ C $\qquad\qquad\qquad$ D
tion. No error
$\qquad$ E

2. A person may study diligently , but without ade-
$\qquad\qquad\qquad$ A
quate sleep you can hardly expect to do well. No
$\qquad$ B $\qquad$ C $\qquad$ D
error

(C) The singular subject "emigration" requires a singular verb, "was gradually reducing."

(B) Do not switch from the third person ("person")
to the second person ("you") in the middle of a sentence.

Note that punctuation marks, as well as words and phrases, may be underlined.

As you can see, this type of question is rather short and usually doesn't take long to answer. In fact, it is recommended that you use only ten minutes for all twenty-five of these questions.

The second type of multiple-choice question presents sentences in which only one part is underlined. Beneath the sentence are five answer choices. The first choice, (A), always duplicates exactly what is in the original sentence. The other choices offer rewrites of the underlined part. If you think that the original sentence is superior to any of the rewrites, choose (A) as your answer. If you feel that one of the rewrites is better, choose the letter of that option as your answer. Since questions of this type are typically longer and more complex than questions of the earlier type, you should expect to spend about twenty minutes of the allotted testing time on them, or about a minute on each.

Here is an example of this type of question:

1. Had he not remembered his jacket and turned back, they might never have met.

    (A) Had he not remembered
    (B) If he didn't remember
    (C) Unless he had remembered
    (D) He had not remembered
    (E) Hadn't he remembered

(A) The writer is simultaneously telling us what *did* happen as well as what *might* have happened. The first clause is a supposition: suppose, it says in effect, he had *not* gone back for his jacket. The second clause speculates on the consequence of the supposition. This neat feat of language is made possible, in English, by the use of the subjunctive mood in the contrary-to-fact clause and the use of the *conditional* mood in the consequence clause. The sentence is in the past tense, which means that the form for the subjunctive is in the past perfect, *Had . . . not remembered,* and the form for the conditional is the past tense of a modal auxiliary plus the present perfect: *might not have met.* (B) is a trap. It's a vague echo of another form for the past subjunctive, not offered as a choice: *If he had not remembered. . . .* (C) is illiterate.

Note that you do not need to know grammatical terminology in order to answer the questions, although learning some of the grammatical terms and definitions explained in the "Writing Skills Review" chapter will enable you to better understand the explanatory answers.

Both types of multiple-choice questions ask you to act as an editor, first by detecting errors and then by choosing among different possibilities in order to correct errors. When you perform these editing tasks on the test, you should be careful to choose answers that are not only grammatically correct, but that also do not change the meaning of the original sentences. After all, an editor's primary role is to clarify meaning, not to create it.

You should also take care to read through all the available choices before you select your answer. Choice (B), for instance, might correct grammatical errors in the original sentence but might be stylistically inferior to (D), which also corrects those errors. In this case, (D) would be the better choice.

Section 2: The Essay

Unlike the multiple-choice section of the Writing Test, which asks you to be the editor of someone else's writing, the essay section asks *you* to do the writing. You will be presented with an assigned topic to which you must respond, but beyond that, the ideas, organization, and words will be all your own. Also unlike the multiple-choice section, which consists of separate and unconnected sentences, the essay gives you the chance to work your skills on a developed and sustained piece of prose, one that you create. Since the essay counts for 50 percent of your total Writing score, it is clearly considered an important component of the PPST.

You will have only thirty minutes from the time you see the topic to the time your paper must be handed in. Obviously, then, your essay is not expected to have the scope of a research paper or report. The topic may ask you to take a position or develop an argument, but you will be graded on your writing skills, not on your personal beliefs or your knowledge of any particular subject area. To be fair to all test-takers, the topics are designed to be broad enough so that anyone can respond, regardless of his or her background or training. The sample topic below will illustrate this point:

A generation ago, young people took it for granted that they would marry and soon after become parents. Today's young couples seem to be putting off parenthood well into their marriages, and a significant number are not having children at all. Discuss the advantages and disadvantages of having children. Be specific.

Virtually anyone can discuss this subject, and can draw on personal experience or observation to do so. You need not be a parent or intend to become one in order to respond. The essay section within the ''Writing Skills Review'' chapter will show you how you might plan and write an essay on this and other topics.

What standards will be used to judge your effort? No one expects a thirty-minute essay to be a flawless work that serves as the last word on a subject. The readers realize that what they are evaluating is essentially a first draft, and they know that even the best papers will probably contain a few errors and imperfections. Nevertheless, you will have to demonstrate control of the various elements of writing if you intend to achieve a top score. In awarding a high score, readers will look for a work that is well organized and logically developed. They will expect you to present a point of view and to support your position with appropriate examples and details. In addition, your work must demonstrate command of the conventions of standard written English and a sufficiently extensive vocabulary to convey your ideas precisely and effectively. Your sentences should indicate a command of punctuation, grammar, and syntax, as well as your ability to use a variety of sentence structures. Your essay must avoid monotony, oversimplification, awkwardness, and incoherence.

You will not receive separate sub-scores for the different elements of the essay, such as organization or syntax. Instead, your score will represent the readers' evaluation of your essay's *overall* effectiveness.

The scores given by PPST readers range from a 1 (low) to a 6 (high). Each essay is scored independently by two qualified readers; thus, neither knows the score given by the other. The two readers' scores are then added, resulting in a score that falls within a range from 2 to 12. Here is a guide to the levels of writing proficiency represented by each point on the 1–6 scale:

1. These papers lack a clear plan of action and organization. There is also great weakness in basic skills such as grammar, usage, punctuation, spelling, correct sentences and paragraphs, and capitalization. Not only has the writer of a 1 paper not proven his or her point, but he or she has not proven any point at all.

2. These papers have very weak details and examples. The ideas are not fully developed or proven. The level of reasoning is unsophisticated and displays a lack of understanding of the thesis. There are a lot of generalizations that are not backed up with specific details. There may be conflicting purposes rather than one clear plan of action. There are also a great many errors in usage and basic skills, as in the 1 papers.

3. These papers are not well organized and simply list details rather than developing supporting examples. While the purpose may be correctly *stated* (unlike the 1 and 2 papers, which do not make a point at all), the purpose is still not well supported with

details and examples. There is also weakness with basic skills, as in the 1 and 2 papers.

4. These papers show a clear plan and method of organization, although the supporting detail could be stronger. There are errors in usage and basic skills, but they are not intrusive enough to destroy the plan or the point being made.

5. These papers show a very clear organization and enough support for each point being made so that the reader is convinced of the logic of the writer's argument. The writer also shows a maturity of thought as well as writing, and may present ideas that show a level of sophistication beyond the topic, although always clearly *related to the topic*. There may be some minor writing errors, but they do not interrupt the flow of ideas.

6. These papers have a very clear "voice" or point of view. The topic is not only well proven, but there is a fluency and style in word and example choice that clearly demonstrates the writer's ideas and maturity. The supporting details are especially effective because they are specific and very clearly prove the point under discussion. There may be an error or two, but the writer clearly shows an understanding of the rules of English grammar and usage.

If you fail to respond to the assigned topic, either by not writing anything or by writing on a subject of your own choosing, your essay will receive a zero.

How long an essay should you write? There is no set rule concerning length. We are often told that "length is not a valid substitute for strength." In fact, since you must write your essay on one 2-sided sheet of lined paper, you are actually limited to writing *no more than* two pages. Even so, you should not write furiously to fill up all the available space merely to make it appear that you have many ideas. This approach can actually result in needless repetition, rambling, lack of organization, and muddled thinking, all of which can lower your score. By the same token, you don't want your essay to appear skimpy. Obviously, if you write only five or six sentences, the examiner may not get an adequate picture of your writing ability and may penalize you as a result. Many college instructors indicate that a development of at least three paragraphs is desirable. This is not to say that some test-takers may not wish to attempt more in the designated time. Here is where practice before the examination can be of great help. Most people do not have an accurate sense of how much or how little they can write in thirty minutes until they actually sit down and attempt the exercise.

TEST-TAKING STRATEGIES AND TIPS

These important suggestions apply to all the skills tests and can help you improve your scores:

1. Read each question carefully so that you are sure of what is really being asked. Some questions include such phrases as "All of the following except . . ." and "Which of the following does not . . ." If you read carelessly and overlook the "except" or the "not," you will misunderstand the question.

2. Read through all the given answer choices for a question before you mark your answer. Frequently one choice will seem right until you consider a later choice among the options that you then realize is more precise or appropriate.

3. Do not spend too much time on any one question. Bring a watch to the test center and be sure that you work at a reasonable pace. If you hit a particularly baffling question and you cannot figure it out within a minute, leave it, and see if you can return to it later. Some questions will seem to be and are harder than others, but if you spend an inordinate amount of time laboring over a few difficult questions, you will not have enough

time to answer many of the other questions that you could probably handle quite easily.

4. If you don't know an answer, *guess*. Because only your right answers are used to figure your score, and there is *no* deduction of points for wrong answers, *it always pays to guess*. Eliminate the choices you think are wrong—even if you can only eliminate one or two—and take a guess from among the choices left. If you realize that you are not going to be able to finish all the questions on a particular test—and this happens to many people—then before you are instructed to put your pencil down, you should simply fill in answers randomly on the answer sheet for those questions that you didn't have time to answer. You have at least a chance of getting some of them right. You should never leave any questions unanswered on the answer sheet if you can possibly avoid it.

5. Bring plenty of sharpened pencils and clean erasers to the test center, and periodically check to make sure that the question number in the test booklet corresponds to the question number you are answering on the answer sheet. The answer sheets are scanned by machine, and a machine may not register marks that are too light, or may mistakenly register smudged erasures. You do not want to lose time or points because of faulty equipment, and you don't want to blunder by inadvertently skipping a line on the answer sheet and thus marking all of your subsequent answers in the wrong spaces.

6. Be well rested on the day of the exam, and try to stay calm without losing your concentration. Fatigue that results from all-night studying or panic at the thought of an exam will probably not translate into better scores.

HOW TO USE THIS BOOK

The PPST tests skills that are typically acquired and developed over a significant period of time. You can best prepare yourself for the exam by practicing the skills it seeks to measure, becoming familiar with its format, and analyzing your own strengths and weaknesses. This book can help you do all these things. We recommend the following study plan:

1. Reread the descriptions of each of the skills tests from the preceding pages. Make sure that you understand what each of the different question types requires you to do.

2. Work through the "Skills Review" chapters for each of the tests you plan to take. Work as slowly as is necessary for you to absorb and understand the material thoroughly. You may choose to skim through certain sections that contain material you are confident you already know well, but remember—it never hurts to reinforce skills or knowledge.

3. Take the practice tests under conditions as close to those of the real exam as possible. That means no distractions, no interruptions, no snacking, no smoking, and no outside assistance. Find a quiet place where you can work with full concentration. Most importantly, *strictly observe the time limits established for each test*. You will *not* get an accurate idea of how well you can do on the real PPST if you allow yourself an hour for the Math Test or 45 minutes for the Essay. Although the PPST is not designed primarily to be a test of speed, the time limits do restrict what you can accomplish and exert significant pressure on you. If you fall into the habit of taking as much time on a practice test section as you like—or even if you only cheat a little—you will be sabotaging your own efforts. If you do observe the time limits and you find that you cannot finish all the questions, you'll know that you have to work faster. Conversely, if you have some time left over, you'll know that you can afford to work more deliberately.

   As part of the simulation of test conditions, you should cut or carefully tear out the answer sheet provided with each practice test and mark your answers on it in pencil. It does take slightly longer to work through a test by filling in a separate answer sheet rather than merely circling your chosen answers in the book, but since this is what you have to do for the real test, it's best to become accustomed to it. Use your own lined paper for each practice essay, but remember that the real test allows you only two pages for the essay—the front and back of a single sheet of paper.

4. Refer to the answer keys to identify your right and wrong answers. Then, study the explanatory answers to *all* the questions—to make sure you got the right answers for the right reasons, and to figure out why you missed the questions you got wrong. See if you can find a pattern in the questions you missed that might indicate a particular weakness to which you must attend. If, for instance, you find that in the multiple-choice Writing sections you are missing a number of questions that involve subject-verb agreement, you can return to the ''Writing Skills Review'' chapter and study the rules governing agreement again.

It is not a good idea to take the complete set of practice tests in one sitting. You will probably experience fatigue and a loss of concentration that will adversely affect your performance. For maximum results, take only one complete practice test a day. Ideally, you should take the first practice test, study its explanatory answers, and refer back to relevant sections of the ''Skills Review'' chapters before you take the second practice test. You should then repeat this procedure with tests 2 and 3, monitoring changes in your performance from test to test.

By getting the most out of this book, you will get the most out of yourself. It's well worth trying to do your best on an exam that can have such a great impact on both your academic and professional careers. A little work can make luck unnecessary—but, for good measure, we nevertheless do wish you the best of luck on the PPST and on your future endeavors.

Part II
PPST Skills Review

READING SKILLS REVIEW

It is more difficult to develop a structured study plan for the PPST Reading Test than for the Writing or Math tests. You can learn and review the rules for subject-verb agreement and for converting a fraction to a percent, but there are few rules you can learn or follow to improve your reading skills. Ultimately, the most effective way to become a better reader is to read frequently and widely, and with full attention. Reading often makes you a more comfortable reader and increases your speed. Reading material about a variety of subjects introduces you to new ideas and vocabulary. Of course, you cannot expand your vocabulary or improve your comprehension unless you actually take the trouble to look up the words from your reading that are unfamiliar or confusing to you. Make this practice a habit. And, when time permits, study the roots, prefixes, and suffixes of the words you look up, so that you can apply all that you learn when you encounter other unfamiliar words.

You should also try to read with sustained attention. When you read newspaper or magazine articles, don't be satisfied with just the opening paragraph of each article. Push yourself to read the whole story, and concentrate on it fully as you read. This will help you learn to process information and to deal with complex ideas. If your mind wanders as you read or if you never read beyond the headlines, you may have only a sketchy understanding of the issues involved, or you may miss the point altogether.

As beneficial as it may be, the kind of preparation recommended above may not seem practical to someone facing an important exam in a few days' or weeks' time. That is why this Reading Skills Review focuses not on how you learn to read but on the particular demands and features of the Reading Test itself. What follow are an expanded description of the Reading Test and an illustration of techniques that will help you perform the required tasks and achieve your best score.

PPST READING SKILLS

It is important to bear in mind that Reading Test questions are designed to test not whether you know certain facts, but how well you understand and interpret what you read. A good reader does several things:

A good reader understands the main idea of the material.
A good reader pays attention to details.
A good reader can ''read between the lines.''
A good reader understands the logical structure of the selection.
A good reader can evaluate the material.
A good reader can determine from the written material what attitude the author holds about
   a topic.

Every Reading Test question is designed to test one of these reading skills.

Some questions test whether you understand the main idea of the selection. These questions usually have one of the following forms:

What is the main idea of the selection?
The author is primarily concerned with . . . .
Which of the following best summarizes the main point of the selection?
Which of the following titles best summarizes the content of the passage?

These are called "main idea" questions.

Other questions ask about specific points made in the passage. These questions often take one of the following forms:

Which of the following is stated in the passage?
According to the author, which of the following . . . ?
According to the selection, ...
The author makes which of the following points about . . . ?

These are called "specific idea" questions.

Another type of question asks about ideas that are not explicitly stated in the passage but that can be inferred from the material. They often have the following form:

The author implies that . . . .
It can be inferred from the passage that . . . .
Which of the following statements can be inferred from the passage?

These are called "inference" questions.

A fourth type of question asks you about the logical structure of the passage. These questions can ask about the overall organization of the selection or about the logical significance of a particular point:

The author is primarily concerned with . . . .
Why does the author introduce . . . at line 15?

As you can see, the first form is like that of a main idea question. But the correct answer to a "logical structure" question that asks about the overall organization of the selection will describe the *form* of the passage rather than the *content*. The second question above is related to the specific detail content. However, a question about logical detail asks not about *what* the author said but about *why* the author said it.

Some questions ask that you critically evaluate the material in the passage. These often have the following forms:

With which of the following statements would the author be likely to agree?
The selection most likely appeared in which of the following contexts?
Which of the following topics would be the most logical one for the author to take up next?

"Evaluation" questions take you beyond the text of the selection. To find the correct answer, you must apply what you have learned in the selection to a new situation.

Finally, some questions ask about the author's attitude or about the tone of the selection. For example:

The author's attitude toward . . . can best be described as one of . . . .
Which of the following best describes the tone of the selection?

And we will call these "tone/attitude" questions.

Learning to recognize the different kinds of questions will make it easier for you to recognize the right (and wrong) answers.

Since every Reading Test is designed along these lines, there are some procedures you can follow regardless of the content of the selection.

First do selections that are familiar to you. Save until last the selection that seems most difficult.

Even though a selection may treat a topic that seems familiar to you, the selection will probably still seem difficult for several reasons. First, though the general topic is familiar, the specific treatment given the topic by the author may be unusual. Second, the selection will seem to begin in the middle of nowhere. Third, the selection has been carefully edited to contain many ideas in very few words. A good technique for getting over these difficulties is "previewing" (after deciding on the "easiest" passage to do first).

Begin your attack on a reading test question by reading the question stems.

The "stem" of the question is the part that introduces the answer choices; in other words, the stem is everything but the choices. Why should you read the stem before you read the selection? For two reasons. First, some stems will actually tell you what the selection is about. Second, some stems will tell you what specific points to be looking for as you read the selection.

Here are six question stems. (On the actual PPST you would not have more than five questions per selection. Here you have one example of each of the six kinds of questions.) Later you will see the passage on which the questions are based. Now read the question stems to see what you can learn from them. This is previewing the question stems before reading the passage.

The author is primarily concerned with
According to the author, Aristotle warned against
The selection suggests that zoology would have developed more rapidly if
The author describes the 'fantastic journey' of zoology (line 18) in order to
A discussion of which of the following would be the most logical continuation of the selection?
The author's attitude toward Aristotle's approach to zoology can best be described as

The first and fifth question stems really don't provide any information:

The author is primarily concerned with
A discussion of which of the following would be the most logical continuation of the selection?

These are stock question stems that could be used with any selection. They don't refer specifically to any ideas discussed in the passage. The other stems, however, do refer to the content of the specific passage you will see below.

The second stem—"According to the author, Aristotle warned against"—tells you that Aristotle will be mentioned in the selection and that the author will note that Aristotle warned against something. As you read the passage, look for the section where the author mentions Aristotle's warning.

The third stem—"The selection suggests that zoology would have developed more rapidly if"—tells you that the author discusses the development of zoology. It also lets you know that you must understand why zoology did not develop very rapidly.

The fourth stem—"The author describes the 'fantastic journey' of zoology (line 18) in order to"—reinforces an idea mentioned in the third stem: the passage discusses the development of zoology. The fourth stem tells you to ask yourself as you read why the author describes a "fantastic journey."

The sixth stem—"The author's attitude toward Aristotle's approach to zoology can best be described as"—mentions Aristotle and tells you to ask yourself about the author's attitude toward him.

After you have previewed the question stems, you should next read the first sentence of each paragraph.

Before reading the passage, preview the first sentence of each paragraph.

The first sentence of a paragraph is often the topic sentence, so you may get a better idea of the content and structure of the selection by previewing the first sentence of each paragraph. (Of course, if the selection is only one paragraph long, this advice doesn't apply.) Here are the first sentences from the three paragraphs that make up the selection you will see later:

If a fascination with the workings of nature and a desire to understand them defines mankind as an intellectual or reasoning race, then a genuine regard for the animals of nature makes us a compassionate, even estimable species.
As they did with nearly all the sciences, the Greeks set zoology off on the right road.

The sensitive subject of man's own physical nature and origin had a great deal to do with zoology's late development.

The first sentence is a bit cryptic and so not all that helpful. But the other two sentences confirm what was suggested by our preview of the stems, namely, that the passage deals with the development of zoology.

When you have finished your preview, read the selection. Don't try to go through it too quickly. The Reading Test is not a speed-reading test.

Do not merely skim the passage, and do not try to "speed read."

This part of the PPST tests reading *comprehension,* not reading *speed*. The selections are carefully edited so that they are not too long. Even if you read slowly, you should be able to complete the longest selections in less than two minutes.

Of course, since this is a test of comprehension rather than speed, make sure you understand what you read. Read actively, not passively.

As you read, ask yourself: What is the main theme of this passage? How do the specific ideas relate to the main theme? What is the author's attitude toward the subject?

But don't get stuck on specific details. This is particularly true if there is some technical point in the selection that you don't understand. Even if you don't understand a technicality, you can still answer most of the questions so long as you do understand *why* the technical point is in the selection.

Using your pencil, draw a box around points that are difficult to understand.

Don't spend a lot of time trying to figure out a technical idea that may not even be the basis of a question.

Finally, once you have completed your reading of the selection, pause briefly and ask yourself about what you have just read.

Before attacking the questions, summarize in your own words the main idea and general development of the passage.

Ask yourself about what you have just read. If you are clear in your own mind about the passage, the wrong answer choices will be less likely to distract your attention from the correct answer.

Now read the section, which concerns the development of zoology.

If a fascination with the workings of nature and a desire to understand them defines mankind as an intellectual or reasoning race, then a genuine regard for the animals of nature makes us a com-
(5) passionate, even estimable species. Well over two millennia ago, Aristotle warned against easy patronizing of the animal world: "We must not betake ourselves to the consideration of the meaner animals with a bad grace, as though we
(10) were children; since in all natural things there is somewhat of the marvelous." Interestingly, Aristotle likens man's feelings of superiority over the animal world to a child's natural but incorrect assumption that the world exists for his pleasure.
(15) His simile is especially apt, for with both a child

and a scientific discipline, the process of maturing involves the recognition, understanding, and acceptance of things as they are. As the branch of biology dealing with the animal world, zoology
(20) took a long time to grow up. And unlike some disciplines, it had no real unifying theory until a little over a century ago. Until Darwin, the history of zoology was an incomplete tale—a story rich in detail with a great many characters but one
(25) with no recurring theme or unifying plot.

As they did with nearly all the sciences, the Greeks set zoology off on the right road, but with their decline, the scientific pathways became overgrown and were finally lost. Zoology then
(30) set upon a sometimes fantastic journey from the

mythical, moralizing bestiaries of medieval times through the rigid classifying methods of the eighteenth century and the charm and naiveté of its popular natural history phase to the broader,
(35) sounder science of more modern times. Despite these scientific ups and downs and the vagaries and trends of scientific fashion, the core phenomenon of zoology has remained constant throughout—the phenomenon of life. Life and its perpet-
(40) uation was what the animal world seemed to be about—indeed, the only thing it seemed to be about—and until Darwin, there was no one, large, encompassing idea under which the great variety of animal life could be gathered and relat-
(45) ed.
　　The sensitive subject of man's own physical nature and origin had a great deal to do with zoology's late development, since religious dogma dictated an essential distinction between animal
(50) and man, placing animals in a separate and decidedly inferior position. The conceptual revolution implicit in Darwinism was its renunciation of this distinction and its espousal of the opposite notion that all the varied forms and phenomena
(55) of life are part of a connected whole. The implications of Darwin's theory outside of science are broad and deeply felt—morally, socially, and politically. His removal of mankind from its self-created position of superiority returned the study
(60) of animal life to the sound footing it had enjoyed when zoology as a scientific discipline was first practiced by the ancient Greeks.

　　Did you read actively? Did you box material? To illustrate our advice concerning technical material, look back at the second paragraph. What do you suppose is the meaning of "bestiaries"? Why would a natural history have "charm and naiveté"? What type of classifying system would be "rigid"? These are questions that you don't have to answer in order to understand most of the selection. To prove this, look at the second paragraph with that material deleted:

As they did with nearly all the sciences, the Greeks set zoology off on the right road, but with their decline, the scientific pathways became overgrown and were finally lost. Zoology then set upon sometimes fantastic journey from xxx xxxxxxxx, xxxxxxxxxx xxxxxxxxxx of medieval times through xxx xxxxx xxxxxxxxxxx xxxxxxx of the eighteenth century and xxx xxxxx xxx xxxxxxx xx xxx xxxxxxx xxxxxxx xxxxxxx xxxxx to xxx xxxxxxx, xxxxxxx science of more modern times. Despite these scientific ups and downs and the vagaries and trends of scientific fashion, the core phenomenon of zoology has remained constant throughout—the phenomenon of life. Life and its perpetuation was what the animal world seemed to be about—indeed, the only thing it seemed to be about—and until Darwin, there was no one, large, encompassing idea under which the great variety of animal life could be gathered and related.

　　The significance of the paragraph should be clear to you even without all the detail.
　　Now you can attack the questions based on the passage:

　　　　The author's primary concern is to

　　　　(A) report on Darwin's theory of evolution
　　　　(B) outline Aristotle's idea of zoology
　　　　(C) describe the development of zoology
　　　　(D) encourage the reader to study zoology
　　　　(E) report on recent advances in zoology

This is a main idea question, and the correct answer to a main idea question must capture the main theme of the selection without going beyond the scope of the selection.

For a main idea question, eliminate choices that refer to small parts of the passage.

　　The author does mention Aristotle's approach to zoology in the first paragraph, and he or she does mention Darwin's theory in the third paragraph. But these ideas are only parts of the greater whole. So (A) and (B) must be wrong answers.
　　Other wrong answers to main idea questions take you beyond the scope of the selection.

For a main idea question, eliminate choices that go beyond the scope of the passage.

This tip helps you eliminate (D) and (E). As for (D), while a reader might become interested in zoology after reading the selection, that is not the author's main intention. As for (E), the author does refer to modern zoology in the last paragraph. But he or she does not report on any "advances."

The correct answer to our main idea question is (C). The author describes the development of zoology from the ancient Greeks, through medieval times and the eighteenth and nineteenth centuries, to modern times.

The correct answer to a main idea question describes the *overall* point of the selection without going beyond the scope of the selection.

Our second question is a specific idea question:

According to the author, Aristotle warned against

(A) viewing animals as objects of scientific study
(B) regarding animals as inferior to human beings
(C) teaching children about zoology
(D) allowing scientific findings to affect political institutions
(E) expecting too much from an infant science

Notice that this specific idea question refers you to a specific part of the selection, the part where the author discusses Aristotle.

Use the referential words of a specific idea question to find the material you need to answer the question.

The referential words of this question are "Aristotle" and "warning." And those ideas are found in the first paragraph. There the author tells us that Aristotle warns against treating animals as inferior to human beings. So the correct answer must be (B).

Our third question is an inference question:

The selection suggests that zoology would have developed more rapidly if

(A) religious organizations had not opposed the use of animals in experiments
(B) Darwin had been able to demonstrate that all forms of animal life are interconnected
(C) the ancient Greeks had not regarded animals as below humans on the evolutionary scale
(D) animals were a more stable, enduring phenomenon like the atoms and molecules studied by physics and chemistry
(E) dominant religious organizations had not insisted on the superiority of humans over animals

Notice that this question also refers you to a specific part of the selection.

Look for referential words in an inference question.

The referential words here are "developed more rapidly." That idea is discussed in the first sentence of the final paragraph. There the author states that zoology developed more slowly than did other sciences because of the influence of a particular religious doctrine. But, you object, the author doesn't say anything specific about how zoology might have developed more rapidly! That's true.

For an inference question, you must read between the lines.

The author says that zoology developed slowly because of a certain religious influence. We can infer, therefore, that had religion not had this effect, zoology would have developed more rapidly. Thus, the correct answer to our inference question is (E).

Our next question is a logical structure question.

Logical structure questions ask not about what the author said but about why the author said it.

The author describes the "fantastic journey" of zoology (line 18) in order to

(A) demonstrate that zoology as a science went through different phases
(B) show that modern zoology is fundamentally different from Aristotle's study of animals
(C) suggest that zoologists have employed the same methods of study since medieval times
(D) prove that Darwin's theory of evolution corrected early misconceptions about zoology
(E) remind the reader that it is impossible to study zoology without a knowledge of history

Here you are referred to a particular part of the selection, line 18. The development of the second paragraph is chronological: from the ancient Greeks, through the middle centuries, to modern times. Therefore, the author mentions this "journey" in order to demonstrate that zoology developed over the centuries, as answer choice (A) correctly points out.

Our fifth question is an evaluation question:

A discussion of which of the following would be the most logical continuation of the selection?

(A) Methods used by zoologists in the eighteenth century to classify animals
(B) Aristotle's reasons for believing that there is something marvelous about nature
(C) Religious doctrines concerning the relationship between man and other animals
(D) Various scientific principles that are the basis of the modern science of zoology
(E) Approaches taken by ancient Greeks to the study of other natural phenomena

Evaluation questions are the most difficult type of question.

With an evaluation question, there is often very little in the actual passage on which to base an answer. Here the correct answer is (D). The passage describes the rise of zoology and is arranged chronologically. You would expect, therefore, that the author would continue along this line and discuss modern zoology next. It is not impossible that the author would return to Aristotle or to the eighteenth century; but, on balance, it seems more likely that he or she would continue to discuss modern zoology.

Our last question is a tone/attitude question.

> The author's attitude toward Aristotle's study of animals can best be described as:
>
> (A) critical
> (B) admiring
> (C) outraged
> (D) neutral
> (E) adoring

The correct answer to this question is (B).

For a tone/attitude question, try to arrange the answers on a scale from negative to positive.

The answer choices suggest various negative or positive attitudes:

− outraged   critical   neutral   admiring   adoring   +

The author specifically states that Aristotle and other ancient Greeks were "on the right road." This is clearly a positive attitude. So we eliminate choices (A), (C), and (D). Now we must decide whether the positive attitude is so extreme as to be considered "adoring." The treatment of Aristotle, while approving, is not so emotional as to warrant the description "adoring."

Here are three additional points to be made about the Reading Test:

Read all five answer choices.

Do not rush to choose the first answer that might be correct. One answer might be partially correct, but it might not be the *best* answer among the choices given; another answer may be more exact.

Avoid inserting your own judgments into your answers.

Even if you disagree with the author or if you spot a factual error in the passage, you must answer on the basis of what is stated or implied *in the passage*.

Do not spend too much time on any one question!

If you labor too long over one difficult question, you may miss the opportunity to answer three easier questions. And *always* guess rather than not answering at all.

MATHEMATICS SKILLS REVIEW

Many people find that once they stop taking math classes in school, they forget a great deal of even the basic math they learned in earlier years. Although the PPST does not test mathematics more advanced than high school math, many people nevertheless need a refresher course to bring back to mind the terminology, concepts, and operations covered by the Mathematics Test. What follows is a comprehensive review of math from basic arithmetic through algebra and geometry. Also included are sections on word problems, measurement, and graphs, since these kinds of problems appear frequently on the PPST. As you go through the various sections of the Mathematics Skills Review, skim the topics that you already know well and focus on the topics that you either never learned or no longer remember completely. Make sure that you understand all of the steps involved in solving the example problems; while the PPST stresses mathematical reasoning rather than elaborate computations, facility with certain numerical operations and formulas can make the logic underlying them more readily apparent.

PPST MATHEMATICS SKILLS

The Number Line

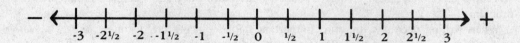

A number line is a convenient concept to keep as a mental picture. The number line above shows whole numbers and fractions greater than zero and less than zero. Numbers increase in size as you move to the right, and decrease in size as you move to the left. The number line above has an arrow at each end, meaning that the number line goes on infinitely in both positive and negative directions.

Number lines can be drawn up to aid in basic mathematical calculations. Either fractions, whole numbers, or decimals can be used to name the intervals on the line. You may want to use number lines when dealing with signed $(+, -)$ numbers and inequalities.

Here is a list of a few basic rules that must be mastered for speed and accuracy in mathematical computation. You should memorize these rules.

Any number multiplied by $0 = 0$.
$5 \times 0 = 0.$
If 0 is divided by any number, the answer is 0.
$0 \div 2 = 0$
If 0 is added to any number, the number does not change.
$7 + 0 = 7$
If 0 is subtracted from any number, that number does not change.
$4 - 0 = 4$
If a number is multiplied by 1, that number does not change.
$3 \times 1 = 3$

23

If a number is divided by 1, that number does not change.

$6 \div 1 = 6$

A number added to itself is doubled.

$4 + 4 = 8$

If a number is subtracted from itself, the answer is 0.

$9 - 9 = 0$

If a number is divided by itself, the answer is 1.

$8 \div 8 = 1$

When multiplying a number by 10, 100, 1000, etc., move the decimal point to the right a number of spaces equal to the number of zeros in the multiplier. If the number being multiplied is a whole number, push the decimal point to the right by inserting the appropriate number of zeros.

$$.36 \times 100 = 36.$$
$$1.2 \times 10 = 12.$$
$$5. \times 10 = 50.$$
$$60.423 \times 100 = 6042.3$$

When dividing a number by 10, 100, 1000, etc., again count the zeros, but this time move the decimal point to the left.

$$123. \div 100 = 1.23$$
$$352.8 \div 10 = 35.28$$
$$16. \div 100 = .16$$
$$7. \div 1000 = .007$$

Decimals

Decimals are a way of writing fractions using tenths, hundredths, thousandths, and so forth. If you can count money, make change, or understand a batting average, decimals should present no problem.

When writing decimals, the most important step is placing the decimal point. The whole system is based on its location. Remember the decimal places?

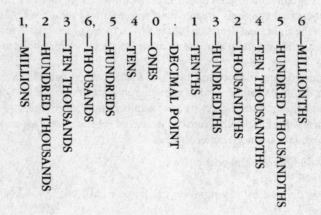

When adding or subtracting decimals, it is most important to keep the decimal points in line. Once the decimal points are aligned, proceed with the problem in exactly the same way as with whole numbers, simply maintaining the location of the decimal point.

Example: Add 36.08 + 745 + 4.362 + 58.6 + .0061.

Solution:

36.08	If you find it easier, you may fill in the spaces	036.0800
745.	with zeros. The answer will be unchanged.	745.0000
4.362		004.3620
58.6		058.6000
+ .0061		+ 000.0061
844.0481		844.0481

Example: Subtract 7.928 from 82.1.

Solution:

$$\begin{array}{r} 82.1 \\ -\ 7.928 \\ \hline 74.172 \end{array} \qquad \begin{array}{r} 82.100 \\ -\ 7.928 \\ \hline 74.172 \end{array}$$

When multiplying decimals, you can ignore the decimal points until you reach the product. Then the placement of the decimal point is dependent on the sum of the places to the right of the decimal point in both the multiplier and number being multiplied.

$$\begin{array}{r} 1.482 \\ \times\ .16 \\ \hline 8892 \\ 14820 \\ \hline .23712 \end{array}$$

(3 places to right of decimal point)
(2 places to right of decimal point)

(5 places to right of decimal point)

You cannot divide by a decimal. If the divisor is a decimal, you must move the decimal point to the right until the divisor becomes a whole number, an integer. Count the number of spaces by which you moved the decimal point to the right and move the decimal point in the dividend (the number being divided) the same number of spaces to the right. The decimal point in the answer should be directly above the decimal point in the dividend.

$$.06_{\wedge}\overline{)4.21_{\wedge}2} \qquad \dfrac{70.2}{}$$ Decimal point moves two spaces to the right.

Rounding decimals

To round a number to a given decimal place, locate the given place. If the digit to the right is less than 5, omit all digits following the given place. If the digit to the right is 5 or more, raise the given place by 1 and omit all digits following the given place.

$$4.27 = 4.3 \text{ to the nearest tenth}$$
$$.71345 = .713 \text{ to the nearest thousandth}$$

In problems involving money, answers are usually rounded to the nearest cent.

Fractions

Fractions are used when we wish to indicate parts of things. A fraction consists of a numerator and a denominator.

$$\dfrac{3}{4} \begin{array}{l} \leftarrow\text{numerator}\rightarrow \\ \leftarrow\text{denominator}\rightarrow \end{array} \dfrac{7}{8}$$

The denominator tells you how many equal parts the object or number has been divided into, and the numerator tells how many of those parts which we are concerned with.

Examples: Divide a baseball game, a football game, and a hockey game into convenient numbers of parts. Write a fraction to answer each equation.

1. A baseball game has nine innings. If a pitcher played two innings, how much of the whole baseball game did he play?
2. A football game has four quarters. If a quarterback played three parts of a football game, how much of the whole game did he play?
3. A hockey game has three periods. If a goalie played two parts of a hockey game, how much of the whole game did he play?

Solution 1: A baseball game is conveniently divided into nine parts (each an inning). The pitcher pitched two innings. Therefore, he played $\frac{2}{9}$ of the game. The denominator represents the nine parts the game is divided into; the numerator, the two parts which we are concerned with.

Solution 2: Similarly, there are four quarters in a football game, and a quarterback playing three of those quarters plays in $\frac{3}{4}$ of the game.

Solution 3: There are three periods in hockey, and the goalie played in two of them. Therefore, he played in $\frac{2}{3}$ of the game.

Equivalent fractions

Fractions having different denominators and numerators may actually represent the same amount. Such fractions are equivalent fractions.

For example, the circle below is divided into two equal parts. Write a fraction to indicate that half of the circle is shaded.

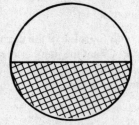

$$\frac{1 \text{ shaded}}{2 \text{ parts}} = \tfrac{1}{2} \text{ of circle is shaded}$$

The circle below is divided into four equal parts. Write a fraction to indicate how much of the circle is shaded.

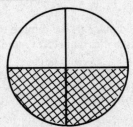

$$\frac{2 \text{ shaded}}{4 \text{ parts}} = \tfrac{2}{4} \text{ of the circle is shaded}$$

The circle below is divided into eight equal parts. Write a fraction to indicate how much of the circle is shaded.

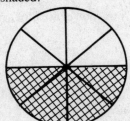

$$\frac{4 \text{ shaded}}{8 \text{ parts}} = \tfrac{4}{8} \text{ of the circle is shaded}$$

In each circle the same amount was shaded. This should show you that there is more than one way to indicate one half of something.

The fractions $\frac{1}{2}$, $\frac{2}{4}$, and $\frac{4}{8}$ that you wrote are *equivalent fractions* because they all represent the same amount. Notice that the denominator is twice as large as the numerator in every case. Any fraction you write that has a denominator that is exactly twice as large as the numerator will be equivalent to $\frac{1}{2}$.

Example 1: Write other fractions equivalent to $\frac{1}{2}$.

Example 2: Write other fractions equivalent to $\frac{1}{4}$.

Example 3: Write other fractions equivalent to $\frac{2}{3}$.

Solution 1: Any fraction that has a denominator that is twice as large as the numerator: $\frac{3}{6}$, $\frac{5}{10}$, $\frac{6}{12}$, $\frac{32}{64}$, etc.

Solution 2: Any fraction that has a denominator that is four times as large as the numerator: $\frac{2}{8}$, $\frac{4}{16}$, $\frac{5}{20}$, $\frac{15}{60}$, etc.

Solution 3: Any fraction that has a denominator that is one-and-one-half times as large as the numerator: $\frac{4}{6}$, $\frac{10}{15}$, $\frac{14}{21}$, $\frac{16}{24}$, etc.

When the numerator and denominator of a fraction cannot be divided evenly by the same whole number (other than 1), the fraction is said to be in lowest terms. In the examples above, $\frac{1}{2}$, $\frac{1}{4}$, and $\frac{2}{3}$ are in lowest terms.

To write equivalent fractions where the numerator is not 1 requires one more step.

Example: What is the equivalent fraction for $\frac{4}{5}$ using 10 as a denominator?

Solution: Each $\frac{1}{5}$ is equivalent to $\frac{2}{10}$; therefore, $\frac{4}{5}$ is equivalent to $\frac{8}{10}$.

The quickest way to find an equivalent fraction is to divide the denominator of the fraction you know *into* the denominator you want. Take the result and multiply it by the numerator of the fraction you know. This becomes the numerator of the equivalent fraction.

Example: Change $\frac{3}{8}$ to an equivalent fraction having 16 as a denominator.

Solution: $16 \div 8 = 2$ $2 \times 3 = 6$ Answer: $\frac{6}{16}$

Example: Change $\frac{3}{4}$ into equivalent fractions having 8, 12, 24, and 32 as denominators.

Solution: $\frac{3}{4} = \frac{6}{8}$ $(8 \div 4 = 2; 2 \times 3 = 6)$

$\qquad \frac{3}{4} = \frac{9}{12}$ $(12 \div 4 = 3; 3 \times 3 = 9)$

$\qquad \frac{3}{4} = \frac{18}{24}$ $(24 \div 4 = 6; 6 \times 3 = 18)$

$\qquad \frac{3}{4} = \frac{24}{32}$ $(32 \div 4 = 8; 8 \times 3 = 24)$

A fraction that has a numerator larger than the denominator is called an *improper fraction*. A number expressed as an integer together with a proper fraction is called a *mixed number*.

Examples of improper fractions include $\frac{3}{2}$, $\frac{12}{7}$, and $\frac{9}{5}$. Note that each is in lowest terms because the numerator and denominator cannot be divided evenly by a number other than 1.

Examples of mixed numbers include $1\frac{1}{2}$, $1\frac{5}{7}$, and $1\frac{4}{5}$. These are called mixed numbers because they have a whole number part and a fractional part. These mixed numbers are equivalent to the improper fractions given above.

To change a mixed number to an improper fraction is easy.

Example: Change $2\frac{1}{4}$ to an improper fraction.

Solution: The whole number 2 contains 8 fourths. Add to it the $\frac{1}{4}$ to write the equivalent fraction $\frac{9}{4}$.

An alternative way of figuring this is to multiply the denominator of the fraction by the whole number and add the numerator.

Example: Change $2\frac{1}{4}$ to an improper fraction.

Solution: $4 \times 2 = \frac{8}{4} + \frac{1}{4} = \frac{9}{4}$

To change an improper fraction to a mixed number, just proceed backwards.

Example: Change $\frac{9}{4}$ to a mixed number.

Solution: Divide the denominator into the numerator and use the remainder (R) as the fraction:

$$9 \div 4 = 2 \text{ R1 or } 9 \div 4 = 2\frac{1}{4}$$

Adding and subtracting fractions

To add fractions with the same denominators, simply add the numerators and keep the same denominator.

Example: Add $\frac{1}{4} + \frac{3}{4} + \frac{3}{4}$.

Solution: The denominators are the same, so just add the numerators to arrive at the answer, $\frac{7}{4}$ or $1\frac{3}{4}$.

To find the difference between two fractions with the same denominators, simply subtract the numerators, leaving the denominators alone.

Example: Find the difference between $\frac{7}{8}$ and $\frac{3}{8}$.

Solution: $\frac{7}{8} - \frac{3}{8} = \frac{4}{8}$ Reduced to lowest terms: $\frac{4}{8} = \frac{1}{2}$

To add or subtract fractions having different denominators, you will have to find a *common denominator*. A common denominator is a number into which the denominators of all the fractions in the problem can be divided without a remainder.

Example: Find a common denominator for $\frac{1}{4}$ and $\frac{1}{3}$.

Solution: Both 4 and 3 can be divided evenly into 12:

$\frac{1}{4}$ is equivalent to $\frac{3}{12}$

$\frac{1}{3}$ is equivalent to $\frac{4}{12}$

We can now add the fractions because we have written equivalent fractions in a common denominator.

$$\frac{3}{12} + \frac{4}{12} = \frac{7}{12}$$

Therefore,

$$\frac{1}{4} + \frac{1}{3} = \frac{7}{12}$$

Seven-twelfths is in lowest terms, because 7 and 12 do not have a whole number (other than 1) that goes into both evenly.

Example: Add $\frac{3}{8}$, $\frac{5}{6}$, $\frac{1}{4}$, and $\frac{2}{3}$.

Solution: Find a number into which all denominators will divide evenly. For 8, 6, 4, and 3, the best choice is 24. Now convert each fraction to an equivalent fraction having a denominator of 24.

$$\frac{3}{8} = \frac{9}{24} \quad (24 \div 8 = 3; 3 \times 3 = 9)$$

$$\frac{5}{6} = \frac{20}{24} \quad (24 \div 6 = 4; 4 \times 5 = 20)$$

$$\frac{1}{4} = \frac{6}{24} \quad (24 \div 4 = 6; 6 \times 1 = 6)$$

$$\frac{2}{3} = \frac{16}{24} \quad (24 \div 3 = 8; 8 \times 2 = 6)$$

Now add the fractions.

$$\frac{9}{24} + \frac{20}{24} + \frac{6}{24} + \frac{16}{24} = \frac{51}{24}$$

The answer, $\frac{51}{24}$, is an improper fraction; that is, the numerator is greater than the denominator. To convert the answer to a mixed number, divide the numerator by the denominator and express the remainder as a fraction.

$$\frac{51}{24} = 51 \div 24 = 2\frac{3}{24} = 2\frac{1}{8}$$

Multiplying and dividing fractions

When multiplying fractions, multiply numerators by numerators and denominators by denominators.

$$\frac{3}{5} \cdot \frac{4}{7} \cdot \frac{1}{5} = \frac{3 \times 4 \times 1}{5 \times 7 \times 5} = \frac{12}{175}$$

In multiplying fractions, try to work with numbers that are as small as possible. You can make numbers smaller by *canceling*. Cancel by dividing the numerator of any one fraction and the denominator of any one fraction by the same number.

$$\frac{\overset{1}{\cancel{3}}}{\underset{2}{\cancel{4}}} \cdot \frac{\overset{1}{\cancel{2}}}{\underset{3}{\cancel{9}}} = \frac{1 \times 1}{2 \times 3} = \frac{1}{6}$$

In this case the numerator of the first fraction and the denominator of the other fraction were divided by 3, while the denominator of the first fraction and the numerator of the other fraction were divided by 2.

To divide by a fraction, invert the fraction following the division sign and multiply.

$$\frac{3}{16} \div \frac{1}{8} = \frac{3}{\underset{2}{\cancel{16}}} \times \frac{\overset{1}{\cancel{8}}}{1} = \frac{3}{2} = 1\frac{1}{2}$$

Conversion of Decimals and Fractions

Since a decimal point indicates a number having a denominator that is a power of 10, a decimal can be expressed as a fraction, the numerator of which is the number itself and the denominator of which is the power indicated by the number of decimal places in the decimal.

$$.3 = \frac{3}{10} \quad .47 = \frac{47}{100}$$

When dealing with whole numbers, do not change the decimal. In the problem $12 \times .14$, it is better to keep the decimal.

$$12 \times .14 = 1.68$$

When dealing with fractions, change the decimal to a fraction. In the problem $\frac{3}{5} \times .17$ it is best to change the decimal to a fraction.

$$\frac{3}{5} \times .17 = \frac{3}{5} \times \frac{17}{100} = \frac{51}{500}$$

The line in a fraction means ''divided by.'' To change a fraction to a decimal follow through on the division.

$$\frac{4}{5} = 4 \div 5 = .8$$

To change a decimal to a percent, move the decimal point two places to the right and add a percent sign.

$$.8 = 80\%$$

Because decimal equivalents of fractions are often used, it is helpful to be familiar with the most common conversions.

$\frac{1}{2}$	$= .5$	$\frac{1}{3}$	$= .3333$
$\frac{1}{4}$	$= .25$	$\frac{2}{3}$	$= .6667$
$\frac{3}{4}$	$= .75$	$\frac{1}{6}$	$= .1667$
$\frac{1}{5}$	$= .2$	$\frac{1}{7}$	$= .1429$
$\frac{1}{8}$	$= .125$	$\frac{1}{9}$	$= .1111$
$\frac{1}{16}$	$= .0625$	$\frac{1}{12}$	$= .0833$

Note that the left column contains exact values. The values in the right column have been rounded to the nearest ten-thousandth.

Percentage

One percent is one one-hundredth of something. The last syllable of the word *percent, -cent,* is the name we give to one one-hundredth of a dollar.

One percent of $1.00, then, is one cent. Using decimal notation, we can write one cent as $.01, five cents as $.05, twenty-five cents as $.25, and so forth.

Twenty-five cents represents twenty-five one-hundredths of a dollar. Rather than say that something is so many one-hundredths of something else, we use the word *percent*. Twenty-five cents, then, is twenty-five percent of a dollar. We use the symbol % to stand for percent.

Percentage ("hundredths of") is a convenient and widely used way of measuring all sorts of things. By measuring in hundredths, we can be very precise and notice very small changes.

Percentage is not limited to comparing other numbers to 100. You can divide any number into hundredths and talk about percentage.

Example: Find 1% of 200.

Solution: 1% of 200 is one one-hundredth of 200.

$$200 \div 100 = 2$$

Using decimal notation, we can calculate one percent of 20

$$200 \times .01 = 2$$

Similarly, we can find a percentage of any number we choose by multiplying it by the correct decimal notation.

Five percent of fifty: $.05 \times 50 = 2.5$
Three percent of 150: $.03 \times 150 = 4.5$
Ten percent of 60: $.10 \times 60 = 6.0$

All percentage measurements are not between one percent and 100 percent. We may wish to consider less than one percent of something, especially if it is very large.

For example, if you were handed a book 1,000 pages long and were told to read one percent of it in five minutes, how much would you have to read?

$$1000 \times .01 = 10 \text{ pages}$$

Quite an assignment! You might bargain to read one-half of one percent, or one-tenth of one percent, in the five minutes allotted to you.

Using decimal notation, we write one-tenth of one percent as .001, the decimal number for one one-thousandth. If you remember that a percent is one one-hundredth of something, you can see that one-tenth of that percent is equivalent to one one-thousandth of the whole.

In percent notation, one-tenth of one percent is written as .1%. Students often mistakenly think that .1% is equal to .1. As you know, .1% is really equal to .001.

Sometimes we are concerned with more than 100% of something. But, you may ask, since 100% constitutes all of something, how can we speak of *more* than all of it?

Where things are growing, or increasing in size or amount, we may want to compare their new size to the size they once were. For example, suppose we measured the heights of three plants to be 6 inches, 9 inches, and 12 inches one week, and discover a week later that the first plant is still 6 inches tall but the second and third ones are now 18 inches tall.

- The 6-inch plant grew *zero percent,* because it didn't grow at all.
- The second plant *added* 100% to its size. It doubled in height.
- The third plant *added* 50% to its height.

We can also say:

- The first plant is 100% of its original height.
- The second plant grew to 200% of its original height.
- The third plant grew to 150% of its original height.

Here are some common percentage and fractional equivalents you should remember:

- Ten percent (10%) is one tenth ($\frac{1}{10}$), or (.10).
- Twelve and one-half percent (12.5%) is one-eighth ($\frac{1}{8}$), or (.125).
- Twenty percent (20%) is one fifth ($\frac{1}{5}$), or (.20).
- Twenty-five percent (25%) is one quarter ($\frac{1}{4}$), or (.25).
- Thirty-three and one-third percent (33 $\frac{1}{3}$%) is one third ($\frac{1}{3}$), or (.333).
- Fifty percent (50%) is one half ($\frac{1}{2}$), or (.50).
- Sixty-six and two-thirds percent (66 $\frac{2}{3}$%) is two thirds ($\frac{2}{3}$), or (.666).
- Seventy-five percent (75%) is three quarters ($\frac{3}{4}$), or (.75).

Warning

When solving problems involving percentages, be careful of common errors:

- **Read the notation carefully.** .50% is *not* fifty percent, but one-half of one percent.
- When solving problems for percentage increases or decreases in size, **read the problem carefully.**
- **Use common sense.** If you wish to find less than 100% of a number, your result will be smaller than the number you started with. For example, 43% of 50 is less than 50.
- **Using common sense works in the other direction as well.** For example, 70 is 40% of what number? The number you are looking for must be larger than 70, since 70 is only $\frac{40}{100}$ of it. Moreover, you can estimate that the number you are looking for will be a little more than twice as large as 70, since 70 is almost half (50%) of that number.

To find a percent of a number, change the percent to a decimal and multiply the number by it.

Example: What is 5% of 80?

Solution: 5% of 80 = 80 × .05 = 4

To find out what a number is when a percent of it is given, change the percent to a decimal and divide the given number by it.

Example: 5 is 10% of what number?

Solution: 5 ÷ .10 = 50

To find what percent one number is of another number, create a fraction by putting the part over the whole. Reduce the fraction if possible, then convert it to a decimal (remember: the line means divided by, so divide the numerator by the denominator) and change to a percent by multiplying by 100, moving the decimal point two places to the right.

Example: 4 is what percent of 80?

Solution: $\frac{4}{80} = \frac{1}{20} = .05 = 5\%$

Operations With Algebraic Expressions

Vocabulary

In addition, the numbers that are being added are called the *addends*. The solution to an addition problem is the *sum* or *total*.

There are several ways to express an addition problem such as 10 + 2:

the sum of 10 and 2	2 more than 10
the total of 10 and 2	2 greater than 10
2 added to 10	10 increased by 2

In subtraction, the number from which something is subtracted is the *minuend,* the number being subtracted is the *subtrahend,* and the answer is the *difference.*

In 25 − 22 = 3, the minuend is 25, the subtrahend is 22, and the difference is 3.

A subtraction problem such as 25 − 22 may be expressed as:

25 minus 22	from 25 take 22
25 less 22	25 decreased by 22
the difference of 25 and 22	22 less than 25
subtract 22 from 25	

In multiplication, the answer is called the *product* and the numbers being multiplied are the *factors* of the product.

In the multiplication 3 · 5 = 15 [which may also be written as 3(5) = 15 or (3)(5) = 15] all of the following expressions apply:

15 is the product of 3 and 5	15 is a multiple of 3
3 is a factor of 15	15 is a multiple of 5
5 is a factor of 15	

In division, the number being divided is the *dividend,* the number the dividend is divided by is the *divisor,* and the answer is the *quotient.* Any number left over in the division is the *remainder.*

In 12 ÷ 2 = 6, the dividend is 12, the divisor is 2, and the quotient is 6.

$$
\begin{array}{r}
7 \\
3\overline{)22} \\
\underline{21} \\
1
\end{array}
$$

In 3)22   22 is the dividend

         3 is the divisor

         1 is the remainder

The division problem $12 \div 2$ may be expressed as:

$$12 \text{ divided by } 2 \qquad 2 \text{ divided into } 12$$
$$\text{the quotient of } 12 \text{ and } 2$$

Because $12 \div 2 = 6$ with no remainder, 2 is called a *divisor* of 12, and 12 is said to be *divisible* by 2.

Properties

Addition is a *commutative* operation; this means that two numbers may be added in either order without changing their sum.

$$2 + 3 = 3 + 2$$
$$a + b = b + a$$

Multiplication is also commutative.

$$4 \cdot 5 = 5 \cdot 4$$
$$ab = ba$$

Subtraction and division problems are *not* commutative; changing the order within a subtraction or division problem may affect the answer.

$$10 - 6 \neq 6 - 10$$
$$8 \div 4 \neq 4 \div 8$$

Addition and multiplication are *associative;* that is, if a problem involves only addition or only multiplication, the parentheses may be changed without affecting the answer. Parentheses are grouping symbols that indicate work to be done first.

$$(5 + 6) + 7 = 5 + (6 + 7)$$
$$(2 \cdot 3) \cdot 4 = 2 \cdot (3 \cdot 4)$$
$$(a + b) + c = a + (b + c)$$
$$(ab)c = a(bc)$$

Subtraction and division are *not* associative. Work within parentheses *must* be performed first.

$$(8 - 5) - 2 \neq 8 - (5 - 2)$$
$$(80 \div 4) \div 2 \neq 80 \div (4 \div 2)$$

Multiplication is *distributive* over addition. If a sum is to be multiplied by a number, instead of adding first and then multiplying, each addend may be multiplied by the number and the products added.

$$5(6 + 3) = 5 \cdot 6 + 5 \cdot 3$$
$$a(b + c) = ab + ac$$

Multiplication is also distributive over subtraction.

$$8(10 - 6) = 8 \cdot 10 - 8 \cdot 6$$
$$a(b - c) = ab - ac$$

The distributive property may be used in both directions.

$$5a + 3a = (5 + 3)a = 8a$$
$$847 \cdot 94 + 847 \cdot 6 = 847(94 + 6) = 847(100) = 84{,}700$$

Signed Numbers

The number line exists to both sides of zero. Each positive number on the right of zero has a negative counterpart to the left of zero. The number line on the following page shows the location of some pairs of numbers $(+4, -4; +2, -2; +1, -1)$.

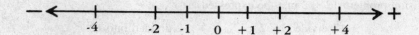

Because each number of a pair is located the same distance from zero (though in different directions), each has the same absolute value. Two vertical bars symbolize absolute value.

$$| +4 | = | -4 | = 4$$

The absolute value of +4 equals the absolute value of −4. Both are equivalent to 4. If you think of absolute value as distance from zero, regardless of direction, you will understand it easily. The absolute value of any number, positive or negative, is always expressed as a positive number.

Addition of signed numbers

When two oppositely signed numbers with the same absolute value are added, the sum is zero.

$$+10 + -10 = 0$$
$$-1.5 + +1.5 = 0$$
$$-.010 + +.010 = 0$$
$$+\tfrac{3}{4} + -\tfrac{3}{4} = 0$$

If one of the two oppositely signed numbers is larger in absolute value the sum is equal to the amount of that excess and carries the same sign as the number having the larger absolute value.

$$+2 + -1 = +1$$
$$+8 + -9 = -1$$
$$-2.5 + +2.0 = -.5$$
$$-\tfrac{3}{4} + +\tfrac{1}{2} = -\tfrac{1}{4}$$

Subtraction of signed numbers

Subtraction is the operation that finds the difference between two numbers, including the difference between signed numbers.

When subtracting signed numbers, it is helpful to refer to the number line.

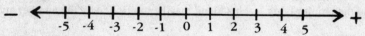

For example, if we wish to subtract +2 from +5, we can use the number line to see that the difference is +3. We give the sign to the difference that represents the direction we are moving along the number line, from the number being subtracted to the number from which you are subtracting. In this case, because we are subtracting +2 from +5, we count three units in a positive direction from +2 to +5 on the number line.

When subtracting signed numbers:

- The distance between the two numbers gives you the absolute value of the difference.
- The direction you have to move from the number being subtracted, to get to the number from which you are subtracting, gives you the sign of the difference.

Example: Subtract −3 from +5.

Solution: Distance on number line between −3 and +5 is 8 units. Direction is from negative to positive—a positive direction. Answer is +8.

Example: Subtract −6 from −8.

Solution: Distance on number line between −6 and −8 is 2 units. Direction is from −6 to −8—a negative direction. Answer is −2.

Example: Subtract $+1.30$ from -2.70.

Solution: Distance between them on the number line is 4.0. Direction is from $+1.30$ to -2.70—a negative direction. Answer is -4.0

A quick way to subtract signed numbers accurately involves placing the numbers in columns, reversing the sign of the number being subtracted, and then adding the two.

Example: Subtract $+26$ from $+15$.

Solution:

$$\begin{array}{r} +15 \\ -\ +26 \end{array} = \begin{array}{r} +15 \\ -26 \\ \hline -11 \end{array}$$

Example: Subtract -35 from $+10$.

Solution:

$$\begin{array}{r} +10 \\ -\ -35 \end{array} = \begin{array}{r} +10 \\ +35 \\ \hline +45 \end{array}$$

Notice that in each of the examples, the correct answer was found by reversing the sign of the number being subtracted and then adding.

Mutliplication of signed numbers

Signed numbers are mutliplied as any other numbers would be, with the following exceptions:

- The product of two negative numbers is positive.
- The product of two positive numbers is positive.
- The product of a negative and positive number is negative.

$$-3 \times -6 = +18$$
$$+3.05 \times +6 = +18.30$$
$$+4\tfrac{1}{2} \times -3 = -13\tfrac{1}{2}$$
$$+1 \times -1 \times +1 = -1$$

Division of signed numbers

As with multiplication, the division of signed numbers requires you to observe three simple rules:

- When dividing a positive number by a negative number, the result is negative.
- When dividing a negative number by a positive number, the result is negative.
- When dividing a negative number by a negative number, or a positive number by a positive number, the result is positive.

$$+6 \div -3 = -2$$
$$-6 \div +3 = -2$$
$$-6 \div -3 = +2$$
$$+6 \div +3 = +2$$

Equations, Problems, and Inequalities in Algebra

Equations

An *equation* states that two quantities are equal.

The solution to an equation is a number that can be substituted for the letter, or *variable*, to give a true statement.

In the equation $x + 7 = 10$, if 5 is substituted for x, the equation becomes $5 + 7 = 10$, which is false. If 3 is substituted for x, the equation becomes $3 + 7 = 10$, which is true. Therefore, $x = 3$ is a solution for the equation $x + 7 = 10$.

To *solve an equation* means to find all solutions for the variables.

An equation has been solved when it is transformed or rearranged so that a variable is isolated on one side of the equal sign and a number is on the other side.

There are two basic principles that are used to transform equations. The first principle is that the same quantity may be added to, or subtracted from, both sides of an equation.

Example: Solve the equation $x - 3 = 2$.

Solution: Add 3 to both sides:

$$\begin{array}{rr} x - 3 = & 2 \\ + 3 & + 3 \\ \hline x \quad = & 5 \end{array}$$

Adding 3 isolates x on one side and leaves a number on the other side. The solution to the equation is $x = 5$.

Example: Solve the equation $y + 4 = 10$.

Solution: Subtract 4 from both sides (adding -4 to both sides will have the same effect):

$$\begin{array}{rr} y + 4 = & 10 \\ - 4 & - 4 \\ \hline y \quad = & 6 \end{array}$$

The variable has been isolated on one side of the equation. The solution is $y = 6$.

The second basic principle is that both sides of an equation may be multiplied by, or divided by, the same quantity.

Example: Solve $2a = 12$.

Solution: Divide both sides by 2:

$$\frac{2a}{2} = \frac{12}{2}$$
$$a = 6$$

Example: Solve $\dfrac{b}{5} = 10$.

Solution: Multiply both sides by 5:

$$5 \cdot \frac{b}{5} = 10 \cdot 5$$
$$b = 50$$

To solve equations containing more than one operation, first eliminate any number that is being added to or subtracted from the variable. Then eliminate any number that is multiplying or dividing the variable.

Example: Solve

$$\begin{array}{rr} 3x - 6 = & 9 \\ + 6 & +6 \\ \hline 3x \quad = & 15 \end{array}$$

$$\frac{3x}{3} = \frac{15}{3}$$

$$x = 5$$

Solution:

Adding 6 eliminates -6.

Dividing by 3 eliminates the 3 which is multiplying the x.

The solution to the original equation is $x = 5$.

A variable term may be added to, or subtracted from, both sides of an equation. This is necessary when the variable appears on both sides of the original equation.

Example: Solve

$$6y + 9 = 2y + 1$$
$$-2y \quad\quad -2y$$

Solution:

Eliminate the y term from the right side by subtracting $2y$ from both sides.

$$\overline{4y + 9 = \quad + 1}$$
$$-9 \quad\quad -9$$

Eliminate 9 from the left side by subtracting 9 from both sides.

$$\overline{4y \quad = \quad -8}$$
$$\frac{4y}{4} \quad = \quad \frac{-8}{4}$$
$$y \quad\quad -2$$

Divide both sides by 4 to eliminate the multiplication by 4 and isolate the y.

It may be necessary to first *simplify* the expression on each side of an equation by removing parentheses or combining like terms.

Example: Solve

$$5z - 3(z - 2) = 8$$
$$5z - 3z + 6 = 8$$
$$2z + 6 = 8$$
$$-6 = -6$$
$$\frac{2z}{2} = \frac{2}{2}$$
$$z = 1$$

Solution:

Remove parentheses first.
Combine like terms.
Subtract 6 from both sides.

Divide by 2 to isolate the z.

To check the solution to any equation, replace the variable with the solution in the original equation, perform the indicated operations, and determine whether a true statement results.

Example: Earlier it was found that $x = 5$ is the solution for the equation $3x - 6 = 9$.

Solution: To check, substitute 5 for x in the equation:

$$(3 \cdot 5) - 6 = 9 \quad\quad \text{Perform the operations on the left side.}$$
$$15 - 6 = 9$$
$$9 = 9 \quad\quad \text{A true statement results; therefore the solution is correct.}$$

Solving problems

Many types of problems can be solved by using algebra. To solve a problem:

- Read it carefully. Determine what information is given and what information is unknown and must be found.
- Represent the *unknown* quantity with a letter.
- Write an equation that expresses the relationship given in the problem.
- Solve the equation.

Example: If 7 is added to twice a number, the result is 23. Find the number.

Solution: Let $x =$ the unknown number. Then write the equation:

$$7 + 2x = 23$$
$$-7 \quad\quad -7$$
$$\frac{2x}{2} = \frac{16}{2}$$
$$x = 8$$

Example: There are 6 more women than men in a group of 26 people. How many women are there?

Solution: Let m = the number of men. Then, $m + 6$ = the number of women.

$$(m + 6) + m = 26$$
$$m + 6 + m = 26 \quad \text{Remove parentheses.}$$
$$2m + 6 = 26 \quad \text{Combine like terms.}$$
$$\underline{- 6 \quad -6}$$
$$\frac{2m}{2} = \frac{20}{2}$$
$$m = 10$$
$$m + 6 = 16$$

Example: Josh is 3 years older than Norm. If the sum of their ages is 39, how old is Norm?

Solution: Let n = Norm's age. Then, $n + 3$ = Josh's age. The sum of their ages is 39.

$$n + (n + 3) = 39$$
$$n + n + 3 = 39$$
$$2n + 3 = 39$$
$$2n = 36$$
$$n = 18$$

Consecutive Integer Problems

Consecutive integers are integers that follow one another.

7, 8, 9, and 10 are consecutive integers.
$-5, -4, -3, -2$ and -1 are consecutive integers.

Consecutive integers may be represented in algebra as:
$$x, x + 1, x + 2, x + 3, \ldots$$

Example: Find three consecutive integers whose sum is 39.

Solution: Let x = first consecutive integer. Then, $x + 1$ = second consecutive integer, and $x + 2$ = third consecutive integer.

$$x + (x + 1) + (x + 2) = 39$$
$$x + x + 1 + x + 2 = 39$$
$$3x + 3 = 39$$
$$\underline{- 3 \quad -3}$$
$$\frac{3x}{3} = \frac{36}{3}$$
$$x = 12$$

The integers are 12, 13, and 14.

Consecutive even and consecutive odd integers are both represented as $x, x + 2, x + 4, x + 6, \ldots$

If x is even, then $x + 2, x + 4, x + 6, \ldots$ will all be even.
If x is odd, then $x + 2, x + 4, x + 6, \ldots$ will all be odd.

Example: Find four consecutive odd integers such that the sum of the largest and twice the smallest is 21.

Solution: Let $x, x + 2, x + 4$, and $x + 6$ be the four consecutive odd integers. Here, x is the smallest and $x + 6$ is the largest. The largest integer plus twice the smallest is 21.

$$x + 6 + 2x = 21$$
$$3x + 6 = 21$$
$$\underline{- 6 \quad -6}$$
$$\frac{3x}{3} = \frac{15}{3}$$
$$x = 5$$

The integers are 5, 7, 9, and 11.

Perimeter Problems

To solve a perimeter problem, express each side of the figure algebraically. The *perimeter* of the figure is equal to the sum of all of the sides.

Example: A rectangle has four sides. One side is the length, and the side next to it is the width. The opposite sides of a rectangle are equal. In a particular rectangle, the length is one less than twice the width. If the perimeter is 16, find the length and the width.

Solution:

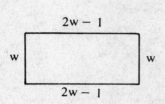

Let w = width

Then $2w - 1$ = length

The sum of the four sides is 16.

$$w + (2w - 1) + w + (2w - 1) = 16$$
$$w + 2w - 1 + w + 2w - 1 = 16$$
$$6w - 2 = 16$$
$$\underline{+2 \quad +2}$$
$$\frac{6w}{6} = \frac{18}{6}$$
$$w = 3$$
$$2w - 1 = 2(3) - 1 = 5$$

The width is 3 and the length is 5.

Ratio and Proportion Problems

A ratio is the quotient of two numbers. The ratio of 2 to 5 may be expressed $2 \div 5$, $\frac{2}{5}$, 2 is to 5, $2:5$, or algebraically as $2x:5x$.

The numbers in a ratio are called the *terms* of the ratio.

Example: Two numbers are in the ratio $3:4$. Their sum is 35. Find the numbers.

Solution:

Let $3x$ = the first number

$4x$ = the second number

Note that $\dfrac{3x}{4x} = \dfrac{3}{4} = 3:4$

The sum of the numbers is 35.

$$3x + 4x = 35$$
$$\frac{7x}{7} = \frac{35}{7}$$
$$x = 5$$
$$3x = 15$$
$$4x = 20$$

The numbers are 15 and 20.

A ratio involving more than two numbers may also be expressed algebraically. The ratio $2:3:7$ is equal to $2x:3x:7x$. The individual quantities in the ratio are $2x$, $3x$, and $7x$.

A *proportion* states that two ratios are equal.

In the proportion $a:b = c:d$ (which may also be written $\frac{a}{b} = \frac{c}{d}$), the inner terms, b and c, are called the *means;* the outer terms, a and d, are called the *extremes*.

In $3:6 = 5:10$, the means are 6 and 5; the extremes are 3 and 10.

In any proportion the product of the means equals the product of the extremes. $a:b = c:d \rightarrow bc = ad$.

$$3:6 = 5:10 \rightarrow \tfrac{3}{6} = \tfrac{5}{10} \rightarrow 6 (5) = 3(10)$$

In many problems, the quantities involved are in proportion. If three quantities are given in a problem and the fourth quantity is unknown, determine whether the quantities should form a proportion. The proportion will be the equation for the problem.

Example: A tree that is 20 feet tall casts a shadow 12 feet long. At the same time, a pole casts a shadow 3 feet long. How tall is the pole?

Solution: Let p = height of pole. The heights of objects and their shadows are in proportion.

$$\frac{\text{tree}}{\text{tree's shadow}} = \frac{\text{pole}}{\text{pole's shadow}}$$

$$\frac{20}{12} = \frac{p}{3}$$ The product of the means equals the

$$12p = 60$$ product of the extremes.

$$\frac{12p}{12} = \frac{60}{12}$$

$$p = 5$$

The pole is 5 feet tall.

Example: The scale on a map is 3 cm = 500 km. If two cities appear 15 cm apart on the map, how far apart are they actually?

Solution: Let d = actual distance. The quantities on maps and scale drawings are in proportion with the quantities they represent.

$$\frac{\text{first map distance}}{\text{first actual distance}} = \frac{\text{second map distance}}{\text{second actual distance}}$$

$$\frac{3 \text{ cm}}{500 \text{ km}} = \frac{15 \text{ cm}}{d \text{ km}}$$

$$3d = 7500$$

$$\frac{3d}{3} = \frac{7500}{3}$$ The product of the means equals the

         product of the extremes.

$$d = 2500$$

The cities are 2500 km apart.

Percent Problems

Percent problems may be solved algebraically by translating the relationship in the problem into an equation. The word ''of'' means multiplication, and ''is'' means equal to.

Example: 45% of what number is 27?

Solution: Let n = the unknown number. 45% of n is 27.

$$.45n = 27$$ Change the % to a decimal (45% = .45)

$$45n = 2700$$ Multiplying both sides by 100

$$\frac{45n}{45} = \frac{2700}{45}$$ eliminates the decimal.

$$n = 60$$

Example: Mr. Jones receives a salary raise from \$15,000 to \$16,200. Find the percent of increase.

Solution: Let p = percent. The increase is $16,200 - 15,000 = 1,200$. What percent of 15,000 is 1,200?

$$p \cdot 15,000 = 1,200$$

$$\frac{15000p}{15000} = \frac{1200}{15000}$$

$$p = .08$$

$$p = 8\%$$

Interest is the price paid for the use of money in loans, savings, and investments. Interest problems are solved using the formula $I = prt$, where:

I = interest
p = principal (amount of money bearing interest)
r = rate of interest, in %
t = time, in years

Example: How long must $2000 be invested at 6% to earn $240 in interest?

Solution:

Let t = time
I = $240
p = $2000
r = 6% or .06
$240 = 2000(.06)t$
$$\frac{240}{120} = \frac{120t}{120}$$
$2 = t$

The $2000 must be invested for 2 years.

A *discount* is a percent that is deducted from a marked price. The marked price is considered to be 100% of itself. If an item is discounted 20%, its selling price is 100% − 20%, or 80%, of its marked price.

Example: A radio is tagged with a sale price of $42.50, which is 15% off the regular price. What is the regular price?

Solution: Let r = regular price. The sale price is 100% − 15%, or 85%, of the regular price. 85% of r = $42.50

$.85r = \$42.50$
$$\frac{85r}{85} = \frac{4250}{85}$$ Multiply by 100 to eliminate the decimals.
$r = 50$

The regular price was $50.

If two discounts are given in a problem, an intermediate price is computed by taking the first discount on the marked price. The second discount is then computed on the intermediate price.

Example: An appliance company gives a 15% discount for purchases made during a sale, and an additional 5% discount if payment is made in cash. What will the price of an $800 refrigerator be if both discounts are taken?

Solution: First discount: 100% − 15% = 85%.

After the first discount, the refrigerator will cost:

85% of $800 = .85($800)
= $680

The intermediate price is $680.

Second discount: 100% − 5% = 95%.

After the second discount, the refrigerator will cost:

95% of $680 = .95($680)
= $646

The final price will be $646.

Profit is the amount of money added to the dealer's cost of an item to find the selling price. The cost price is considered 100% of itself. If the profit is 20% of the cost, the selling price must be 100% + 20%, or 120% of the cost.

Example: A furniture dealer sells a sofa at $870, which represents a 45% profit over the cost. What was the cost to the dealer?

Solution: Let c = cost price. 100% + 45% = 145%. The selling price is 145% of the cost.

$$145\% \text{ of } c = \$870$$
$$1.45c = 870$$
$$\frac{145c}{145} = \frac{87000}{145}$$
$$c = 600$$

The sofa cost the dealer $600.

If an article is sold at a *loss,* the amount of the loss is deducted from the cost price to find the selling price. An article that is sold at a 25% loss has a selling price of 100% − 25%, or 75%, of the cost price.

Example: Mr. Charles bought a car for $8000. After a while he sold it to Mr. David at a 30% loss. What did Mr. David pay for the car?

Solution: The car was sold for 100% − 30%, or 70%, of its cost price.

$$70\% \text{ of } \$8000 = .70(\$8000)$$
$$= \$5600$$

Mr. David paid $5600 for the car.

Tax is computed by finding a percent of a base amount.

Example: A homeowner pays $2500 in school taxes. What is the assessed value of her property if school taxes are 3.2% of the assessed value?

Solution: Let v = assessed value.

$$3.2\% \text{ of } v = 2500$$
$$.032v = 2500$$
$$\frac{32v}{32} = \frac{2500000}{32} \quad \text{(Multiply by 1000 to eliminate decimals)}$$
$$v = 78125$$

The value of the property is $78,125.

Distance problems and work problems

Two kinds of word problems that you may encounter on the PPST that can also be solved with algebra are *rate, time, and distance problems* and *work problems*.

Rate, Time, and Distance Problems

The basic formula used in solving problems for distance is:

$$d = rt \text{ (distance = rate} \times \text{time)}$$

Use this form when you know rate (speed) and time.

To find rate, use:

$$r = \frac{d}{t} \quad \text{(rate = distance} \div \text{time)}$$

To find time, use:

$$t = \frac{d}{r} \quad \text{(time = distance} \div \text{rate)}$$

Study the following problems:

Example: Two hikers start walking from the city line at different times. The second hiker, whose speed is 4 miles per hour, starts 2 hours after the first hiker, whose speed is 3 miles per hour. Determine the amount of time and distance that will be consumed before the second hiker catches up with the first.

Solution 1: Since the first hiker has a 2-hour head start and is walking at the rate of 3 miles per hour, he is 6 miles from the city line when the second hiker starts.

$$\text{Rate} \times \text{Time} = \text{Distance}$$

Subtracting 3 miles per hour from 4 miles per hour gives us 1 mile per hour, or the difference in the rates of speed of the two hikers. In other words, the second hiker gains one mile on the first hiker every hour.

Since there is a 6-mile difference to cut down and it is cut down one mile every hour, it is clear that the second hiker will need 6 hours to overtake his companion.

In this time, he will have traveled $4 \times 6 = 24$ miles. The first hiker will have been walking 8 hours, since he had a 2-hour head start, $8 \times 3 = 24$ miles.

or

Solution 2: One excellent way to solve distance (or mixture) problems is to organize all of the data in a chart. For distance problems, make columns for Rate, Time, and Distance, and separate lines for each moving object. In the problem about the two hikers, the chart technique works like this:

Step 1: Draw the chart.

$$\text{Rate} \times \text{Time} = \text{Distance}$$

	Rate	Time	Distance
Hiker 1			
Hiker 2			

Step 2: Since the problem states that Hiker 1 is traveling at 3 miles per hour and Hiker 2 is traveling at 4 miles per hour, enter these two figures in the Rate column.

$$\text{Rate} \times \text{Time} = \text{Distance}$$

	Rate	Time	Distance
Hiker 1	3 mph		
Hiker 2	4 mph		

Step 3: The problem does not tell us how long each hiker traveled, but it does say that Hiker 1 started 2 hours before Hiker 2. Therefore, if we use the unknown "x" to represent the number of hours Hiker 2 traveled, we can set Hiker 1's time as $x + 2$. Enter these two figures in the Time column.

$$\text{Rate} \times \text{Time} = \text{Distance}$$

	Rate	Time	Distance
Hiker 1	3 mph	$x + 2$	
Hiker 2	4 mph	x	

Step 4: Using the formula $D = R \times T$, we can easily find each hiker's distance by multiplying the figures for rate and time already in the chart.

For Hiker 1: $3(x + 2) = 3x + 6$
For Hiker 2: $4(x) = 4x$

$$\text{Rate} \times \text{Time} = \text{Distance}$$

	Rate	Time	Distance
Hiker 1	3 mph	$x + 2$	$3x + 6$
Hiker 2	4 mph	x	$4x$

Step 5: When the two hikers meet, each will have covered the same distance. Using this information, we can set up an equation:

$$\begin{array}{ccc} \text{Distance covered} & & \text{Distance covered} \\ \text{by Hiker 1} & & \text{by Hiker 2} \\ 3x + 6 & = & 4x \end{array}$$

Solving this equation for x, we find that $x = 6$. This means that Hiker 2 has walked for $6 + 2 = 8$ hours when Hiker 2 catches up to him.

Step 6: Since Hiker 1 started 2 hours earlier than Hiker 2, he will have walked for 6 hours to catch up to Hiker 1.

Step 7: Using this information, we can determine that Hiker 1 walked 8 hours at 3 miles per hour to cover 24 miles. Hiker 2 walked for 6 hours at 4 miles per hour to cover the same 24 miles.

Example: The same two hikers start walking toward each other along a road connecting two cities that are 60 miles apart. Their speeds are the same as in the preceding example, 3 and 4 miles per hour respectively. How much time will elapse before they meet?

Solution 1: In each hour of travel toward each other, the hikers will cut down a distance equal to the sum of their speeds, $3 + 4 = 7$ miles per hour. To meet they must cut down 60 miles, and at 7 miles per hour this would be:

$$\frac{D}{R} = T \frac{60}{7} = 8\frac{4}{7} \text{ hours}$$

or

Solution 2: In this problem we know that the distance traveled by Hiker 1 plus the distance traveled by Hiker 2 equals 60 miles, and that the two hikers will have been traveling for the same length of time when they meet. Therefore, we set up an equation to represent this information and solve for x to find the time that will have elapsed before the two hikers meet:

$$3x + 4x = 60$$
$$7x = 60$$
$$x = 8\frac{4}{7} \text{ hours}$$

The problem might also have asked:"How much distance must the slower hiker cover before the two hikers meet?" In such a case, we go through the same steps plus one additional step: The time consumed before meeting was $8\frac{4}{7}$ hours. To find the distance covered by the slower hiker, we merely multiply his rate by the time elapsed.

$$R \times T = D \qquad 3 \times 8\frac{4}{7} = 25\frac{5}{7}$$

Work Problems

Work problems generally involve two or more workers doing a job at different rates. The aim of work problems is to predict how long it will take to complete a job if the number of workers is increased or decreased. Work problems may also involve determining how fast pipes can fill or empty tanks. In solving pipe and tank problems, you must think of the pipes as workers.

In most work problems, a job is broken up into several parts, each representing a fractional portion of the entire job. For each part represented, the numerator should represent the time actually spent working, while the denominator should represent the total time needed for the worker to do the job alone. The sum of all the individual fractions must be 1 if the job is completed. The easiest way to understand this procedure is to carefully study the examples that follow. By following the step-by-step solutions, you will learn how to make your own fractions to solve the practice problems that follow the problems you may find on the Mathematics Test.

Example: If A does a job in six days, and B does the same job in three days, how long will it take the two of them, working together, to do the job?

Solution:

Step 1:   Write the fractions as follows.

$$\frac{\text{Time actually spent}}{\substack{\text{Time needed to do}\\ \text{entire job alone}}} \qquad \overset{A}{\frac{x}{6 \text{ days}}} + \overset{B}{\frac{x}{3 \text{ days}}} = 1$$

The variable x represents the amount of time each worker will work when both work together. 1 represents the completed job.

Step 2:   Multiply all the terms by the same number (in this case 6) in order to clear the fractions so as to work with whole numbers.

$$x + 2x = 6$$

Step 3:   Solve for x.

$$3x = 6$$
$$x = 2 \text{ days}$$

Working together, A and B will get the job done in 2 days.

Example: A and B, working together, do a job in $4\frac{1}{2}$ days. B, working alone, is able to do the job in 10 days. How long would it take A to do the job working alone?

Solution:

Step 1:   Write the fractions as follows.

$$\frac{\text{Time actually spent}}{\substack{\text{Time needed to do}\\ \text{entire job alone}}} \qquad \overset{A}{\frac{4.5 \text{ days}}{x}} + \overset{B}{\frac{4.5 \text{ days}}{10 \text{ days}}} = 1$$

Step 2:   Multiply all the terms by $10x$ to clear the fractions.

$$45 + 4.5x = 10x$$

Step 3:   Solve for x.

$$45 = 5.5x$$
$$x = 8.18 \text{ or } 8\frac{2}{11} \text{ days}$$

It would take A nearly $8\frac{1}{4}$ days to do the job alone.

Example: If A can do a job in 6 days that B can do in 5 days, and C can do in 3 days, how long would the job take if A, B, and C were working together?

Solution:

Step 1:   This example is very similar to the first one. The number of workers is greater, but the procedure is the same. First write the fractions as follows.

$$\frac{\text{Time actually spent}}{\substack{\text{Time needed to do}\\ \text{entire job alone}}} \qquad \overset{A}{\frac{x}{6 \text{ days}}} + \overset{B}{\frac{x}{5 \text{ days}}} + \overset{C}{\frac{x}{3 \text{ days}}} = 1$$

Remember that 1 represents the completed job regardless of the number of days involved.

Step 2: Multiply all terms by 30 to clear the fractions.

$$5x + 6x + 10x = 30$$

Step 3: Solve for x.

$$21x = 30$$
$$x = 1.428 \text{ days}$$

A, B, and C all working together at their usual rates would get the job done in about $1\frac{1}{2}$ days.

Example: One pipe can fill a pool in 20 minutes, a second pipe can fill the pool in 30 minutes, and a third pipe can fill it in 10 minutes. How long would it take the three pipes together to fill the pool?

Solution:

Step 1: Treat the pipes as workers and write the fractions as follows.

$$\frac{\text{Time actually spent}}{\substack{\text{Time needed to do} \\ \text{entire job alone}}} \quad \overset{\text{A}}{\frac{x}{20 \text{ mins.}}} + \overset{\text{B}}{\frac{x}{30 \text{ mins.}}} + \overset{\text{C}}{\frac{x}{10 \text{ mins}}} = 1$$

Step 2: Multiply all terms by 60 to clear the fractions.

$$3x + 2x + 6x = 60$$

Step 3: Solve for x.

$$11x = 60$$
$$x = 5\frac{5}{11} \text{ minutes}$$

If the water flows from all three pipes at once, the pool will be filled in $5\frac{5}{11}$ minutes.

Inequalities

The = symbol indicates the relationship between two equal quantities. The symbols used to indicate other relationships between two quantities are:

$\neq$ not equal to
$>$ greater than
$<$ less than
$\geq$ greater than or equal to
$\leq$ less than or equal to

A number is *greater* than any number appearing to its left on the number line. A number is *less* than any number appearing to its right on the number line.

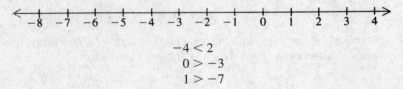

$$-4 < 2$$
$$0 > -3$$
$$1 > -7$$

An *inequality* states that one quantity is greater than, or less than, another quantity.

Inequalities are solved in the same way as equations, except that in multiplying or dividing both sides of an inequality by a negative quantity, the inequality symbol is reversed.

Example: Solve for x:

Solution:

$$3x - 4 > 11$$
$$\underline{+4 \quad +4}$$

Add 4 to both sides.

$$\frac{3x}{3} > \frac{15}{3}$$

Divide both sides by 3. Since 3 is positive, the inequality symbol remains the same.

$$x > 5$$

The solution $x > 5$ means that all numbers greater than 5 are solutions to the inequality.

Example: Solve for y:

Solution:

$$2y + 3 > 7y - 2$$
$$\underline{-7y \qquad -7y}$$

Subtract $7y$ from both sides.

$$-5y + 3 > -2$$
$$\underline{-3 \qquad -3}$$

Subtract 3 from both sides.

$$-5y > -5$$
$$y < 1$$

Divide both sides by -5. When dividing both sides by a negative number, reverse the inequality symbol.

Exponents

It is frequently beneficial to use shorthand methods of writing numbers in mathematics. One of the most common is the use of *exponents*.

An exponent is a number that tells you how many times the number it refers to (called the *base*) is used as a factor in a given calculation.

$$10^3 \longleftarrow \text{exponent}$$
$$ \longleftarrow \text{base}$$

10^3 is a shorthand way of writing $10 \cdot 10 \cdot 10$, or $1,000$. Note that the exponent is written to the right and above the base, and, to avoid confusion, the numeral is smaller in size.

Exponents are most useful in certain scientific realms where very large or very small numbers are involved. For example, it is much easier to write 10^9 rather than $1,000,000,000$.

Geometry is another subject that has frequent use for exponents. Area and surface area are measured in *square* units such as square feet, square inches, and so forth. Volume is measured in cubic feet, cubic inches, or in other *cubic* units.

For example, the area of a floor might be 200 square feet. Using an exponent, we can write 200 ft.^{2}. The volume of a cube might be 8 cubic feet. We can write this as 8 ft.^{3}.

The exponent "2" is read "square" or "squared." The exponent "3" is read "cube" or "cubed."

For exponents other than 2 and 3, we use the phrase "to the —— power." For example, 5^6 would be read "five to the sixth power."

When the exponent is not written, as when we write most numbers, the exponent is understood to be equal to 1. Any number to the first power is equivalent to itself.

For example, $10 = 10^1$. We do not write 1 as an exponent.

There are two major rules to help you calculate numbers written in exponential form. Both require that the bases of the numbers be the same.

The *first rule* involves **multiplying numbers in exponential form having the same base.** In such instances, the product may be found by adding the exponents.

Example: Multiply 10^3 by 10^5.

Solution: $10^3 \cdot 10^5 = 10^{3+5} = 10^8$

Example: Multiply 2^3 by 2^4.

Solution: $2^3 \cdot 2^4 = 2^{3+4} = 2^7$

Example: Multiply x^2 by x^3.

Solution: $x^2 \cdot x^3 = x^{2+3} = x^5$

Example: Multiply 3^3 by 3.

Solution: $3^3 \cdot 3 = 3^{3+1} = 3^4$

It is very important to note that the bases were equal in each of the preceding problems. The exponents may be different.

The *second rule* involves **division of numbers in exponential form having the same base.** In finding the product of numbers in exponential form, we added the exponents. To find their quotient, we subtract the exponent of the divisor from that of the dividend.

Example: Divide 10^3 by 10^2.

Solution: $10^3 \div 10^2 = 10^{3-2} = 10^1 = 10$

Example: Divide 5^6 by 5^3.

Solution: $5^6 \div 5^3 = 5^{6-3} = 5^3$

Example: Divide x^4 by x^2.

Solution: $x^4 \div x^2 = x^{4-2} = x^2$

Example: Divide a^3 by a.

Solution: $a^3 \div a^{3-1} = a^2$

For each of the preceding examples, you may wish to calculate the problem the long way to prove to yourself that it works.

Squares and Square Roots

Squares

The product of a number times itself is called the *square* of that number. For example, 9 is the square of 3; 16 is the square of 4; and 25 is the square of 5. Any number we work with has a square; we simply multiply the number by itself to find it.

Examples: Find the squares of the following numbers:

a) 15   c) $\frac{3}{4}$ e) 125

b) 3.22   d) .01   f) $\frac{7}{6}$

Solutions:

a) $15 \times 15 = 225$s   d) $.01 \times .01 = .0001$

b) $3.22 \times 3.22 = 10.3684$ e) $125 \times 125 = 15,625$

c) $\frac{3}{4} \times \frac{3}{4} = \frac{9}{16}$ f) $\frac{7}{6} \times \frac{7}{6} = \frac{49}{36}$ or $1\frac{13}{36}$

The word *square* is also used to name the process used to find the product of a number times itself. To *square a number* means to multiply it by itself. Special notation is used when working with squares. Rather than write $15 \times 15 = 225$, we use an exponent, $15^2 = 225$.

You will find that test makers and mathematics textbook writers rely on easily recognized squares in many problems. For this reason we think it is very important that you learn to recognize certain common numbers as squares of other numbers.

The table on page 49 lists numbers and their squares. Note that once you learn the link between a number and its square, you can apply that knowledge regardless of where the decimal point is located. For example, if you know that $15^2 = 225$, you also know that $1.5^2 = 2.25$, and $.15^2 = .0225$, and $150^2 = 22,500$.

Study the table carefully. It is a good idea to memorize the squares of the numbers 1 through 25, 30, 40, 50, 60, 70, 80, 90, and 100, though you should not spend a great deal of time on it. The important thing is to understand the relationships in the table and to link in your mind a whole number with its square.

Square roots

Every number that is a square has a *square root*. The number multiplied by itself to find the square is the *square root* of the square.

For example, 15 is the square root of 225, 1.5 is the square root of 2.25, and .15 is the square root of .0225.

A special notation called a *radical* ($\sqrt{}$) is used when working with square roots. For example, $\sqrt{9} = 3$ is read: "The square root of nine equals three." The radical over the number nine is read "square root of."

If you are asked to find the square root of a fraction, simply consider the numerator and denominator as separate numbers, and find the square root of each.

Example: Find: $\sqrt{\frac{9}{16}}$

Solution: $\frac{\sqrt{9}}{\sqrt{16}} = \frac{3}{4}$. The square root of $\frac{9}{16}$ is $\frac{3}{4}$.

Check: $(\frac{3}{4})^2 = \frac{3}{4} \cdot \frac{3}{4} = \frac{9}{16}$

Related numbers and their squares

WHOLE NUMBER	SQUARE		
1	1	$.1^2 = .01$	$10^2 = 100$
2	4	$.2^2 = .04$	$20^2 = 400$
3	9	$.3^2 = .09$	$30^2 = 900$
4	16	$.4^2 = .16$	$40^2 = 1600$
5	25	$.5^2 = .25$	$50^2 = 2500$
6	36	$.6^2 = .36$	$60^2 = 3600$
7	49	$.7^2 = .49$	$70^2 = 4900$
8	64	$.8^2 = .64$	$80^2 = 6400$
9	81	$.9^2 = .81$	$90^2 = 8100$
10	100	$1.0^2 = 1$	$100^2 = 10,000$
11	121	$1.1^2 = 1.21$	$110^2 = 12,100$
12	144	$1.2^2 = 1.44$	$120^2 = 14,400$
13	169	$1.3^2 = 1.69$	$130^2 = 16,900$
14	196	$1.4^2 = 1.96$	$140^2 = 19,600$
15	225	$1.5^2 = 2.25$	$150^2 = 22,500$
16	256	$1.6^2 = 2.56$	$160^2 = 25,600$
17	289	$1.7^2 = 2.89$	$170^2 = 28,900$
18	324	$1.8^2 = 3.24$	$180^2 = 32,400$
19	361	$1.9^2 = 3.61$	$190^2 = 36,100$
21	441	$2.1^2 = 4.41$	$210^2 = 44,100$
22	484	$2.2^2 = 4.84$	$220^2 = 48,400$
23	529	$2.3^2 = 5.29$	$230^2 = 52,900$
24	576	$2.4^2 = 5.76$	$240^2 = 57,600$
25	625	$2.5^2 = 6.25$	$250^2 = 62,500$

You can refer to the table to find the square roots of some commonly used numbers.

Summary of Kinds of Numbers

The numbers that have been used in this review are called *real numbers* and may be grouped into special categories.

The *natural* numbers, or counting numbers, are:

$$1, 2, 3, 4, 5, 6, 7, 8, 9, 10, 11, 12, \ldots$$

A natural number (other than 1) is a *prime* number if it can be exactly divided only by itself and 1. If a natural number has other divisors it is a *composite* number. The numbers 2, 3, 5, 7, and 11 are prime numbers, while 4, 6, 8, 9, and 12 are composites.

The *whole* numbers consist of 0 and the natural numbers:

$$0, 1, 2, 3, \ldots$$

The *integers* consist of the natural numbers, the negatives of the natural numbers, and zero:

$$\ldots -3, -2, -1, 0, 1, 2, 3, 4, \ldots$$

Even integers are exactly divisible by 2:

$$\ldots -6, -4, -2, 0, 2, 4, 6, 8, \ldots$$

Odd integers are not exactly divisible by 2:

$$\ldots -5, -3, -1, 1, 3, 5, 7, 9, \ldots$$

The *rational* numbers are numbers that can be expressed as the quotient of two integers (excluding division by 0). Rational numbers include integers, fractions, terminating decimals (such as 1.5 or .293), and repeating decimals (such as .333 . . . or .74867676767 . . .).

The *irrational* numbers cannot be expressed as the quotient of two integers, but can be written as nonterminating, nonrepeating decimals. The numbers $\sqrt{2}$ and π are irrational.

Statistics and Probability

Statistics

The *averages* used in statistics include the *arithmetic mean*, the *median*, and the *mode*.

The most commonly used average of a group of numbers is the *arithmetic mean*. It is found by adding the numbers given and then dividing this sum by the number of items being averaged.

Example: Find the arithmetic mean of 2, 8, 5, 9, 6, and 12.

Solution: There are 6 numbers.

$$\text{Arithmetic mean} = \frac{2 + 8 + 5 + 9 + 6 + 12}{6}$$
$$= \frac{42}{6}$$
$$= 7$$

If a problem calls for simply the "average" or the "mean," it is referring to the arithmetic mean.

If a group of numbers is arranged in order, the middle number is called the *median*. If there is no single middle number (this occurs when there is an even number of items), the median is found by computing the arithmetic mean of the two middle numbers.

Example: The median of 6, 8, 10, 12, and 14 is 10.

Example: The median of 6, 8, 10, 12, 14, and 16 is the arithmetic mean of 10 and 12.

$$\frac{10 + 12}{2} = \frac{22}{2} = 11.$$

The *mode* of a group of numbers is the number that appears most often.

Example: The mode of 10, 5, 7, 9, 12, 5, 10, 5, and 9 is 5.

To obtain the arithmetic mean of quantities that are *weighted:*

- Set up a table listing the quantities, their respective weights, and their respective values.
- Multiply the value of each quantity by its respective weight.
- Add up these products.
- Add up the weights.
- Divide the sum of the products by the sum of the weights.

Example: Assume that the weights for the following subjects are: English 3, History 2, Mathematics 2, Foreign Languages 2, and Art 1. What would be the average of a student whose marks are: English 80, History 85, Algebra 84, Spanish 82, and Art 90?

Solution:

Subject	Weight	Mark
English	3	80
History	2	85
Algebra	2	84
Spanish	2	82
Art	1	90

English	$3 \times 80 =$	240
History	$2 \times 85 =$	170
Algebra	$2 \times 84 =$	168
Spanish	$2 \times 82 =$	164
Art	$1 \times 90 =$	90
		832

Sum of the weights: $3 + 2 + 2 + 2 + 1 = 10$

$$832 \div 10 = 83.2$$

Probability

The study of probability deals with predicting the outcome of chance events; that is, events in which one has no control over the results. Tossing a coin, rolling dice, and drawing concealed objects from a bag are chance events.

The probability of a particular outcome is equal to the number of ways that outcome can occur, divided by the total number of possible outcomes. In tossing a coin, there are 2 possible outcomes: heads or tails. The probability that the coin will turn up heads is $1 \div 2$ or $\frac{1}{2}$. If a bag contains 5 balls of which 3 are red, the probability of drawing a red ball is $\frac{3}{5}$. The probability of drawing a non-red ball is $\frac{2}{5}$.

If an event is certain, its probability is 1. If a bag contains only red balls, the probability of drawing a red ball is 1.

If an event is impossible, its probability is 0. If a bag contains only red balls, the probability of drawing a green ball is 0.

Probability may be expressed in fractional, decimal, or percent form. An event having a probability of $\frac{1}{2}$ is said to be 50% probable.

A probability determined by random sampling of a group of items is assumed to apply to other items in that group and in other similar groups.

Example: A random sampling of 100 items produced in a factory shows that 7 are defective. How many items of the total production of 50,000 can be expected to be defective?

Solution: The probability of an item being defective is $\frac{7}{100}$, or 7%. Of the total production, 7% can be expected to be defective.

$$7\% \times 50{,}000 = .07 \times 50{,}000 = 3500$$

Sequences

A *sequence* is a list of numbers based on a certain pattern. There are three main types of sequences: If each term in a sequence is being increased or diminished by the same number to form the next term, then it is an *arithmetic sequence*. The number being added or subtracted is called the *common difference*.

2, 4, 6, 8, 10 . . . is an arithmetic sequence in which the common difference is 2.
14, 11, 8, 5, 2 . . . is an arithmetic sequence in which the common difference is 3.

If each term of a sequence is being multiplied by the same number to form the next term, then it is a *geometric sequence*. The number multiplying each term is called the *common ratio*.

2, 6, 18, 54 . . . is a geometric sequence in which the common ratio is 3.
64, 16, 4, 1 . . . is a geometric sequence in which the common ratio is $\frac{1}{4}$.

If the sequence is neither arithmetic nor geometric, it is a *miscellaneous sequence*. Such a sequence may have each term a square or a cube, or the difference may be squares or cubes; or there may be a varied pattern in the sequence that must be determined.

A sequence may be ascending, that is, the numbers increase; or descending, that is, the numbers decrease.

To determine whether the sequence is arithmetic:

- If the sequence is ascending, subtract the first term from the second, and the second term from the third. If the difference is the same in both cases, the sequence is arithmetic.
- If the sequence is descending, subtract the second term from the first, and the third term from the second. If the difference is the same in both cases, the sequence is arithmetic.

To determine whether the sequence is geometric, divide the second term by the first, and the third term by the second. If the ratio is the same in both cases, the sequence is geometric.

To find a missing term in an arithmetic sequence that is ascending:

- Subtract any term from the one following it to find the common difference.
- Add the common difference to the term preceding the missing term.
- If the missing term is the first term, it may be found by subtracting the common difference from the second term.

Example: What number follows $16\frac{1}{3}$ in this sequence:

$$3, \, 6\frac{1}{3}, \, 9\frac{2}{3}, \, 13, \, 16\frac{1}{3}. \, . \, .$$

Solution: $6\frac{1}{3} - 3 = 3\frac{1}{3}, \, 9\frac{2}{3} - 6\frac{1}{3} = 3\frac{1}{3}$

The sequence is arithmetic; the common difference is $3\frac{1}{3}$.

$$16\frac{1}{3} + 3\frac{1}{3} = 19\frac{2}{3}$$

The missing term, which is the term following $16\frac{1}{3}$, is $19\frac{2}{3}$.

To find a missing term in an arithmetic sequence that is descending:

- Subtract any term from the one preceding it to find the common difference.
- Subtract the common difference from the term preceding the missing term.
- If the missing term is the first term, it may be found by adding the common difference to the second term.

Example: Find the first term in the sequence:

$$-, \ 16, \ 13\tfrac{1}{2}, \ 11, \ 8\tfrac{1}{2}, \ 6 \ldots$$

Solution: $16 - 13\tfrac{1}{2} = 2\tfrac{1}{2}, \ 13\tfrac{1}{2} - 11 = 2\tfrac{1}{2}$

The sequence is arithmetic; the common difference is $2\tfrac{1}{2}$.

$$16 + 2\tfrac{1}{2} = 18\tfrac{1}{2}$$

The term preceding 16 is $18\tfrac{1}{2}$

To find a missing term in a geometric sequence:

- Divide any term by the one preceding it to find the common ratio.
- Multiply the term preceding the missing term by the common ratio.
- If the missing term is the first term, it may be found by dividing the second term by the common ratio.

Example: Find the missing term in the sequence:

$$2, \ 6, \ 18, \ 54, \ -$$

Solution: $6 \div 2 = 3, \ 18 \div 6 = 3$

The sequence is geometric; the common ratio is 3.

$$54 \times 3 = 162$$

The missing term is 162.

Example: Find the missing term in the sequence:

$$-, \ 32, \ 16, \ 8, \ 4, \ 2$$

Solution: $16 \div 32 = \tfrac{1}{2}$ (common ratio)

$$32 \div \tfrac{1}{2} = 32 \times \tfrac{2}{1}$$
$$= 64$$

The first term is 64.

If, after trial, a sequence is neither arithmetic nor geometric, it must be one of a miscellaneous type. Test to see whether it is a sequence of squares or cubes or whether the difference is the square or the cube of the same number; or the same number may be first squared, then cubed, etc.

Geometry

Geometry is that part of mathematics that studies lines, curves, and angles and the various shapes they create when put together in different ways. Usually, geometry is divided into two subgroups: *plane geometry* and *solid geometry*.

Plane geometry studies any shapes and angles that can be drawn in one plane. This means that shapes that can be measured in only one or two dimensions, or directions, are studied. For example:

- A line has only one dimension, its length.
- A triangle, a square, or a circle drawn on a piece of paper can be measured in only two directions, or dimensions: length and width.

Solid geometry studies shapes that have three dimensions: length, width, and thickness. For example:

- An object such as a brick or a shoebox is a rectangular solid that can be measured in three directions or dimensions.

- Cubes, cones, spheres, cylinders, pyramids, or tetrahedrons are examples of shapes that are three dimensional and as such require the use of the principles of solid geometry.

First we will review some basics of plane geometry.

Points, lines, and angles

A *point* is an exact location and has no dimensions.

By placing lots of points in a row, we build a *line*. A line has infinite length in both directions, and has a symbol like this:

The arrowhead at each end indicates that the line is infinite. Usually, we select two points on the line, give them names, and name the line the same way:

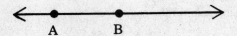

Note that we need a minimum of two points to make a line. There is no *maximum* number of points on a line, however.

A *ray* is a line that has one end point, and goes infinitely in one direction. We refer to a ray by its end point and one other point along it.

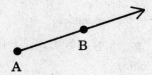

A *line segment* is a piece of a line having two end points. We name it by naming the end points:

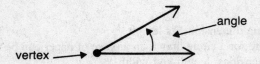

read: "line segment AB"

Because their length is infinite, lines and rays cannot be measured. Line segments, on the other hand, are finite and *can* be measured.

Angles

Where lines, line segments, or rays meet or cross each other, *angles* are formed. The simplest angle is that formed by two rays having the same end point but going in different directions. The end point that these two rays share is called the *vertex* of the angle.

angle

vertex

Angles are measured in units called *degrees*. A degree is $\frac{1}{360}$ of a complete revolution around the point called the vertex.

For example, the drawings below show one ray of an angle going through one complete revolution around the vertex. In each case, the measure of the angle is shown.

a.

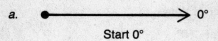

Start 0°

e.

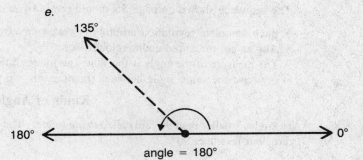

angle = 180°

b.

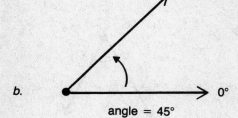

angle = 45°

f.

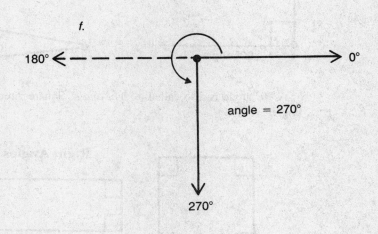

angle = 270°

c.

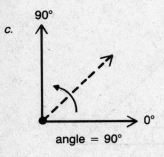

angle = 90°

d.

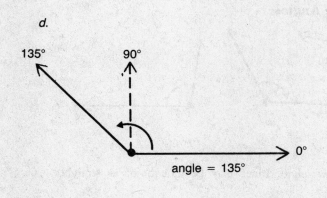

angle = 135°

g.

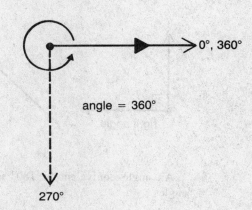

angle = 360°

The sequence shown on page 55 should remind you of a number of things:

- Each complete revolution around the vertex creates an angle of 360°.
- Angles are measured counterclockwise.
- The measure of the angle is the same, no matter how long the rays are. The tips of each ray have the same angle between them, as do two points closer to the vertex.

Kinds of Angles

Angles smaller than 90° are called *acute angles*. The measure of an acute angle is greater than zero, but less than 90°.

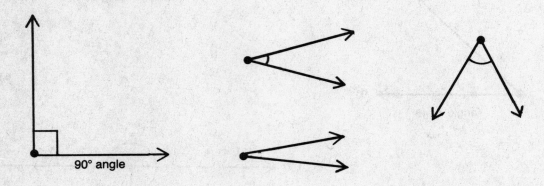

A 90° angle is also called a *right angle*. Squares, rectangles, and some triangles have right angles.

Right Angles

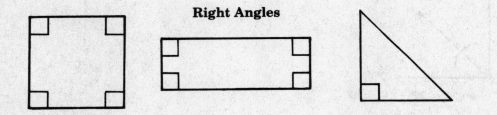

An angle measured greater than 90° but less than 180° is called an *obtuse angle*.

Obtuse Angles

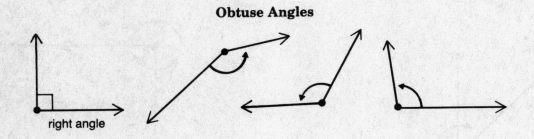

An angle equivalent to 180° is a *straight angle*. Lines may be thought of as straight angles.

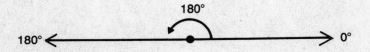

Angles whose sum is 180° are *supplementary angles*. For example, the sum of 60° and 120° is 180°. Each angle is a supplement of the other.

A line intersecting a straight angle cuts it into supplementary angles.

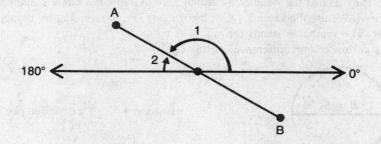

Angle 1 and angle 2 are supplementary angles.

Angles whose sum is 90° are *complementary angles*. For example, the sum of 60° and 30° is 90°. Each angle is a complement of the other.

Perimeter

The *perimeter* of an object is the distance around it. For example, if you walked all the way around the "outside" of a football field, a track, or a building, you would have walked along its perimeter.

Perimeters are usually easy to compute. We simply add up the lengths of the sides.

Example: What is the perimeter of the object below?

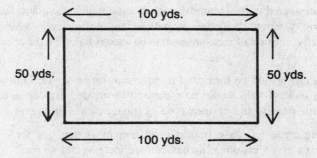

Solution: Just add the length of each side:

$$
\begin{array}{r}
100 \text{ yards} \\
100 \text{ yards} \\
50 \text{ yards} \\
+\ 50 \text{ yards} \\
\hline
300 \text{ yards} = \text{perimeter}
\end{array}
$$

Frequently, objects are much more irregular than the one shown above. For an object such as the one below, for example, you must find the length of each small segment of the perimeter. Then add the lengths together to find the perimeter.

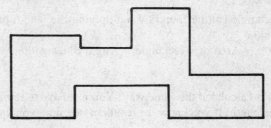

The perimeter of a circle is called its *circumference,* which is computed in a special way.

Ancient Greek mathematicians discovered an important fact about circles. No matter how large the circle was, they found that its circumference (perimeter) was almost exactly 3.14 times its diameter. They named the number by which they multiplied a circle's diameter to get its circumference *pi*. We use the value 3.14, or the fraction $^{22}/_7$, to represent pi, though its value is slightly larger. The symbol π stands for pi.

To find the perimeter (circumference) of this circle:

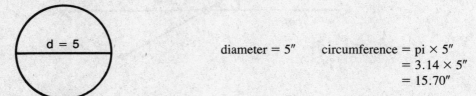

diameter = 5″   circumference = pi × 5″
= 3.14 × 5″
= 15.70″

We can also work backward to find the diameter of a circle from its circumference. For example, if the circumference of a circle is 21.98 inches, what is its diameter?

Since the circumference is the product of π and the diameter, divide the circumference by π to find the diameter.

$$21.98 \div 3.14 = 7″ \text{ (diameter)}$$

Area of plane figures

When a plane figure such as a rectangle, triangle, or circle lies flat, it covers a certain amount of area. When it is necessary to buy carpeting, grass seed, paint, and many other things, the area of the place to be covered must be calculated.

Area is always measured in square units, such as square inches, square feet, square yards, or square miles. Metric system units for area include square centimeters, square meters, and square kilometers. Generally, the unit of measurement to be used is based on the area of the object being measured.

- The area of a city would be measured in square miles or square kilometers.
- The area of a football field would be measured in square yards or square meters.
- The area of this page would be measured in square inches or square centimeters.

When calculating area, it is most important to remember that you are dealing with *square units*. Area is always given in square inches, square meters, and so on.

Area of squares and rectangles

The area of squares and rectangles is found by multiplying the length of any one side by the length of the side adjoining it.

8 cm.

3 cm.   3 cm.

8 cm.

The area of this rectangle is the product of
8 cm. × 3 cm. = 24 sq. cm.

The area of any rectangle can be found by multiplying the length of its longest side by the length of its shortest side.

Area of a rectangle = length times width

$$A = l \times w$$

The area of squares is calculated the same way. You just have to remember that the sides of a square are all the same length. If you know the length of one side, you know the lengths of all the sides.

6″

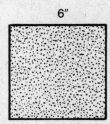

The area of the square is
6 in. × 6 in. = 36 sq. in.

Area of triangles

Triangles may be *acute*, if each of their angles is less than 90°:

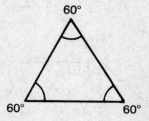

If each angle is 60°, the triangle is called *equilateral*, because all angles are equal in measure.

Triangles may be *right*, if one angle is 90°:

Triangles may be *obtuse*, if one angle is larger than 90°:

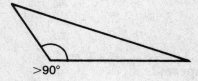

Familiarize yourself with these kinds of triangles, because finding their area requires you to be very careful about one thing: *measuring the altitude correctly.*

We find the area of triangles by using the following formula:

Area = one half the product of the base and the altitude
$$A = \frac{1}{2} \times b \times a \quad or \quad A = \frac{1}{2}ba$$

The *altitude* of a triangle is the distance from a point on the base to a point directly above, or perpendicular to, the base.

These drawings show how to measure altitude correctly.

In a right triangle:

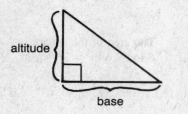

In an obtuse triangle:

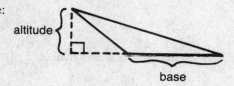

In an acute triangle:

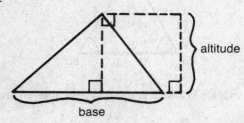

Notice that in each case, the altitude or height of a triangle *must* be measured along a line that makes a right angle with the base.

Example: Find the area of the triangle shown below.

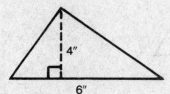

Solution: $A = \frac{1}{2} ba$

$A = \frac{1}{2} \cdot 4'' \cdot 6''$

$A = 12$ sq. in.

Parallelograms and trapezoids

A *parallelogram* is a four-sided figure with opposite sides parallel to each other. The area of a parallelogram can be found by multiplying the length of the base by the altitude.

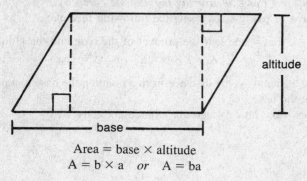

Area = base × altitude

$A = b \times a$ *or* $A = ba$

Here again, you *must* be careful to measure the altitude perpendicular to the base, just as you did when finding the areas of triangles.

A *trapezoid* is a four-sided figure with one pair of sides parallel, and one pair nonparallel. The parallel sides are called the *bases,* and we find the area as follows:

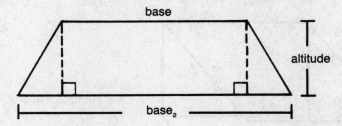

$$\text{Area} = \tfrac{1}{2} \times \text{altitude} \times (\text{length of base 1} + \text{length of base 2})$$
$$A = \tfrac{1}{2} \times a \times (b_1 + b_2) \quad or \quad A = \tfrac{1}{2}a\,(b_1 + b_2)$$

Be sure to measure the altitude of the trapezoid along a line that makes a right angle with the base.

Area of a circle

The area of a circle is easily calculated, if you remember two things:

- Use the number pi ($\pi = 3.14$, or $\tfrac{22}{7}$).
- Use the radius of the circle in the calculation instead of the diameter.

To find the area of a circle, use the following formula:

$$\text{Area} = \pi \times \text{length of radius} \times \text{length of radius}$$
$$A = \pi\, r^2$$

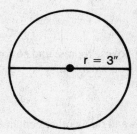

For example, this circle has a radius of $3''$. Thus, its area is:

$$A = \pi r^2$$
$$= 3.14 \times 3'' \times 3''$$
$$= 28.26 \text{ sq. in.}$$

Sometimes, to avoid the extra calculation, areas of circles are written in pi. In the example above, we would write:

$$A = \pi \times 3'' \times 3''$$
$$= 9\,\pi \text{ sq. in.}$$

Volume of solid figures

Three-dimensional figures such as cubes, cones, spheres, and rectangular solids take up space. The amount of space an object or substance takes up is called its *volume.*

Because we purchase items and plan the sizes of buildings, homes, ships, and so forth according to our needs for a certain volume of something, volume is one of the most important measurements that we make. In this section, you will review how to calculate the volume of certain easy-to-measure shapes.

Volume of rectangular solids

A familiar rectangular solid is a shoe box. Its volume is calculated by multiplying its length times its width times its thickness or depth. The formula is:

$$\text{volume} = 1 \times w \times h, \textit{ or } V = lwh.$$

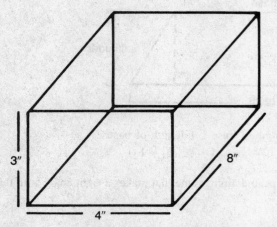

For example, the box shown to the left has the volume:
$V = 3'' \times 4'' \times 8''$
$V = 96$ cubic inches

Notice that we multiplied the measurement of each dimension of the box only once. The units that we use in measuring volume are *cubic* units.

A special rectangular solid is a *cube*. A cube has all of its dimensions the same length, so you need only the length of one edge to find its volume.

For example, the drawing below shows a cube with an edge 4″ long.

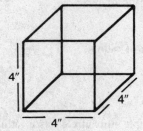

Its volume is calculated:
$V = 4'' \times 4'' \times 4''$
$\quad = 64$ cu. in.

When you are calculating the volume of rectangular solids, shoe boxes, rooms, and so forth, be certain that you have measurements for each dimension before you calculate.

Volume of a cylinder

Cylinders are objects we deal with all of the time. Soft drink cans and many other containers, as well as pipes and smokestacks, are cylinders.

In many ways, a cylinder resembles a stack of coins; or a stack of round, thin objects such as cocktail coasters, or slices of bologna. By thinking of a cylinder as a stack of slices or coins, it is easy to remember how to calculate its volume.

The volume of a cylinder can be calculated by first finding the area of the circular base, and multiplying that value by the height.

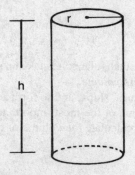

$$\text{Volume} = \underset{\text{area of base}}{\pi r^2} \times \underset{\substack{\text{height or length} \\ \text{of cylinder}}}{h}$$

By finding the area of the base, you are finding the area of one "slice" of the cylinder. When you multiply that by the height or length, you are calculating volume by counting all of the "slices" that you could make.

For example, find the volume of the cylinder below:

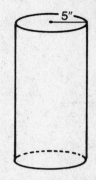

The radius of the base is 5″. The height, or length, is 10″.

$V = \pi r^2 h$
$V = \pi \times 5″ \times 5″ \times 10″$
$V = \pi \times 250$ cu. in.
  $= 3.14 \times 250$ cu. in.
Volume $= 785$ cu. in.

As with area, you may find that the answer can be left in terms of pi. That is, it may not be necessary to multiply by 3.14. In the example above, the answer $V = 250\pi$ cubic inches is acceptable.

Coordinate geometry

Coordinate geometry is used to locate and to graph points and lines on a plane.

The coordinate system is made up of two perpendicular number lines that intersect at 0. Any point on the plane has two numbers, or coordinates, that indicate its location relative to the number lines.

The *x*-coordinate (abscissa) is found by drawing a vertical line from the point to the horizontal number line (the *x*-axis). The number found on the *x*-axis is the abscissa.

The *y*-coordinate (ordinate) is found by drawing a horizontal line from the point to the vertical number line (the *y* axis). The number found on the *y*-axis is the ordinate.

The two coordinates are always written in the order (*x*, *y*).

Example:

The *x*-coordinate of point *A* is 3.
The *y*-coordinate of point *A* is 2.
The coordinates of point *A* are given by the ordered pair (3, 2).
Point *B* has coordinates (−1, 4).
Point *C* has coordinates (−4, −3).
Point *D* has coordinates (2, −3).

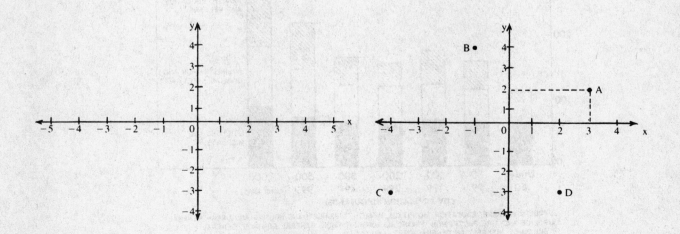

To graph a point whose coordinates are given, first locate the *x*-coordinate on the *x*-axis, then from that position move vertically the number of spaces indicated by the *y*-coordinate.

Example: To graph (4, −2), locate 4 on the *x*-axis, then move −2 spaces vertically (2 spaces down) to find the given point.

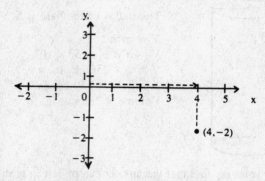

The point at which the *x*-axis and the *y*-axis meet has coordinates (0, 0) and is called the origin. Any point on the *y*-axis has 0 as its *x*-coordinate. Any point on the *x*-axis has 0 as its *y*-coordinate.

Graphs

Graphs illustrate comparisons and trends in statistical information. The most commonly used graphs are *bar graphs, line graphs, circle graphs,* and *pictographs*.

Bar graphs

Bar graphs are used to compare various quantities. Each bar may represent a single quantity or may be divided to represent several quantities.

Bar graphs may have horizontal or vertical bars:

Municipal Expenditures, Per Capita

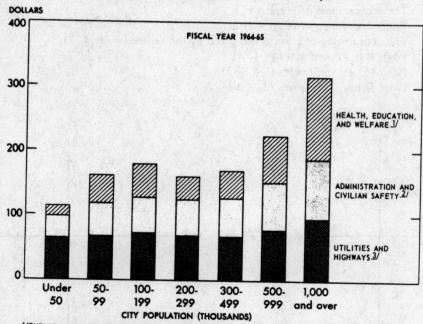

Question: What was the approximate municipal expenditure per capita in cities having populations of 200,000 to 299,000?

Answer: The middle bar of the seven shown represents cities having populations from 200,000 to 299,000. This bar reaches about halfway between 100 and 200. Therefore, the per capita expenditure was approximately $150.

Question: Which cities spent the most per capita on health, education, and welfare?

Answer: The bar for cities having populations of 1,000,000 and over has a larger striped section than the other bars. Therefore, those cities spent the most.

Question: Of the three categories of expenditures, which was least dependent on city size?

Answer: The expenditures for utilities and highways, the darkest part of each bar, varied least as city size increased.

Line graphs

Line graphs are used to show trends, often over a period of time.

A line graph may include more than one line, with each line representing a different item.

The graph below indicates at 5-year intervals the number of citations issued for various offenses from the year 1960 to the year 1980:

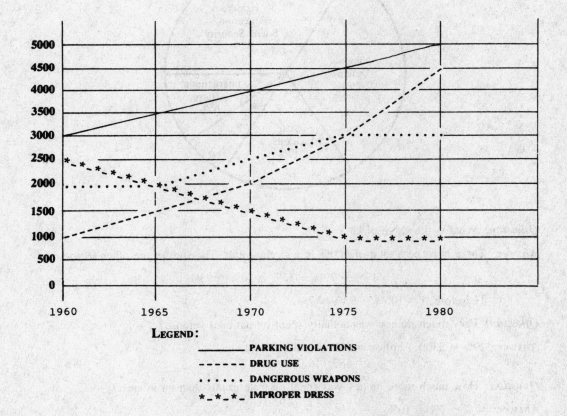

LEGEND:

——————— PARKING VIOLATIONS

– – – – – – DRUG USE

· · · · · · DANGEROUS WEAPONS

––*– IMPROPER DRESS

Question: Over the 20-year period, which offense shows an average rate of increase of more than 150 citations per year?

Answer: Drug use citations increased from 1000 in 1960 to 4500 in 1980. The average increase over the 20-year period is $\frac{3500}{20} = 175$.

Question: Over the 20-year period, which offense shows a constant rate of increase or decrease?

Answer: A straight line indicates a constant rate of increase or decrease. Of the four lines, the one representing parking violations is the only straight one.

Question: Which offense shows a total increase or decrease of 50% for the full 20-year period?

Answer: Dangerous weapons citations increased from 2000 in 1960 to 3000 in 1980, which is an increase of 50%.

Circle graphs

Circle graphs are used to show the relationship of various parts of a quantity to each other and to the whole quantity.

Percents are often used in circle graphs. The 360 degrees of the circle represent 100%. Each part of the circle graph is called a *sector*.

The following circle graph shows how the federal budget of $300.4 billion was spent:

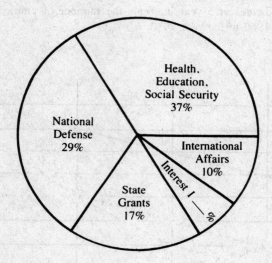

Question: What is the value of I?

Answer: There must be a total of 100% in a circle graph. The sum of the other sectors is:

$$17\% + 29\% + 37\% + 10\% = 93\%$$

Therefore, I = 100% − 93% = 7%.

Question: How much money was actually spent on national defense?

Answer: 29% × $300.4 billion = $87.116 billion
= $87,116,000,000

Question: How much more money was spent on state grants than on interest?

Answer: 17% − 7% = 10%
10% × $300.4 billion = $30.04 billion
= $30,040,000,000

Pictographs

Pictographs allow comparisons of quantities by using symbols. Each symbol represents a given number of a particular item:

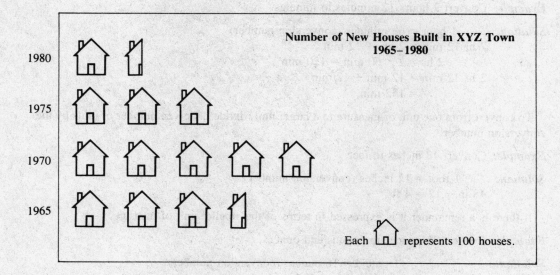

**Number of New Houses Built in XYZ Town
1965–1980**

Each ⌂ represents 100 houses.

Question: How many more new houses were built in 1970 than in 1975?

Answer: There are two more symbols for 1970 than for 1975. Each symbol represents 100 houses. Therefore, 200 more houses were built in 1970.

Question: How many new houses were built in 1965?

Answer: There are $3\frac{1}{2}$ symbols shown for 1965; $3\frac{1}{2} \times 100 = 350$ houses.

Question: In which year were half as many houses built as in 1975?

Answer: In 1975, $3 \times 100 = 300$ houses were built. Half of 300, or 150, houses were built in 1980.

Denominate Numbers (Measurement)

A *denominate number* is a number that specifies a given measurement. The unit of measure is called the *denomination*.

7 miles, 3 quarts, and 5 grams are denominate numbers.

The English system of measurement uses such denominations as pints, ounces, pounds, and feet. The metric system of measurement uses such denominations as grams, liters, and meters.

English system of measurement

To convert from one unit of measure to another, find in the Table of Measures how many units of the smaller denomination equal one unit of the larger denomination. This number is called the *conversion number*.

To convert from one unit of measure to a smaller unit, multiply the given number of units by the conversion number.

Example: Convert 7 yards to inches.

Solution: 1 yard = 36 inches (conversion number)
          7 yards = 7 × 36 inches
                    = 252 inches

Example: Convert 2 hours 12 minutes to minutes.

Solution: 1 hour = 60 minutes (conversion number)

2 hr 12 min = 2 hr + 12 min

2 hr = 2 × 60 min = 120 min

2 hr 12 min = 12 min + 12 min

= 132 min

To convert from one unit of measure to a larger unit, divide the given number of units by the conversion number.

Example: Convert 48 inches to feet.

Solution: 1 foot = 12 inches (conversion number)

48 in ÷ 12 = 4 ft

If there is a remainder it is expressed in terms of the smaller unit of measure.

Example: Convert 35 ounces to pounds and ounces.

Solution: 1 pound = 16 ounces (conversion number)

$$35 \text{ oz} \div 16 = 16\overline{)35 \text{ oz}}$$
$$\begin{array}{r} 2 \text{ lb} \\ \hline 35 \text{ oz} \\ 32 \\ \hline 3 \text{ oz} \end{array}$$

= 2 lb 3 oz

To add denominate numbers, arrange them in columns by common unit, then add each column. If necessary, simplify the answer, starting with the smallest unit.

Example: Add 1 yd 2 ft 8 in., 2 yd 2 ft 10 in, and 3 yd 1 ft 9 in.

Solution:
```
  1 yd 2 ft  8 in
  2 yd 2 ft 10 in
+ 3 yd 1 ft  9 in
  6 yd 5 ft 27 in
```
= 6 yd 7 ft 3 in (since 27 in = 2 ft 3 in)

= 8 yd 1 ft 3 in (since 7 ft = 2 yd 1 ft)

To subtract denominate numbers, arrange them in columns by common unit, then subtract each column starting with the smallest unit. If necessary, borrow to increase the number of a particular unit.

Example: Subtract 2 gal 3 qt from 7 gal 1 qt.

Solution:
```
  7 gal 1 qt =    6 gal 5 qt
− 2 gal 3 qt = −  2 gal 3 qt
                  4 gal 2 qt
```
Note that 1 gal was borrowed from 7 gal.

1 gal = 4 qt

Therefore, 7 gal 1 qt = 6 gal 5 qt

To multiply a denominate number by a given number, if the denominate number contains only one unit, multiply the numbers and write the unit.

3 oz × 4 = 12 oz

If the denominate number contains more than one unit of measurement, multiply the number of each unit by the given number and simplify the answer, if necessary.

Example: Multiply 4 yd 2 ft 8 in by 2.

Solution:
$$\begin{array}{l} 4 \text{ yd } 2 \text{ ft } 8 \text{ in} \\ \underline{\times \qquad\qquad 2} \\ 8 \text{ yd } 4 \text{ ft } 16 \text{ in} \end{array}$$

= 8 yd 5 ft 4 in (since 16 in = 1 ft 4 in)
= 9 yd 2 ft 4 in (since 5 ft = 1 yd 2 ft)

To divide a denominate number by a given number, convert all units to the smallest unit, then divide. Simplify the answer, if necessary.

Example: Divide 5 lb 12 oz by 4.

Solution:
1 lb = 16 oz, therefore
5 lb 12 oz = 92 oz
92 oz ÷ 4 = 23 oz
= 1 lb 7 oz

Alternate method of division:

- Divide the number of the largest unit by the given number.
- Convert any remainder to the next largest unit.
- Divide the total number of that unit by the given number.
- Again convert any remainder to the next unit and divide.
- Repeat until no units remain.

Example: Divide 9 hr 21 min 40 sec by 4.

Solution:
$$\begin{array}{l} \ 2 \text{ hr} \quad 20 \text{ min} \quad 25 \text{ sec} \\ 4\overline{)\ 9 \text{ hr} \quad 21 \text{ min} \quad 40 \text{ sec}} \\ \ \underline{8 \text{ hr}} \\ \ 1 \text{ hr} = \underline{60 \text{ min}} \\ \qquad\qquad 81 \text{ min} \\ \qquad\qquad \underline{80 \text{ min}} \\ \qquad\qquad 1 \text{ min} = \underline{60 \text{ sec}} \\ \qquad\qquad\qquad\qquad 100 \text{ sec} \\ \qquad\qquad\qquad\qquad \underline{100 \text{ sec}} \\ \qquad\qquad\qquad\qquad 0 \text{ sec} \end{array}$$

Metric measurement

The basic units of the metric system are the meter (m), which is used for length; the gram (g), which is used for weight: and the liter (l), which is used for capacity, or volume.

The prefixes that are used with the basic units, and their meanings, are:

PREFIX	ABBREVIATION	MEANING
micro	**m**	one millionth of (.000001)
milli	m	one thousandth of (.001)
centi	c	one hundredth of (.01)
deci	d	one tenth of (.1)
deka	da or dk	ten times (10)
hecto	h	one hundred times (100)
kilo	k	one thousand times (1000)
mega	M	one million times (1,000,000)

To convert *to* a basic metric unit from a prefixed metric unit, multiply by the number indicated in the prefix.

Example: Convert 72 millimeters to meters.

Solution: 72 millimeters = 72 × .001 meters
= .072 meters

Example: Convert 4 kiloliters to liters.

Solution: 4 kiloliters = 4 × 1000 liters
= 4000 liters

To convert *from* a basic unit to a prefixed unit, divide by the number indicated in the prefix.

Example: Convert 300 liters to hectoliters.

Solution: 300 liters = 300 ÷ 100 hectoliters
= 3 hectoliters

Example: Convert 4.5 meters to decimeters.

Solution: 4.5 meters = 4.5 ÷ .1 decimeters
= 45 decimeters

To convert from any prefixed metric unit to another prefixed unit, first convert to a basic unit, then convert the basic unit to the desired unit.

Example: Convert 420 decigrams to kilograms.

Solution: 420 dg = 420 × .1 g = 42 g
42 g = 42 ÷ 1000 kg = .042 kg

To add, subtract, multiply, or divide using metric measurement, first convert all units to the same unit, then perform the desired operation.

Example: Subtract 1200 g from 2.5 kg.

Solution:

$$
\begin{array}{rcr}
2.5 \text{ kg} = & & 2500 \text{ g} \\
- 1200 \text{ g} = & & - 1200 \text{ g} \\
\hline
& & 1300 \text{ g}
\end{array}
$$

To convert from a metric measure to an English measure, or the reverse:

- In the Table of English–Metric Conversions on page 71, find how many units of the desired measure are equal to one unit of the given measure.
- Multiply the given number by the number found in the table.

Example: Find the number of pounds in 4 kilograms.

Solution: From the table, 1 kg = 2.2 lb.
4 kg = 4 × 2.2 lb
= 8.8 lb

Example: Find the number of meters in 5 yards.

Solution: 1 yd = .9 m
5 yd = 5 × .9 m
= 4.5 m

Temperature measurement

The temperature measurement currently used in the United States is the degree Fahrenheit (°F). The metric measurement for temperature is the degree Celsius (°C), also called degree Centigrade.

Degrees Celsius may be converted to degrees Fahrenheit by the formula:

$$°F = \frac{9}{5}°C + 32°$$

Example: Water boils at 100°C. Convert this to °F.

Solution: $°F = \dfrac{9}{\cancel{5}} \times \overset{20}{\cancel{100°}} + 32°$
$$= 180° + 32°$$
$$= 212°$$

Degrees Fahrenheit may be converted to degrees Celsius by the formula:

$$°C = \frac{5}{9}(°F - 32°)$$

In using this formula, perform the subtraction in the parentheses first, then multiply by $\frac{5}{9}$.

Example: If normal body temperature is 98.6°F, what is it on the Celsius scale?

Solution: $°C = \dfrac{5}{9}(98.6° - 32°)$
$$= \frac{5}{9} \times 66.6°$$
$$= \frac{333°}{9}$$
$$= 37°$$

Table of English—Metric Conversions (Approximate)

English to Metric

1 inch = 2.54 centimeters
1 yard = .9 meters
1 mile = 1.6 kilometers
1 ounce = 28 grams
1 pound = 454 grams
1 fluid ounce = 30 milliliters
1 liquid quart = .95 liters

Metric to English

1 centimeter = .39 inches
1 meter = 1.1 yards
1 kilometer = .6 miles
1 kilogram = 2.2 pounds
1 liter = 1.06 liquid quart

Table of Metric Conversions*

1 liter = 1000 cubic centimeters (cm^3)
1 milliliter = 1 cubic centimeter
1 liter of water weighs 1 kilogram
1 milliliter of water weighs 1 gram

---

*These conversions are exact only under specific conditions. If the conditions are not met, the conversions are approximate.

WRITING SKILLS REVIEW

This Writing Skills chapter is designed to help you prepare for both the multiple-choice and the essay sections of the PPST Writing Test. The first section, "Correct English Usage," will help you recognize diction and idiom errors in the multiple-choice section and should enable you to avoid many such errors in your essay. The "Punctuation Review" will remind you of important punctuation and capitalization rules, and will help you recognize and practice good mechanics. The section called "The Essentials of English Grammar" will help you understand sentence structure and logic, and the section on "The Essay" will help you generate and organize your ideas for that very important part of the exam. Together, these sections will help you review the principles of effective written communication and the conventions of standard written English, and should leave you ready to tackle both the Practice Writing Tests and the actual PPST.

Correct English Usage

The ability to choose and use the right word is an important part of the PPST Writing Test. The list that follows presents some of the most commonly misused words in the English language. Study it well and you will be rewarded with higher test scores.

accede—means *to agree with*.
concede—means *to yield*, but not necessarily in agreement.
exceed—means *to be more than*.
  We shall *accede* to your request for more evidence.
  To avoid delay, we shall *concede* that more evidence is necessary.
  Federal expenditures now *exceed* federal income.

access—means *availability*.
excess—means *too much*.
  The lawyer was given *access* to the grand jury records.
  The expenditures this month are far in *excess* of income.

accept—means *to take when offered*.
except—means *excluding*. (preposition)
except—means to leave out. (verb)
  The draft board will *accept* all seniors as volunteers before graduation.
  All eighteen-year-olds *except* seniors will be called.
  The draft board will *except* all seniors until after graduation.

adapt—means *to adjust to change*.
adopt—means *to take as one's own*.
adept—means *skillful*.
  Children can *adapt* to changing conditions very easily.
  The war orphan was *adopted* by the general and his wife.
  Proper instruction makes children *adept* in various games.
  NOTE: adapt *to*, adopt *by*, adept *in* or *at*.

adapted to—implies *original or natural suitability*.
  The gills of the fish are *adapted* to underwater breathing.

adapted for—implies *created suitability*.
  Atomic energy is constantly being *adapted for* new uses.

adapted from—implies *changes to be made suitable*.
  Many of Richard Wagner's opera librettos *were adapted from* old Norse sagas.

affect—means *to influence*. (verb)
effect—means *an influence*. (noun)
effect—means *to bring about*. (verb)

Your education must *affect* your future.

The *effect* of the last war is still being felt.

A diploma *effected* a tremendous change in his attitude.

NOTE: *Affect* also has a meaning of *pretend*. She had an *affected* manner.

all ready—means *everybody or everything ready*.

already—means *previously*.

They were *all ready* to write when the teacher arrived.

They had *already* begun writing when the teacher arrived.

alright—is *unacceptable*.

all right—is *acceptable*.

all together—means *everybody or everything together*.

altogether—means *completely*.

The boys and girls sang *all together*.

This was *altogether* strange for a person of his type.

all ways—means *in every possible way*.

always—means *at all times*.

He was in *all ways* acceptable to the voters.

His reputation had *always* been spotless.

alongside of—means *side by side with*.

Bill stood *alongside of* Henry.

alongside—means *parallel to the side*.

Park the car *alongside* the curb.

alot—is *unacceptable*. It should always be written as two words: *a lot*.

among—is used with *more than two persons or things*.

NOTE: *Amongst* should be avoided.

between—is used with *two persons or things*.

The inheritance was equally divided *among* the four children.

The business, however, was divided *between* the oldest and youngest one.

amount—applies to quantities *that cannot be counted one by one*.

number—applies *to quantities that can be counted one by one*.

A large *amount* of grain was delivered to the storehouse.

A large *number* of bags of grain was delivered.

annual—means *yearly*.

biannual—means *twice a year*. (*Semiannual* means the same.)

biennial—means *once in two years* or *every two years*.

anywheres—is *unacceptable*.

anywhere—is *acceptable*.

SAY we can't find it *anywhere*.

ALSO SAY *nowhere* (NOT nowheres), *somewhere* (NOT somewheres)

apt—suggests *habitual behavior*.

likely—suggests *probable behavior*.

liable—suggests an exposure to something *harmful*.

Teenagers are *apt* to be rather lazy in the morning.

A cat, if annoyed, is *likely* to scratch.

Cheating on a test may make one *liable* to expulsion from school.

as—(used as a conjunction) is followed by a verb.

like—(used as a preposition) is NOT followed by a verb.

Do *as* I do, not *as* I say.

Try not to behave *like* a child.

Unacceptable: He acts *like* I do.

as far as—expresses *distance*.

so far as—indicates *a limitation*.

We hiked *as far as* the next guest house.

So far as we know, the barn was adequate for a night's stay.

as if—is correctly used in this expression, "He talked *as if* his jaw hurt him."

Unacceptable: "He talked *like* his jaw hurt him."

as regards to—is *unacceptable*. So is *in regards to*.

SAY: *in regard to* or *as regards*.

The teacher would say nothing *in regard to* the student's marks.

as to whether—is *unacceptable*. *Whether* includes the unnecessary words *as to*.

Acceptable: I don't know *whether* it is going to rain.

at—should be avoided where it does not contribute to the meaning.

SAY: Where shall I meet you? (DON'T add the word *at*)

attend to—means *to take care of*.
tend to—means *to be inclined to*.
> One of the clerks will *attend to* mail in my absence.
> Lazy people *tend* to gain weight.

back—should NOT be used with such words as *refer* and *return* since the prefix *re* means *back*.
> *Unacceptable:* Refer back to the text, if you have difficulty recalling the facts.

backward ⎫ Both are *acceptable* and may be used
backwards ⎭ interchangeably as an adverb.
> We tried to run *backward*. (or *backwards*)
> *Backward* as an adjective means *slow in learning*. (DON'T say *backwards* in this case)
> A *backward* pupil should be given every encouragement.

being that—is *unacceptable* for *since* or *because*.
> SAY: *Since* (or *Because)* you have come a long way, why not remain here for the night?

beside—means *close to*.
besides—refers *to something that has been added*.
> He lived *beside* the stream.
> He found wild flowers and weeds *besides*.

both—means *two considered together*.
each—means *one of two or more*.
> *Both* of the applicants qualified for the position.
> *Each* applicant was given a generous reference.
> NOTE: Avoid using such expressions as the following:
> *Both* girls had a new typewriter. (Use *each girl* instead.)
> *Both* girls tried to outdo the other. (Use *each girl* instead.)
> They are *both* alike (Omit *both*).

breath—means *an intake of air*.
breathe—means *to draw air in and give it out*.
breadth—means *width*.
> Before you dive in, take a very deep *breath*.
> It is difficult to *breathe* under water.
> In a square, the *breadth* should be equal to the length.

can—means *physically able*.
may—implies *permission*.
> I *can* lift this chair over my had.
> You *may* leave after you finish your work.

cannot help—must be followed by an *ing* form.
> We cannot help *feeling* (NOT *feel*) distressed about this.
> NOTE: *cannot help but is unacceptable*.

can't hardly—is a *double negative*. It is *unacceptable*.
> SAY: The child *can hardly* walk in those shoes

capital—is *the city*.
capitol—is the *building*.
> Paris is the *capital* of France.
> The Capitol in Washington is occupied by the Congress. (The Washington *Capitol* is capitalized.)
> NOTE: *Capital* also means wealth.

cease—means *to end*.
seize—means *to take hold of*.
> Will you please *cease* making those sounds?
> *Seize* him by the collar as he comes around the corner.

certainly—(and *surely*) is an *adverb*.
sure—is an *adjective*.
> He was *certainly* learning fast.
> *Unacceptable:* He *sure* was learning fast.

cite—means *to quote*.
sight—means *seeing*.
site—means *a place for a building*.
> He was fond of *citing* from the Scriptures.
> The *sight* of the wreck was appalling.
> The Board of Education is seeking a *site* for the new school.

coarse—means *vulgar* or *harsh*.
course—means a *path* or a *study*.
> He was shunned because of his *coarse* behavior.
> The ship took its usual *course*.
> Which *course* in English are you taking?

come to be—should NOT be replaced with the expression *become to be*, since *become* means *come to be*.
> True freedom will *come to be* when all tyrants have been overthrown.

compare to—means *to liken to something that has a different form*.
compare with—means to *compare persons or things with each other when they are of the same kind*.

contrast with—means *to show the difference between two things*.
> A minister is sometimes *compared to* a shepherd.
> Shakespeare's plays are often *compared with* those of Marlowe.
> The writer *contrasted* the sensitivity of the dancer *with* the grossness of the pugilist.

complement—means *a completing part*.
compliment—is *an expression of admiration*.
> His wit was a *complement* to her beauty.
> He *complimented* her attractive hairstyle.

comprehensible—means *understandable*.
comprehensive—means *including a great deal*.
> Under the circumstances, your doubts were *comprehensible*.
> Toynbee's *comprehensive* study of history covers many centuries.

conscience—means *sense of right*.
conscientious—means *faithful*.
conscious—means *aware of one's self*.
> Man's *conscience* prevents him from becoming completely selfish.
> We all depend on him because he is *conscientious*.
> The injured man was completely *conscious*.

considerable—is properly used *only as an adjective*, NOT as a noun.

consistently—means in *harmony*.
constantly—means *regularly, steadily*.
> If you choose to give advice, act *consistently* with that advice.
> Doctors *constantly* warn against overexertion after forty-five.

continual—means *happening again and again at short intervals*.
continuous—means *without interruption*.
> The teacher gave the class *continual* warnings.
> Noah experienced *continuous* rain for forty days.

convenient to—should be followed by a *person*.
convenient for—should be followed by a *purpose*.
> Will these plans be *convenient to* you?
> You must agree that they are *convenient for* the occasion.

credible—means *believable*.
creditable—means *worthy of receiving praise*.

credulous—means *believing too easily*.
> The pupil gave a *credible* explanation for his lateness.
> Considering all the handicaps, he gave a *creditable* performance.
> Politicians prefer to address *credulous* people.

could of—is *unacceptable*. (*Should of* is also *unacceptable*.)
could have—is *acceptable*. (*Should have* is acceptable.)
> *Acceptable:* You *could have* done better with more care.
> *Unacceptable:* I *could of* won.
> ALSO AVOID: *must of, would of*.

desert—(pronounced DEZZ-ert) means *an arid area*.
desert—(pronounced di-ZERT) means *to abandon; also a reward of punishment*.
dessert—(pronounced di-ZERT) means *the final course of a meal*.
> The Sahara is the world's most famous *desert*.
> A husband must not *desert* his wife.
> Execution was a just *desert* for his crime.
> We had plum pudding for *dessert*.

differ from—is used when there is a difference *in appearance*.
differ with—is used when there is a difference *in opinion*.
> A coat *differs from* a cape.
> You have the right to *differ with* me on public affairs.

different from—is *acceptable*.
different than—is *unacceptable*.
> *Acceptable:* Jack is *different from* his brother.
> *Unacceptable:* Florida climate is *different than* New York climate.

due to—is *unacceptable* at the beginning of a sentence. Use *because of, on account of*, or some similar expression instead.
> *Unacceptable: Due to* the rain, the game was postponed.
> *Acceptable: Because of* the rain, the game was postponed.
> *Acceptable:* The postponement was *due to* the rain.

disinterested—means *impartial*.

uninterested—means *not interested*.
>The judge must always be a *disinterested* party in a trial.
>An *uninterested* observer, he was inclined to yawn at times.

each other—refers to *two persons*.
one another—refers to *more than two persons*.
>The two girls have known *each other* for many years.
>Several of the girls have known *one another* for many years.

either . . . or—is used when referring to choices.
neither . . . nor—is the *negative form*.
>*Either* your *or* I will win the election.
>*Neither* Bill *nor* Henry is expected to have a chance.

eligible—means *fit to be chosen*.
ineligible—means *not fit to be chosen*.
illegible—means *impossible to read* or *hard to read*.
>Not all thirty-five-year-old persons are *eligible* to be President.
>His handwriting was *illegible*.

emigrate—means *to leave one's country for another*.
immigrate—means *to enter another country*.
>Many Norwegians *emigrated* from their homeland to America in the mid-1860's.
>Today government restrictions make it more difficult for foreigners to *immigrate* to this country.

everyone—is written as one word when it is a *pronoun*.
every one—(two words) is used when each individual is stressed.
>*Everyone* present voted for the proposal.
>*Every one* of the voters accepted the proposal.
>NOTE: *Everybody* is written as one word.

everywheres—is *unacceptable*.
everywhere—is *acceptable*.
>We searched *everywhere* for the missing book.
>NOTE: *Everyplace* (one word) is likewise *unacceptable*.

excessively—means *beyond acceptable limits*.
exceedingly—means *to a very great degree*.
>In view of our recent feud, he was *excessively* friendly.
>The weather in July was *exceedingly* hot.

expand—means *to spread out*.
expend—means *to use up*.
>As the staff increases, we shall have to *expand* our office space.
>Don't *expend* all your energy on one project.

farther—is used to describe *concrete distance*.
further—is used to describe *abstract ideas*.
>Chicago is *farther* from New York than Cincinnati is.
>I'll explain my point of view *further*.

feel bad—means *to feel ill*.
feel badly—means *to have a poor sense of touch*.
>I *feel bad* about the accident I saw.
>The numbness in his limbs caused him to *feel badly*.

feel good—means *to be happy*.
feel well—means *to be in good health*.
>I *feel* very *good* about my recent promotion.
>Spring weather always made him *feel well*.

fewer—refers to *persons or things that can be counted*.
less—refers to *something considered as a mass*.
>We have *fewer* customers this week than last week.
>I have *less* money in my pocket than you have.

flowed—is the past participle of *flow*.
flown—is the past participle of *fly*.
>The flood waters had *flowed* over the levee before nightfall.
>He had *flown* for 500 hours before he crashed.

formally—means *in a formal way*.
formerly—means *at an earlier time*.
>The letter of reference was *formally* written.
>He was *formerly* a delegate to the convention.

former—means *the first of two*.
latter—means *the second of two*.
>The *former* half of the book was in prose.
>The *latter* half of the book was in poetry.

forth—means *forward*
fourth—*comes after third*.
>They went *forth* like warriors of old.
>The *Fourth* of July is our Independence Day.
>NOTE: spelling of *forty* (40) and *fourteen* (14).

hanged—is used in reference to a *person*.
hung—is used in reference to a *thing*.
>The prisoner was *hanged* at dawn.
>The picture was *hung* above the fireplace.

however—means *nevertheless*.
how ever—means *in what possible way*.
> We are certain, *however*, that you will like this class.
> We are certain that, *how ever* you decide to study, you will succeed.

if—introduces a *condition*.
whether—introduces a *choice*.
> I shall go to Europe *if* I win the prize.
> He asked me *whether* I intended to go to Europe. (not *if*)

if it was—implies that *something might have been true in the past*.
if it were—implies *doubt*, or indicates *something that is contrary to fact*.
> *If you book was* there last night, it is there now.
> *If it were* summer now, we would all go swimming.

imply—means *to suggest* or *hint at*. (The speaker *implies*)
infer—means *to deduce* or *conclude*. (The listener *infers*)
> Are you *implying* that I have disobeyed orders?
> From your carefree attitude, what else are we to *infer?*

in—usually refers to *a state of being*. (no motion)
into—is used for *motion from one place to another*.
> The records are *in* that drawer.
> I put the records *into* that drawer.
> NOTE: "We were walking in the room" is correct even though there is motion. The motion is *not* from one place to another.

infect—means *to contaminate with germs*.
infest—means *to be present in large numbers* (in a *bad sense*)
> The quick application of an antiseptic can prevent *infection*.
> The abandoned barn was *infested* with field mice.

irregardless—is *unacceptable*.
regardless—is *acceptable*.
> *Unacceptable: Irregardless* of the weather, I am going to the game.
> *Acceptable: Regardless* of his ability, he is not likely to win.

its—means *belonging to it*.
it's—means *it is*.
> The house lost *its* roof.
> *It's* an exposed house, now.

kind of }
sort of } are *unacceptable* for *rather*.
> SAY: We are *rather* disappointed in you.

last—refers to *the final member in a series*.
latest—refers to *the most recent in time*.
latter—refers to *the second of two*.
> This is the *last* bulletin. There won't be any other bulletins.
> This is the *latest* bulletin. There will be other bulletins.
> Of the two most recent bulletins, the *latter* is more encouraging.

lay—means *to place*.
lie—means *to recline*.
> Note the forms of each verb:

TENSE	LIE (RECLINE)
Present	The child *is lying* down.
Past	The child *lay* down.
Pres. Perf.	The child *has lain* down.

TENSE	LAY (PLACE)
Present	He *is laying* the book on the desk.
Past	He *laid* the book on the desk.
Pres. Perf.	He *has laid* the book on the desk.

least—means *the smallest*.
less—means *the smaller of two*.
> This was the *least* desirable of all the locations we have seen.
> This is the *less* violent of the two movies playing.

many—refers to *a number*.
much—refers to *a quantity in bulk*.
> How *many* inches of rain fell last night?
> I don't know; but I would say *much* rain fell last night.

may—is used in the *present tense*.
might—is used in the *past tense*.
> We are hoping that he *may* come today.
> He *might* have done it if you had encouraged him.

it's I—is always *acceptable*.
it's me—is *acceptable* only in colloquial speech or writing.

It's him This is her It was them	always *unacceptable*
It's he This is she It was they	always *acceptable*

more than—is correct. Do not add *rather* to this construction.

SAY: I depend *more* on you *than* (NOT *rather than*) on him.

BUT: I depend on you *rather than* on him.

most—is an adjective in the *superlative degree*.
almost—is an adverb, meaning *nearly*.

He is the *most* courteous boy in the class.

It's *almost* time to go to school.

myself—is *unacceptable* for *I* or *me*.

SAY: My son and *I* will play.

He is a better player than *I*.

They gave my son and *me* some berries.

NOTE: *Myself* may be used if the subject of the verb is I.

Since I know *myself* better, let me try it my way.

near—is an adjective meaning *close*.
nearly—is an adverb meaning *almost*.

Before 1933, only *near* beer was available.

Unacceptable: It is *near* a week since you called. (SAY: *nearly*)

neither—means *not either of two,* and should NOT be used for *none* or *not one*.

Neither of his two books was very popular.

Of the many plays he has written, *not one* (or *none*) was very popular.

never—means *at no time*. DO NOT use it for *not*.

SAY: Shakespeare was *never* in Italy.

Shakespeare was *not* very fond of France.

nevertheless—means *notwithstanding*.
none the less—means *not any the less,* and is always followed by an adjective.

I have often warned you; *nevertheless*, you have persisted in doing the wrong thing.

I am *none the less* willing to give you a second chance.

number—is singular *when the total is intended*.

The *number* (of pages in the book) is 500.

number—is plural *when the individual units are referred to*.

A *number of pages* (in the book) were printed in italic type.

one . . . one—is the acceptable construction in such expressions as: The more *one* listens to his speeches, the more *one* (NOT *he*) wonders how a young man can be so wise.

other—is an adjective and means *different*.
otherwise—is an adverb and means *in a different way*.

What you did was *other* (NOT *otherwise*) than what you had promised.

I cannot look *otherwise* (NOT *other*) than with delight at the improvement in your work.

SAY: All students, *except* (NOT *other than*) those exempted, should take the examination.

All students, *unless* they have been exempted (NOT *otherwise*), will take the examination.

outdoor—(and *out-of-door*) is an adjective.
outdoors—is an adverb.

We spent most of the summer at an *outdoor* music camp.

Most of the time we played string quartets *outdoors*.

NOTE: *Out-of-doors* is *acceptable* in either case.

persecute—means *to make life miserable for someone*. (Persecution is illegal.)
prosecute—means *to conduct a criminal investigation*. (Prosecution is legal.)

Some racial groups insist upon *persecuting* other groups.

The District Attorney is *prosecuting* the racketeers.

precede—means *to come before*.
proceed—means *to go ahead*. (*Procedure* is the noun.)
supersede—means *to replace*.

What were the circumstances that *preceded* the attack?

We can then *proceed* with our plan for resisting a second attack.

It is then possible that Plan B will *supersede* Plan A.

principal—means *chief* or *main* (as an adjective); *a leader* (as a noun).
principle—means *a fundamental truth* or *belief*.

His *principal* supporters came from among the peasants.

The *principal* of the school asked for cooperation from the staff.

Humility was the guiding *principle* of Buddha's life.

NOTE: *Principal* may also mean *a sum placed at interest*.

Part of his monthly payment was applied as interest on the *principal*.

real—meaning *very* or *extremely* is *unacceptable*.

SAY: He is a *very* (NOT *real*) handsome young man.

He is *really* handsome.

respectably—means *in a manner deserving respect*.
respectfully—means *with respect and decency*.
respectively—means *as relating to each, in the order given*.

Young people should dress *respectably* for job interviews.

The students listened *respectfully* to the principal.

John and Bill are the sons *respectively* of Mr. Smith and Mr. Brown.

saw—is the past tense of *see*.
seen—is the past participle of *see*.

We *saw* a play yesterday. (NOT *seen*)

I have never *seen* a live play before. (NOT *saw*)

sit—means *take a seat*. (intransitive verb)
set—Means *place*. (transitive verb)

Note the forms of each verb:

TENSE	SIT (TAKE A SEAT)
Present	He *sits* on a chair.
Past	He *sat* on the chair.
Pres. Perf.	He *has sat* on the chair.

TENSE	SET (PLACE)
Present	He *sets* the lamp on the table.
Past	He *set* the lamp on the table.
Pres. Perf.	He *has set* the lamp on the table.

some time—means *a portion of time*.
sometime—means *at an indefinite time in the future*.
sometimes—means *occasionally*.

I'll need *some time* to make a decision.

Let us meet *sometime* after twelve noon.

Sometimes it is better to hesitate before signing a contract.

somewheres—is *unacceptable*.
somewhere—is *acceptable*.

stationary—means *standing still*.
stationery—means *writing materials*.

In ancient times people thought the earth was *stationary*.

We bought writing paper at the *stationery* store.

stayed—means *remained*.
stood—means *remained upright* or *erect*.

The army *stayed* in the trenches for five days.

The soldiers *stood* at attention for one hour.

sure—for *surely* is *unacceptable*.

SAY: You *surely* (NOT *sure*) are not going to write that!

their—means *belonging to them*.
there—means *in that place*.
they're—means *they are*.

We took *their* books home with us.

You will find your books over *there* on the desk.

They're going to the ballpark with us.

theirselves—is *unacceptable* for *themselves*.

SAY: Most children of school age are able to care for *themselves* in many ways.

these kind—is *unacceptable*.
this kind—is *acceptable*.

I am fond of *this kind* of apples.

NOTE: *These kinds* would be also *acceptable*.

through—meaning *finished* or *completed* is *unacceptable*.

SAY: We'll finish (NOT *be through with*) the work by five o'clock.

try to—is *acceptable*.
try and—is *unacceptable*.

Try to come (NOT *try and* come).

NOTE: *plan on going* is *unacceptable*; *plan to go* is *acceptable*.

two—is the *numeral* 2.
to—means *in the direction of*.
too—means *more than* or *also*.

There are *two* sides to every story.

Three *twos* (or 2's) equal six.

We shall go *to* school.

We shall go, *too*.

The weather is *too* hot for school.

type man—(*type book, type game*, etc.) is *unacceptable* for *type of man, type of book, type of game*, etc.

SAY: He is the right *type of man* for this position.

unique—means *the only one of its kind,* and therefore does not take *very, most, extremely* before it.
> SAY: The First Folio edition of Shakespeare's works is *unique.* (NOT *very unique*)
> NOTE: The same rule applies to *perfect.*

valuable—means *of great worth.*
valued—means *held in high regard.*
invaluable—means *priceless.*
> This is a *valuable* manuscript.
> The expert gave him highly *valued* advice.
> A good name is an *invaluable* possession.

virtually—means *in effect.*
actually—means *in fact.*
> A tie in the final game was *virtually* a defeat for us.
> We had *actually* won more games than they at that time.

was
were } If something is contrary to fact (not a fact), use *were* in every instance.
> I wish I *were* in Bermuda.
> *Unacceptable:* If he *was* sensible, he wouldn't act like that.
> (SAY: If he *were* . . .)

ways—is *unacceptable* for *way.*
> SAY: We climbed a little way (NOT *ways*) up the hill.

when—(and *where*) should NOT be used to introduce a definition of a noun.
> SAY: A tornado *is a* twisting, high wind on land (NOT *is when a twisting, high wind is on land*).
> A pool *is a place for swimming* (NOT *is where people swim*).

whether—should NOT be preceded by *of* or *as to.*
> SAY: The president will consider the question *whether* (NOT *of whether*) it is better to ask for or demand higher taxes now.
> He inquired *whether* (NOT *as to whether*) we were going or not.

which—is used *incorrectly* in the following expressions:
> He asked me to stay, *which I did.* (CORRECT: He asked me to stay and I did.)

It has been a severe winter, *which* is unfortunate. (CORRECT: Unfortunately, it has been a severe winter.)
> You did not write; besides *which* you have not telephoned. (CORRECT: Omit *which*)

while—is *unacceptable* for *and* or *though.*
> SAY: The library is situated on the south side; (OMIT *while*) the laboratory is on the north side.
> *Though* (NOT *while*) I disagee with you, I shall not interfere with your right to express your opinion.
> *Though* (NOT *while*) I am in my office every day, you do not attempt to see me.

who
whom } The following is a method (without going into grammar rules) for determining when to use WHO or WHOM.
> "Tell me (*who, whom*) you think should represent our company?"
> STEP ONE: Change the who—whom part of the sentence to its natural order.
> "You think (*who, whom*) should represent our company?"
> STEP TWO: Substitute HE for WHO, HIM for WHOM.
> "You think (*he, him*) should represent our company?"
> You would say *he* in this case.
> THEREFORE: "Tell me WHO you think should represent our company?" is correct.

who is
who am } Note these constructions.
> It is I who *am* the most experienced.
> It is he who *is* . . .
> It is he or I who *am* . . .
> It is I or he who *is* . . .
> It is he and I who *are* . . .

whose—means *of whom.*
who's—means *who is.*
> *Whose* is this notebook?
> *Who's* in the next office?

would have—is *unacceptable* for *had.*
> SAY: I wish you *had* (NOT *would have*) called earlier.

your—is the possessive of *you.*
you're—is a contraction of *you are.*
> Are these *your* keys?
> If *you're* ready, we should leave now.

PUNCTUATION REVIEW
The Apostrophe

1. Use an apostrophe to indicate possession. Place the apostrophe according to this rule: "The apostrophe, when used to indicate possession, means *belonging to everything to the left of the apostrophe*."

Examples: lady's   = belonging to the lady
ladies'   = belonging to the ladies
children's = belonging to the children

NOTE: To test for correct placement of the apostrophe, read *of the*.

Example: childrens' = of the childrens (obviously incorrect)

The placement rule applies at all times, even with regard to compound nouns separated by hyphens and with regard to entities made up to two or more names.

Example: father-in-law's = belonging to a father-in-law

Example: Lansdale, Jackson, and Roosevelt's law firm = the law firm belonging to Lansdale, Jackson, and Roosevelt

Example: Brown and Sons' delivery truck = the delivery truck of Brown and Sons

2. Use an apostrophe in a contraction in place of the omitted letter or letters.

Examples: haven't   = have not
we're   = we are
let's   = let us
o'clock   = of the clock
class of '85 = class of 1985

NOTE: Do NOT begin a paragraph with a contraction.

3. Use an apostrophe to form plurals of numbers, letters, and phrases referred to as words.

Example: The Japanese child pronounced his *l's* as *r's*.

Example: Solution of the puzzle involves crossing out all the *3's* and *9's*.

Example: His speech was studded with *you know's*.

The Colon

1. Use a colon after the salutation in a business letter.

Example: Dear Board Member:

2. Use a colon to separate hours from minutes.

Example: The eclipse occurred at 10:36 A.M.

3. Use of the colon is optional in the following cases:
   (a) to introduce a list, especially after an expression such as "as follows"
   (b) to introduce a long quotation
   (c) to introduce a question

Example: My question is this: Are you willing to punch a time clock?

The Comma

1. Use a comma after the salutation of a personal letter.

Example: Dear Mary,

2. Use a comma after the complimentary close of a letter.

Example: Cordially yours,

3. Use a comma or pair of commas to set off a noun of address.

Example: When you finish your homework, Jeff, please take out the garbage.

4. Use a pair of commas to set off an appositive, a phrase that follows a noun or pronoun and means the same as that noun or pronoun.

Example: Mr. Burke, our lawyer, gave us some good advice.

5. Use a pair of commas to set off parenthetical expressions, words that interrupt the flow of the sentence, such as *however, though, for instance, by the way.*

Example: We could not, however, get him to agree.

Example: This book, I believe, is the best of its kind.

> NOTE: Test for placement of commas in a parenthetical expression by reading aloud. If you would pause before and after such an expression, then it should be set off by commas.

6. Use a comma between two or more adjectives that modify a noun equally.

Example: The jolly, fat, ruddy man stood at the top of the stairs.

> NOTE: If you can add the word *and* between the adjectives without changing the sense of the sentence, then use commas.

7. Use a comma to separate words, phrases, or clauses in a series. The use of a comma before *and* is optional. If the series ends in *etc.*, use a comma before *etc.*. Do not use a comma after *etc.* in a series, even if the sentence continues.

Example: Coats, umbrellas, and boots should be placed in the closet at the end of the hall.

Example: Pencils, scissors, paper clips, etc. belong in your top desk drawer.

8. Use a comma to separate a short direct quotation from the speaker.

Example: She said, "I must leave work on time today."

Example: "Tomorrow I begin my summer job," he told us.

9. Use a comma after an introductory phrase of five or more words.

Example: Because the prisoner had a history of attempted jailbreaks, he was put under heavy guard.

10. Use a comma after a short introductory phrase whenever the comma would aid clarity.

Example: As a child she was a tomboy. (comma unnecessary)

Example: To Dan, Phil was friend as well as brother. (comma clarifies)

Example: In 1978, 300 people lost their lives in one air disaster. (comma clarifies)

> NOTE: A comma is not generally used before a subordinate clause that ends a sentence, though in long, unwieldy sentences like this one, use of such comma is optional.

11. Use a comma before a coordinating conjunction unless the two clauses are very short.

Example: The boy wanted to borrow a book from the library, but the librarian would not allow him to take it until he had paid his fines.

Example: Roy washed his dishes and Helen dried.

12. Use a pair of commas to set off a nonrestrictive adjective phrase or clause. A nonrestrictive phrase or clause is one that can be omitted without essentially changing the meaning of the sentence.

Example: Our new sailboat, which has bright orange sails, is very seaworthy.

A restrictive phrase or clause is vital to the meaning of a sentence and cannot be omitted. Do NOT set it off with commas.

Example: A sailboat without sails is useless.

13. Use a comma if the sentence might be subject to different interpretations without it.

Example: The banks which closed yesterday are in serious financial difficulty.
[Some banks closed yesterday and those banks are in trouble.]
The banks, which closed yesterday, are in serious financial difficulty.
[All banks closed yesterday and all are in trouble.]

Example: My brother Bill is getting married.
[The implication is that I have more than one brother.]
My brother, Bill, is getting married.
[Here *Bill* is an appositive. Presumably he is the only brother.]

14. Use a comma if a pause would make the sentence clearer and easier to read.

Example: Inside the people were dancing. (confusing)
Inside, the people were dancing. (clearer)

Example: After all crime must be punished. (confusing)
After all, crime must be punished. (clearer)

The pause rule is not infallible, but it is your best resort when all other rules governing use of the comma fail you.

The Dash

1. Use a dash—or parentheses—for emphasis or to set off an explanatory group of words.

Example: The tools of his trade—probe, mirror, cotton swabs—were neatly arranged on the dentist's tray.

NOTE: Unless the set-off expression ends a sentence, dashes, like parentheses, must be used in pairs.

2. Use a dash to break up a thought.

Example: There are five—remember I said five—good reasons to refuse their demands.

3. Use a dash to mark a sudden break in thought that leaves a sentence unfinished.

Example: He opened the door a crack and saw—

The Exclamation Mark

1. Use an exclamation mark only to express strong feeling or emotion, or to imply urgency.

Example: Congratulations! You broke the record.

Example: Rush! Perishable contents.

The Hyphen

1. Use a hyphen to divide a word at the end of a line. Always divide words between syllables.
2. Use a hyphen in numbers from *twenty-one* to *ninety-nine*.
3. Use a hyphen to join two words serving together as a single adjective before a noun.

Example: That baby-faced man is considerably older than he appears to be.

4. Use a hyphen with the prefixes *ex-, self-, all-,* and the suffix *-elect.*

Example: ex-senator, self-appointed, all-state, governor-elect

5. Use a hyphen to avoid ambiguity.

Example: After the custodian recovered the use of his right arm, he re-covered the office chairs.

6. Use a hyphen to avoid an awkward union of letters.

Example: semi-independent, shell-like

The Period

1. Use a period at the end of a sentence that makes a statement, gives a command, or makes a ''polite request'' in the form of a question that does not require an answer.

Example: I am preparing for my exam.

Example: Proofread everything you type.

Example: Would you please hold the script so that I may see if I have memorized my lines.

2. Use a period after an abbreviation and after the initial in a person's name.

Example: Gen. Robert E. Lee led the Confederate forces.

NOTE: Do NOT use a period after postal service state name abbreviations such as AZ (for Arizona) or MI (for Michigan).

The Question Mark

1. Use a question mark after a request for information.

Example: At what time does the last bus leave?

NOTE: A question must end with a question mark even if the question does not encompass the entire sentence.

Example: ''Daddy, are we there yet?'' the child asked.

Quotation Marks

1. Use quotation marks to enclose all directly quoted material. Words not quoted must remain outside the quotation marks.

Example: "If it is hot on Sunday," she said, "we will go to the beach."

NOTE: Do NOT enclose an indirect quote in quotation marks.

Example: She said that we might go to the beach on Sunday.

2. Use quotation marks around words used in an unusual way.

Example: A surfer who "hangs ten" is performing a tricky maneuver on a surfboard, not staging a mass execution.

3. Use quotation marks to enclose the title of a short story, essay, short poem, song, or article.

Example: Robert Louis Stevenson wrote a plaintive poem called "Bed in Summer."

NOTE: Titles of books and plays are NOT enclosed in quotation marks. They are printed in italics. In handwritten or typed manuscript, underscore titles of books and plays.

Example: The song "Tradition" is from *Fiddler on the Roof*.

Placement of Quotation Marks

1. A period *always* goes inside the quotation marks, whether the quotation marks are used to denote quoted material, to set off titles, or to isolate words used in a special sense.

Example: The principal said, "Cars parked in the fire lane will be ticketed."

Example: The first chapter of *The Andromeda Strain* is entitled "The Country of Lost Borders."

Example: Pornography is sold under the euphemism "adult books."

2. A comma ALWAYS goes inside the quotation marks.

Example: "We really must go home," said the dinner guests.

Example: If your skills become "rusty," you must study before you take the exam.

Example: Three stories in Kurt Vonnegut's *Welcome to the Monkey House* are "Harrison Bergeron," "Next Door," and "Epicac."

3. A question mark goes inside the quotation marks if it is part of the quotation. If the whole sentence containing the quotation is a question, the question mark goes outside the quotation marks.

Example: He asked, "Was the airplane on time?"

Example: What did you really mean when you said "I do"?

4. An exclamation mark goes inside the quotation marks if the quoted words are an exclamation, outside if the entire sentence including the quoted words is an exclamation.

Example: The sentry shouted, "Drop your gun!"

Example: Save us from our "friends"!

5. A colon and a semicolon *always* go outside the quotation marks.

Example: He said, "War is destructive"; she added, "Peace is constructive."

6. When a multiple-paragraph passage is quoted, each paragraph of the quotation must begin with quotation marks, but ending quotation marks are used only at the end of the last quoted paragraph.

The Semicolon

1. Use a semicolon to separate a series of phrases or clauses each of which contain commas.

Example: The old gentleman's heirs were Margaret Whitlock, his halfsister; James Bagley, the butler; William Frame, companion to his late cousin, Robert Bone; and his favorite charity, the Salvation Army.

2. Use a semicolon to avoid confusion with numbers.

Example: Add the following: $1.25; $7.50; and $12.89.

3. You may use a semicolon to join two short, related independent clauses.

Example: Anne is working at the front desk on Monday; Ernie will take over on Tuesday.

NOTE: Two main clauses must be separated by a conjunction *or* by a semicolon *or* they must be written as two sentences. A semicolon never precedes a coordinating conjunction. The same two clauses may be written in any one of three ways:

Autumn had come and the trees were almost bare.
Autumn had come; the trees were almost bare.
Autumn had come. The trees were almost bare.

4. You may use a semicolon to separate two independent clauses that are joined by an adverb such as *however, therefore, otherwise,* or *nevertheless.* The adverb must be followed by a comma.

Example: You may use a semicolon to separate this clause from the next; however, you will not be incorrect if you choose to write two separate sentences.

NOTE: If you are uncertain about how to use the semicolon to connect independent clauses, write two sentences instead.

CAPITALIZATION RULES

1. Capitalize the first word of a sentence.

Example: *With* cooperation, a depression can be avoided.

2. Capitalize all proper names.

Example: America, General Motors, Abraham Lincoln, First Congregational Church

3. Capitalize days of the week, months of the year, and holidays.

Example: The check was mailed on *Thursday,* the day before *Christmas.*

NOTE: The seasons are not capitalized. In Florida, *winter* is mild.

4. Capitalize the first word and all nouns in the salutation of a letter.

Example: *Dear* Mr. Jones,
(*but*—My *dear* Mr. Jones,)

5. Capitalize the first word of the complimentary close of a letter.

Example: *Truly* yours,
      (*but*—Very *truly* yours,)

6. Capitalize the first and all other important words in a title.

Example: *The Art of Salesmanship*

7. Capitalize a word used as part of a proper name.

Example: William *Street* (*but*—That *street* is narrow.)

Example: Morningside *Terrace* (*but*—We have a *terrace* apartment).

8. Capitalize titles, when they refer to a particular official or family member.

Example: The report was read by *Secretary* Marshall.
      (*but*—Miss Shaw, our *secretary,* is ill.)

Example: Let's visit *Uncle* Harry.
      (*but*—I have three *uncles*.)

9. Capitalize points of a compass, when they refer to particular regions of a country.

Example: We're going *South* next week. (*but*—New York is *south* of *Albany*.)

NOTE: Write: the Far West, the Pacific Coast, the Middle East, etc.

10. Capitalize the first word of a direct quotation.

Example: It was Alexander Pope who wrote, "A little learning is a dangerous thing."

NOTE: When a direct quotation sentence is broken, the *first* word of the *second half* of the sentence is not capitalized.

Example: "Don't phone," Lilly told me, "*because* it will be too late."

THE ESSENTIALS OF ENGLISH GRAMMAR

Every test of English usage tests your understanding of English grammar. This Grammar and Usage Review is meant to serve as a quick refresher course. It should "bring back" the rules, hints, and suggestions supplied by many teachers over the years.

Parts of Speech

A **noun** is the name of a person, place, thing, or idea: teacher city desk democracy
Pronouns substitute for nouns: he they ours those
An **adjective** describes a noun: warm quick tall blue
A **verb** expresses action or state of being: yell interpret feel are
An **adverb** modifies a verb, an adjective, or another adverb: fast slowly friendly well
Conjunctions join words, sentences, and phrases: and but or
A **preposition** shows position in time or space: in during after behind

Nouns

There are different kinds of nouns:

Common nouns are general: house girl street city
Proper nouns are specific: White House Jane Main Street New York
Collective nouns name groups: team crowd organization Congress

Nouns have *cases*:

Nominative—the subject, noun of address, or predicate noun
Objective—the direct object, indirect object, or object of the preposition
Possessive—the form that shows possession

Pronouns

Antecedent of the pronoun—the noun to which a pronoun refers. A pronoun must agree with its antecedent in gender, person, and number. There are several kinds of pronouns. (Pronouns also have cases.)

Demonstrative pronoun: this, that, these, those
Indefinite pronoun: all, any, anybody
Interrogative pronoun: who, which, what

PERSONAL PRONOUN

		NOMINATIVE CASE	OBJECTIVE CASE	POSSESSIVE CASE
	1st person	I	me	mine
Singular	2nd person	you	you	yours
	3rd person	he, she, it	him, her, it	his, hers, its
	1st person	we	us	ours
Plural	2nd person	you	you	your
	3rd person	they	them	theirs

Adjectives

Adjectives answer the questions "Which one?", "What kind?", and "How many?"

There are three uses of adjectives:

A **noun modifier** is usually placed directly before the noun it describes: He is a *tall* man.
A **predicate adjective** follows an inactive verb and modifies the subject: He is *happy*. I feel *terrible*.
An **article** or **noun marker** are other names for these adjectives: the, a, an

Adverbs

Adverbs answer the questions "Why?", "How?", "Where?", "When?", and "To what degree?". Adverbs should NOT be used to modify nouns. Adverbs modify verbs, adjectives, and other adverbs.

Verbs

Verbs are the most important part of speech. A verb may stand alone, as an imperative sentence such as "Stop!" Conversely, no group of words can function as a sentence without a verb.

Attributes of a verb

Mood	*I laugh.* (indicative—factual)
	If I were laughing . . . (subjunctive—wishful)
	Laugh! (imperative—forceful)
Voice	*I moved the chair.* (active)
	The chair was moved by me. (passive)
Agreement of Persons and Number	

Tense	*I laugh.* (present)
	We had laughed. (past perfect)
	She will be laughing. (future progressive)

Types of verbs

Transitive	completed by a noun or pronoun
	We invited our friends.

Intransitive	completed in itself or by an adverb
	She fell. She fell down.

Copulative	a form of *is* or a sensory/seeming verb
	She is pretty. We felt bad. He appeared depressed.

PRINCIPAL PARTS OF A VERB

	PRESENT	PAST	PRESENT PERFECT
Regular	walk	walked	have walked
	bathe	bathed	have bathed
Irregular	ring	rang	have rung
	eat	ate	have eaten

ENGLISH VERB TIME LINES

SIMPLE TENSES	PAST	PRESENT	FUTURE
Simple	I walked	I walk	I will walk
Progressive	I was walking	I am walking	I will be walking
Emphatic	I did walk	I do walk	

PERFECT TENSES	PAST PERFECT	PRESENT PERFECT	FUTURE PERFECT
	I had walked	I have walked	I will have walked
	I had walked three miles by the time you caught up with me.	I have walked three miles to get here.	I will have walked three miles by the time you catch up with me.
	activity begun and completed in the past before some other past action	activity begun in the past, completed in the present	activity begun at any time and completed in the future

SELECTED RULES OF GRAMMAR

1. The subject of a verb is in the nominative case even if the verb is understood and not expressed.

Example: They are as old as *we*. (As we are)

2. The word *who* is in the nominative case. *Whom* is in the objective case.

Example: The trapeze artist who ran away with the clown broke the lion tamer's heart. (*Who* is the subject of the verb *ran*.)

Example: The trapeze artist whom he loved ran away with the circus clown. (*Whom* is the object of the verb *loved*.)

3. The word *whoever* is in the nominative case. *Whomever* is in the objective case.

Example: Whoever comes to the door is welcome to join the party. (*Whoever* is the subject of the verb *comes*.)

Example: Invite whomever you wish to accompany you. (*Whomever* is the object of the verb *invite*.)

4. Nouns or pronouns connected by a form of the verb *to be* should always be in the nominative case.

Example: It is *I*. (Not *me*)

5. A pronoun that is the object of a preposition or of a transitive verb must be in the objective case.

Example: It would be impossible for *me* to do that job alone. (*Me* is the object of the preposition *for*.)

Example: The attendant gave *me* the keys to the locker. (*Me* is the indirect object of the verb *gave*.)

6. *Each, either, neither, anyone, anybody, somebody, someone, every, everyone, one, no one,* and *nobody* are singular pronouns. Each of these words takes a singular verb and a singular pronoun.

Example: *Neither likes* the pets of the other.
Everyone must wait *his* turn.
Each of the patients *carries* insurance.
Neither of the women *has* completed her assignment.

7. When the correlative conjunctions *either/or* and *neither/nor* are used, the number of the verb agrees with the number of the last subject.

Example: Neither John nor *Greg eats* meat.

Example: Either the cat or the *mice take* charge in the barn.

8. A subject consisting of two or more nouns joined by a coordinating conjunction takes a plural verb.

Example: Paul *and* Sue *were* the last to arrive.

9. The number of the verb is not affected by the addition to the subject of words introduced by *with, together with, no less than, as well as,* etc.

Example: The *captain,* together with the rest of the team, *was delighted* by the victory celebration.

10. A verb agrees in number with its subject. A verb should not be made to agree with a noun that is part of a phrase following the subject.

Example: *Mount Snow,* one of my favorite ski areas, *is* in Vermont.

Example: The *mountains* of Colorado, like those of Switzerland, *offer* excellent skiing.

11. A verb should agree in number with the subject, not with the predicate noun or pronoun.

Example: Poor study *habits are* the leading cause of unsatisfactory achievement in school.

Example: The leading *cause* of unsatisfactory achievement in school *is* poor study habits.

12. A pronoun agrees with its antecedent in person, number, gender, and case.

Example: Since you were absent on Tuesday, you will have to ask Mary or Beth for her notes on the lecture. (Use *her,* not their, because two singular antecedents joined by *or* take a singular pronoun.)

13. *Hardly, scarcely, barely, only* and *but* (when it means *only*) are negative words. Do NOT use another negative in conjunction with any of these words.

Example: He *didn't have but* one hat. (WRONG)
He had *but* one hat. OR He had *only* one hat.

Example: I *can't hardly* read the small print. (WRONG)
I *can hardly* read the small print. OR I *can't* read the small print.

14. *As* is a conjunction introducing a subordinate clause, while *like* is a preposition. The object of a preposition is a noun or phrase.

Example: Winston tastes good *as* a cigarette should. (*Cigarette* is the subject of the clause; *should* is its verb.)

Example: He behaves *like* a fool.

Example: The gambler accepts only hard currency *like* gold coins.

15. When modifying the words *kind* and *sort,* the words *this* and *that* always remain in the singular.

Example: *This kind* of apple makes the best pie.

Example: *That sort* of behavior will result in severe punishment.

16. In sentences beginning with *there is* and *there are,* the verb should agree in number with the noun that follows it.

Example: There isn't an unbroken bone in her body. (The singular subject *bone* takes the singular verb *is*.)

Example: There are many choices to be made. (The plural subject *choices* takes the plural verb *are*.)

17. A noun or pronoun modifying a gerund should be in the possessive case.

Example: Is there any criticism of Arthur's going? (*Going* is a gerund. It must be modified by Arthur's, not by Arthur.)

18. Do NOT use the possessive case when referring to an inanimate object.

Example: He had difficulty with the *store's* management. (WRONG)
He had difficulty with the management of the store.

19. When expressing a condition contrary to fact or a wish, use the subjunctive form *were*.

Example: I wish I *were* a movie star.

20. Statements equally true in the past and in the present are usually expressed in the present tense. The contents of a book are also expressed in the present tense.

Example: He said that Venus is a planet. (Even though he made the statement in the past, the fact remains that Venus *is* a planet.)

Example: In the book *Peter Pan,* Wendy says, "I can fly." (Every time one reads the book, Wendy *says* it again.)

ANTECEDENTS AND MODIFIERS

1. *It,* when used as a relative pronoun, refers to the nearest noun. In your writing, you must be certain that the grammatical antecedent is indeed the intended antecedent.

Example: Since the mouth of the cave was masked by underbrush, *it* provided an excellent hiding place. (Do you really mean that the underbrush is an excellent hiding place, or do you mean the cave?)

2. *Which* is another pronoun that causes reference problems. In fact, whenever using pronouns, you must ask yourself whether or not the reference of the pronoun is clear.

Example: The first chapter awakens your interest in cloning, which continues to the end of the book. (What continues, cloning or your interest?)

Example: Jim told Bill that he was about to be fired. (Who is about to be fired? This sentence can be interpreted to mean that Jim was informing Bill about Bill's impending termination or about his, Jim's, own troubles.)

In your writing, you may find that the most effective way to clear up an ambiguity is to recast the sentence.

Example: The first chapter awakens your interest in cloning. The following chapters build upon this interest and maintain it throughout the book.

Example: Jim told Bill, ''I am about to be fired.'' OR Jim told Bill, ''You are about to be fired.''

3. Adjectives modify only nouns and pronouns. Adverbs modify verbs, adjectives, and other adverbs.

Example: One can swim in a lake as *easy* as in a pool. (WRONG)
One can swim in a lake as *easily* as in a pool. (The adverb *easily* must modify the verb *can swim.*)

Example: I was *real* happy. (WRONG)
I was *really* happy. (The adverb *really* must be used to modify the adjective *happy.*)

Sometimes context determines the use of adjective or adverb.

Example: The old man looked *angry.* (*Angry* is an adjective describing the old man. [angry old man])
The old man looked *angrily* out of the window. (*Angrily* is an adverb describing the man's manner of looking out the window.)

4. Phrases should be placed near the words they modify.

Example: The author says that he intends to influence your life *in the first chapter.* (WRONG)
The author *in the first chapter* says . . . OR *In the first chapter,* the author says . . .

Example: He played the part in *Oklahoma* of Jud. (WRONG)
He played the part of Jud *in Oklahoma.*

5. Adverbs should be placed near the words they modify.

Example: The man was *only* willing to sell one horse. (WRONG)
The man was willing to sell *only* one horse.

6. Clauses should be placed near the words they modify.

Example: *He* will reap a good harvest *who sows early.* (WRONG)
He who sows early will reap a good harvest.

7. A modifier must modify something.

Example: Having excellent control, a no-hitter was pitched. (WRONG)
(*Having excellent control* does not modify anything.)
Having excellent control, the pitcher pitched a no-hitter.
(*Having excellent control* modifies the pitcher.)

Example: The day passed quickly, climbing the rugged rocks. (WRONG)
The day passed quickly as we climbed the rugged rocks.

Example: While away on vacation, the pipes burst. (WRONG) (The pipes were not away on vacation.)
While we were away on vacation, the pipes burst.

Example: To run efficiently, the serviceman should oil the lawnmower. (WRONG)
The serviceman should oil the lawnmower to make it run efficiently.

NOTE: The best test for the placement of modifiers is to read the sentence literally. If you read a sentence literally and it is literally ridiculous, it is WRONG. The meaning of a sentence must be clear to any reader. The words of the sentence *must make sense*.

SENTENCE STRUCTURE

1. Every sentence must contain a verb. A group of words, no matter how long, without a verb is a sentence fragment, not a sentence. A verb may consist of one, two, three, or four words.

Examples: The boy *studies* hard.
The boy *will study* hard.
The boy *has been studying* hard.
The boy *should have been studying* hard.

The words that make up a single verb may be separated.

Examples: It *is* not *snowing*.
It *will* almost certainly *snow* tomorrow.

2. Every sentence must have a subject. The subject may be a noun, a pronoun, or a word or group of words functioning as a noun.

Examples: *Fish* swim. (noun)
Boats are sailed. (noun)
She is young. (pronoun)
Running is good exercise. (gerund)
To argue is pointless. (infinitive)
That he was tired was evident. (noun clause)

In commands, the subject is usually not expressed but is understood to be *you*.

Example: Mind your own business.

3. A phrase cannot stand by itself as a sentence. A phrase is any group of related words that has no subject or predicate and that is used as a single part of speech. Phrases may be built around prepositions, participles, gerunds, or infinitives.

Example: The boy *with curly hair* is my brother. (Prepositional phrase used as an adjective modifying *boy*)

Example: My favorite cousin lives *on a farm*. (Prepositional phrase used as an adverb modifying *lives*)

Example: *Beyond the double white line* is out of bounds. (Prepositional phrase used as a noun, the subject of the sentence)

Example: A thunderstorm *preceding a cold front* is often welcome. (Participial phrase used as an adjective modifying *thunderstorm*)

Example: We eagerly awaited the pay envelopes *brought by the messenger*. (Participial phrase used as an adjective modifying *envelopes*)

Example: *Running a day camp* is an exhausting job. (Gerund phrase used as a noun, subject of the sentence)

Example: The director is paid well for *running the day camp*. (Gerund phrase used as a noun, the object of the preposition *for*)

Example: *To breathe unpolluted air* should be every person's birthright. (Infinitive phrase used as a noun, the subject of the sentence)

Example: The child began *to unwrap his gift*. (Infinitive phrase used as a noun, the object of the verb *began*)

Example: The boy ran away from home *to become a Marine*. (Infinitive phrase used as an adverb modifying *ran away*)

4. A *main, independent,* or *principal* clause can stand alone as a complete sentence or it may be combined with another clause.

Example: The sky darkened ominously and rain began to fall. (Two independent clauses joined by a coordinating conjunction)

A *subordinate* or *dependent* clause must never stand alone. It is not a complete sentence despite the fact that it has a subject and a verb. A subordinate clause usually is introduced by a subordinating conjunction. Subordinate clauses may act as adverbs, adjectives, or nouns.

Subordinate adverbial clauses are generally introduced by the subordinating conjunctions *when, while, because, as soon as, if, after, although, as before, since, than, though, until,* and *unless*.

Example: *While we were waiting for the local,* the express roared past.

Example: The woman applied for a new job *because she wanted to earn more money*.

Example: *Although a subordinate clause contains both subject and verb,* it cannot stand alone *because it is introduced by a subordinating word*.

Subordinate adjective clauses may be introduced by the pronouns *who, which,* and *that*.

Example: The play *that he liked best* was a mystery.

Example: I have a neighbor *who served in the Peace Corps*.

Subordinate noun clauses may be introduced by *who, what,* or *that*.

Example: The stationmaster says *that the train will be late*.

Example: I asked the waiter *what the stew contained*.

Example: I wish I knew *who backed into my car*.

5. Two independent clauses cannot share one sentence without some form of connective. If they do, they form a run-on sentence. Two principal clauses may be joined by a coordinating conjunction, by a comma followed by a coordinating conjunction, or by a semicolon. They may form two distinct sentences. Two main clauses may NEVER be joined by a comma without a coordinating conjunction. This error is called a comma splice.

Example: A college education has never been more important than it is today it has never cost more. (WRONG—run-on sentence)

A college education has never been more important than it is today, it has never cost more. (WRONG—comma splice)

A college education has never been more important than it is today and it has never cost more. (WRONG—The two independent clauses are not equally short, so a comma is required before the coordinating conjunction.)

A college education has never been more important than it is today, and it has never cost more. (correct form)

A college education has never been more important than it is today; and it has never cost more. (WRONG—A semicolon is never used before a coordinating conjunction.

A college education has never been more important than it is today; it has never cost more. (correct form)

A college education has never been more important than it is today. It has never cost more. (correct form)

A college education has never been more important than it is today. And it has never cost more. (correct form)

While a college education has never been more important than it is today, it has never cost more. (correct form—Introductory subordinate clause is separated from the main clause by a comma.)

6. Direct quotations are bound by all the rules of sentence formation. Beware of comma splices in divided quotations.

Example: "Your total is wrong," he said, "add the column again." (WRONG)

"Your total is wrong," he said. "Add the column again." (The two independent clauses form two separate sentences.)

Example: "Are you lost?" she asked, "may I help you?" (WRONG)

"Are you lost?" she asked. "May I help you?" (Two main clauses; two separate sentences)

7. Comparisons must be logical and complete. Train yourself to concentrate on each sentence so that you can recognize errors.

Example: Wilmington is larger than any city in Delaware. (WRONG)

Wilmington is larger than any *other* city in Delaware.

Example: He is as fat, if not fatter, than his uncle. (WRONG)

He is as fat *as*, if not fatter than, his uncle.

Example: I hope to find a summer job other than a lifeguard. (WRONG)

I hope to find a summer job other than *that of* lifeguard.

Example: Law is a better profession than an accountant. (WRONG)

Law is a better profession than accounting. (Parallel)

8. Avoid the "is when" and "is where" construction.

Example: A limerick is when a short poem has a catchy rhyme. (WRONG)

A limerick is a short poem with a catchy rhyme.

Example: To exile is where a person must live in another place. (WRONG)

To exile a person is to force him to live in another place.

9. Errors in parallelism are often quite subtle, but you should learn to recognize and avoid them.

Example: Skiing and to skate are both winter sports. (WRONG)

Skiing and *skating* are both winter sports.

Example: She spends all her time eating, asleep, and on her studies. (WRONG)
She spends all her time *eating, sleeping,* and *studying*.

Example: The work is neither difficult nor do I find it interesting. (WRONG)
The work is neither difficult nor interesting.

Example: His heavy drinking and the fact that he gambles makes him a poor role model. (WRONG)
His heavy *drinking* and *gambling make* him a poor role model.

10. Avoid needless shifts in point of view. A shift in point of view is a change within the sentence from one tense or mood to another, from one subject or voice to another, or from one person or number to another. Shifts in point of view destroy parallelism within the sentence.

Example: After he *rescued* the kitten, he *rushes* down the ladder to find its owner. (Shift from past tense to present tense) CHANGE TO: After he rescued the kitten, he rushed down the ladder to find its owner.

Example: First *stand* at attention and then you *should salute* the flag. (Shift from imperative to indicative mood) CHANGE TO: First *stand* at attention and then *salute* the flag.

Example: Mary especially likes math, but history is also enjoyed by her. (The subject shifts from *Mary* to *history;* the voice shifts from active to passive.) CHANGE TO: Mary especially likes math, but she also enjoys history.

Example: George rowed around the island and soon the mainland came in sight. (The subject changes from *George* to *the mainland.*) CHANGE TO: George rowed around the island and soon came in sight of the mainland.

Example: The captain welcomed *us* aboard, and the crew enjoyed showing *one* around the boat. (The object shifts from first to third person. *Us* may be the object of *showing.*)

Example: *One* should listen to the weather forecast so that *they* may anticipate a hurricane. (The subject shifts from singular to plural.) CHANGE TO: *One* should listen to the weather forecast so that *he or she* may anticipate a hurricane.

THE ESSAY

It's natural to avoid anything that is difficult or unpleasant. Some people stay away from the water, some avoid flying, and some shun crowds. Many people would like to avoid writing, too. But the ability to organize your thoughts and express them effectively in writing is vital to success in school or on the job, and even though it may be difficult, writing cannot—and should not—be avoided. There are few skills that can serve you as well as writing and give you as much satisfaction once mastered.

Of course, improving one's writing skills takes time and dedication. The best way to become a successful writer is to practice writing as much as you can and to read as much as you can. The more you write, the more at ease you will be with the writing experience. And when you read, you should observe the techniques and style of professional writers. Editorials in newspapers and magazines are particularly good to examine. Take note of how the professional writer organizes his or her ideas and how he or she expresses them. When you discover a piece of writing that impresses you, try to analyze it to discover why it is so effective.

The PPST essay measures your ability to gather your ideas and arrange them into an interesting and effective composition. Your work will be evaluated on how clearly you make your point, how well you connect your ideas from sentence to sentence and paragraph to paragraph, and how logical a conclusion you draw based on your ideas and examples. The essay gives you the chance to demonstrate your command of grammar, vocabulary, and writing mechanics such as punctuation and capitalization, as well as your ability to reason clearly under the pressure of a timed test.

Most PPST essay questions fall into two types: Exposition and Persuasion.

What is Exposition?

Exposition means writing designed to convey information. Expository writing is *informative* writing. It explains or gives directions. Most of the practical writing you will do in the years to come—papers and examinations, job applications, business reports, insurance claims, your last will and testament—are examples of expository writing.

What is Persuasion?

Persuasion is the ability to use language to move an audience to action or belief. There are three main ways to persuade someone:

1. Appeal to emotion
2. Appeal to sense of reason
3. Appeal to ethics—the sense of right and wrong

Argumentation is the form of persuasion that appeals to reason. Although an argument may be more concerned with following a line of reasoning than making someone act, it must nonetheless convince its audience that what you have to say is worthwhile.

Whichever type of question you get, expository or persuasive, you will have to logically state your case, answering the question fully with specific details and examples. You should try to keep in mind the following goals to attempt and errors to avoid:

Five positive aims

1. originality of approach
2. clarity of organization

3. freshness of expression
4. logical development
5. variety of sentence patterns

Five errors to avoid

1. technical problems such as mistakes in sentence structure; frequent misspelling; errors in agreement, punctuation, capitalization; misuse of words
2. poor paragraphing
3. unnecessary repetition of material
4. poor level of English—illiteracies, mixed metaphors, trite expressions, overuse of colloquialisms
5. stylistic problems such as oversimplification, incoherent writing, wordiness, restating the obvious

The following pages will take you through the steps involved in crafting an effective essay. You will then be shown the strengths and weaknesses of six sample essays written in response to topics similar to those you may find on the PPST. Read through these sections carefully, and apply what you learn to the essays in the practice Writing Tests that appear later in this book. Remember that when you take the practice tests you should simulate test conditions and allow yourself only thirty minutes for each essay. It is important that you get an accurate idea of not only how much you can write, but also how well you can write, within the thirty-minute time limit.

PLANNING YOUR ESSAY

Getting Started

The first thing you always must do when answering an essay question is to look carefully at the question to see what it asks you to do. This can be one of the most important steps in any paper you write, for if you rush in without fully understanding what the question is asking, you may lose all credit.

Look at this sample question:

> A generation ago, young people took it for granted that they would marry and soon after become parents. Today's young couples seem to be putting off parenthood well into their marriages, and a significant number are not having children at all. Discuss the advantages and disadvantages of having children. Be specific.

You are being asked to discuss *two* things: the advantages *and* disadvantages of having children. You may give greater weight to one side or the other, but you must acknowledge both. Also note that you are asked to "be specific," so you should provide some examples and illustrations of your points.

Now what? There are few things as frightening as staring at a blank sheet of paper, knowing that you have only a few minutes in which to write an essay. This can be really upsetting in a pressured exam, for you do not have the time to reflect about the topic in a leisurely way, and you are not allowed to talk to people to get their help or their reaction to your ideas. There is no time to revise and rewrite the paper; the first draft will have to stand as the final draft.

Is it best just to take a deep breath and plunge right in? Or are you better off planning for a few moments, even though it seems as though everyone around you is already writing?

It is *always* worth the time to set up a plan of action, even though it looks as if you might be left behind. A plan always makes a better finished product, especially in a timed exam, when you will not have the luxury of a revision. The ideas will flow with greater logic and clarity if you have a plan. There are several different ways to plan—choose the one that is best for you.

One of the best ways to set up an essay involves the following steps.

Write down all the possible ideas you can think of on the topic. Do not stop and consider your ideas, and try not to even lift your pen off the paper. Just write as many things as you can think of as fast as you can. This should take no more than *one* or *two* minutes. For example, look back to our question:

> A generation ago, young people took it for granted that they would marry and soon after become parents. Today's young couples seem to be putting off parenthood well into their marriages, and a significant number are not having children at all. Discuss the advantages and disadvantages of having children. Be specific.

Allowing one to two minutes, you might write something like this:

money	fear	love
housing	material things	continuation
families	career	purpose
time	schooling	
travel	responsibilities	

Next, circle the ideas you think are the most important and which you can write about most effectively. Eliminate the items that you think are minor considerations, and items that might be too complex to deal with effectively in a brief essay. Remember, you will have time only to make a few points; you will not be able to explore every possible aspect of the topic.

Now, group the items you have chosen into possible paragraphs. Look back at the question to arrange the groups. Your grouping might look like this:

Advantages of having children	Disadvantages of having children
love	career
families	time

or

Advantages of having children	Disadvantages of having children
continuation	responsibilities
purpose	money
love	

Last, organize the groups into possible ways to answer the questions. Outlines are a convenient and common way to organize. In the outlines below, each Roman numeral (I, II, III, IV, etc.) stands for a paragraph. Each capital letter (A, B, C, etc.) stands for a subheading. Your outline might look like this:

I. Introduction—There are advantages and disadvantages to having children
II. Advantages of having children
   A. Love
   B. Families
III. Disadvantages of having children
   A. Career
   B. Time
IV. Conclusion—pick a side

or

I. Introduction—There are advantages and disadvantages to having children
II. Advantages
   A. Continuation
   B. Purpose
   C. Love

III. Disadvantages
   A. Responsibilities
   B. Money
IV. Conclusion—pick a side

Under some of the subheadings of your outline, you may also want to jot down a few key words to remind you of the details or examples you intend to use to support your points.

Remember, this entire process is designed to be done very quickly. From start to finish, it should only take a few moments. Do not spend more than five minutes organizing your answer, or you may not have time to complete the essay.

The advantages of this method, or any planning, are that you have organized and arranged your thoughts into a unified whole. Your answer will make a great deal more sense, and you won't find that you complete a paragraph and then exclaim, "Oh! I forgot the point about. . ." and have to insert arrows and various messy signs.

WRITING YOUR ESSAY

Topic Sentences Are A Must

In a way, writing a good topic sentence is like aiming a gun: If the topic sentence is aimed correctly, the whole paragraph will hit its mark, and prove your point.

- *Every paragraph should have a topic sentence.*
- The topic sentence expresses the main idea—the topic—of the paragraph.
- The topic sentence joins together all the ideas expressed in the paragraph.
- The topic sentence should be *limited* enough to be developed within a single paragraph but *broad* enough to have all the ideas that you need in that paragraph. The more specific your topic sentence, the more detailed and descriptive your paragraph will be.

Limiting a topic sentence

Remember: A topic sentence has an idea that can be fully proven in one paragraph. For example, the sentence "You can learn a lot about human nature just by observing people" is so broad that it cannot be proven in one single paragraph. But if we write

    "You can learn a lot about human nature by watching people at a bus station"

or

    "You can learn a lot about human nature by watching people at the beach"

we have a topic that we can prove in one paragraph.

Expressing a clear controlling idea

Another way to look at topic sentences is through the *controlling idea*. This is a *key word* or a *group of words* that expresses the basic idea of the sentence. When the controlling idea is clear, the entire sentence will be specific and clear:

Example: An encyclopedia is a handy book for students.
"Handy" is the *controlling idea,* and in the paragraph that follows, you will explain *how* the encyclopedia is handy.

Using specific words

To prove your point and make your writing interesting, you have to use specific words and phrases.

Example: His face was _____ with fright.
colorless   scarlet   chalky   pale

The answer is "chalky," because "colorless" and "pale" are too vague. "Scarlet" is also incorrect, because your face does not become scarlet (red) when you are afraid. "Chalky" is the best word, because in addition to color—a pale, dry white—it implies a *texture*—dry and lifeless. It is the most descriptive word and the one that will make this sentence most effective.

The points about using clear topic sentences and specific words apply to all the paragraphs of the essay. Now, here is a closer look at each part of the essay: the introduction, the development, and the conclusion.

The Introduction

Here are the main items to bear in mind as you write your introduction:

1. Keep in mind the key words of the question, but don't bother repeating the question word-for-word. Paraphrasing is better than just copying.
2. Let the reader know in your first paragraph what your essay is going to cover and what your controlling idea is. This can be accomplished in a clear topic sentence.
3. Establish your tone or attitude. Dullness in writing is not a virtue, and your introduction must help you engage the reader's attention. You should avoid writing in a stilted or artificial style, but so too should you avoid being too cute, too emotional, or too colloquial.
4. Each sentence should advance your topic and provide interest to your reader.

The Development

The heart of the essay is the development, or the middle paragraph or paragraphs. Here you must attempt to support the main idea of your essay through illustrations, details, and examples. The developmental paragraphs must serve as a link in the chain of ideas and contribute directly to the essay's central thought. All the sentences of the development must explain the essential truth of the thesis or topic sentence without digression. You may do this through a style that is descriptive, narrative, or expository, using a factual or anecdotal approach. Whatever approach and style you choose, your writing should be coherent, logical, unified, and well ordered.

Avoid the following pitfalls:

1. sentences that are irrelevant and contain extraneous material
2. sentences that follow no sequence of thought but seem to jump from one idea to another
3. sentences that do not relate to the topic sentence or do not flow from the preceding sentence

The good writer makes use of transitional words or phrases to connect thoughts and to provide for a logical sequence of ideas. Examine the following list of transitional words and phrases. They can help make your method of development clear to your reader.

therefore	first of all	then
moreover	secondly	indeed
however	for example	in any case
consequently	for instance	nevertheless
of course	finally	

Many other good linking expressions can be added to the above list, but if you choose judiciously from these 14, you will find that your development will be more coherent and well ordered.

The Conclusion

The successful writer, like the wise guest, knows that he must not prolong his stay; when he comes to the end of his essay, he must draw his comments together in a strong, clear concluding paragraph.

A good concluding paragraph should give the reader the feeling that the essay has made its point, that the thesis has been explained, and that a point of view has been established. This can be accomplished in about four to six sentences in one of the following ways:

1. through a *restatement* of the main idea
2. through a *summary* of the material covered in the essay
3. through a clear *statement of the writer's opinion* of the issue(s) involved

Just as there are good techniques, there are also a few very ineffective methods that some test takers are tempted to use in drawing a composition to a close. Avoid falling into the following traps:

1. apologizing for your inability to discuss all the issues in the alotted time
2. complaining that the topics did not interest you or that you don't think it was fair to be asked to write on so broad a topic
3. introducing material that you will not develop, rambling on about nonpertinent matters, or using trite material

Keep in mind that a good conclusion is integrally related to the thesis of the essay. Whether it reviews, restates, or leads the reader to think on his or her own, the conclusion must be strong, clear, and effective.

Proofreading Can Raise Your Score

There is a great tendency to stand up the very minute you have finished writing and rush out of the room, relieved that it is all over. Although we all have this feeling, you should allow time for *proofreading*. You can save yourself a great many unnecessary errors if you proofread your essay.

After you finish writing, leave a few minutes to check over what you said. Make sure of the following:

Did you answer the question?
Did you provide good, *specific* detail to support your ideas?
Did you organize your answer in the best possible way to make your point clearly?
Did you check over what you said for errors in spelling, grammar, punctuation, words misused, and so forth?

This is time very well spent. You must check over what you said, but be sure to read what is there, not what you *think* is there. Do not read too quickly, and go back over passages that seem unclear to you. Some find it helpful to put another piece of paper over the lines to help you focus on only one line at a time. In any event, make sure you check what you have said, even if all others are getting up around you. You'll be the winner if you do.

EVALUATING SAMPLE ESSAYS

Read the essays that follow, and see what each writer did that was right and wrong. See where the essay can be improved and where it is fine. See if the writer proved the point, and if so, what details and examples he or she used. If the point was not proved, where did the essay go off the track? Or, did the writer allow his or her ideas and organization to be marred by faulty sentence structure and mechanics?

Sample Essays 1, 2, and 3 are based on the topic below. Form your own opinion of each essay and compare it with the evaluation provided.

There has been a great deal of attention paid recently to the problem of drinking and driving. The laws on DWI have become much stiffer. Discuss the advantages and disadvantages of stiffer penalties for driving while intoxicated. Be specific.

Sample Essay 1

Personally, I think the drinking law should be raised, one reason is there would be less people getting in acccidents, many accidents are caused by drunk drivers. The people usually involved in DWI's are all young kids who are under pressure try to act cool and instead injure someone's life. Many kids drinking are not responsible enough and take other people's lives in there hands this is ruining many peoples lives and also society is getting worse. The problem would almost be solved if the laws was raised, putting drinking in the hands of youngsters is like giving a baby cofee, there not of right mind to make a decision whether to take it or not. I think that many teens are to young and therefore I think that the laws should be raised if it were lowered it would only be more problems. The lawmakers are making a right move in order to make society better if they keep doing things to prevent teens to drink this country will have a better chance at surviving problems. I'm glad that the law was raised so that my life wasn't taken in the hands of one irresponsible teenager. That's why I think drunk driving laws should be raised.

Evaluation: This essay is poorly organized and fails to prove the point. There are far too many serious writing errors, especially in sentence construction. Some examples of poor sentences include:

Personally, I think the drinking law should be raised, one reason is there would be less people getting into accidents, many accidents are caused by drunk drivers.

This is a *run-on*, which means there are several complete sentences tacked together without proper punctuation. The first sentence ends after the word ''raised''; the second, after the word ''accidents.'' After each of these words there should be periods or words that serve as *conjunctions,* such as ''and,'' ''or,'' or ''for.'' In addition to the technical writing problems, the groups of words that are linked do not make the author's point.

Another example of a weak sentence is:

Many kids drinking are not responsible enough and take other people's lives in there hands this is ruining many peoples lives and also society is getting worse.

This is also a *run-on,* and should properly end after the word ''hands.'' The ideas do not prove the point and show a lack of logic.

Because of errors such as these, this paper would probably receive a grade in the 1–2 range as a very weak essay.

Sample Essay 2

Drinking and driving laws need to be stiffer. When a person drinks and drives he or she is not only taking their own lives, but other innocent lives with them. The government should put very strict laws on those who drink and drive because maybe they will have a second thought about stepping into a car while intoxicated.

There are no advantages to drinking and driving. It is a very foolish thing. The disadvantages are that you will be punished if you violate the law, but that is no one else's fault but your own, for you brought it on yourself.

The advantage to stiffer penalties is that maybe people will stay away from alcohol, if they are driving alone. From my own opinion, I think there are no disadvantages to stiffer penalties.

When a person gets behind the wheel of a car, while intoxicated, they are not aware of many things that are going on around them. This causes them to do things that cause accidents, and many times, take people's lives. Drinking and driving is a very serious and foolish thing to do. Intoxicated drivers deserve a harsh penalty so they won't do it again.

Evaluation: You can see that this paper is much better structured than the previous one. First of all, the paragraphs use the words ''advantages'' and ''disadvantages'' and clearly address themselves to the question. Let's take it apart.

Advantages to stiffer DWI laws	Disadvantages to stiffer DWI laws
will prevent deaths (''second thought'') people will stay away from alcohol	you will be punished

There are clear divisions and a clear reasoning going on here. Although there could be far more specific examples, the paper demonstrates control of the subject and a clear understanding of the question. There is also some style, in phrases such as ''There are no advantages to drinking and driving,'' and ''It is a very foolish thing.'' This paper would probably rate a 4 on the scale. With more specific examples, it could very easily achieve a higher score.

Let's try one last essay on this topic:

Sample Essay 3

While all concerned agree that something has to be done about the problem of driving while intoxicated, there are both advantages and disadvantages to increasing the penalties. The advantages include the obvious saving of lives and property, while the disadvantages include providing incentive for those inclined to break laws to continue to show they can do so. There is little doubt, however, that the advantages vastly outweigh the disadvantages.

The main advantage of tightening the punishment for driving while under the influence of alcohol or drugs would be the protection of lives. There are so many innocent people killed every year by intoxicated drivers that citizens have been moved to take matters in their own hands. Candy Lightner, the mother of a sixteen-year-old daughter killed by a drunken driver, formed an organization called M.A.D.D. (Mothers Against Drunken Drivers) to educate people about the dangers of driving while under the influence. The Scandinavian countries, where alcoholism and driving has long been a problem, have greatly increased penalties for those convicted of driving drunk, and they found that the death rate has dropped significantly. They have mandatory jail sentences and publish the names of offenders. If even one life was saved through stiffer legislation, it would be worth it.

The disadvantages could include the portion of society that feels duty-bound to break rules and might take increased DWI penalties as a sign that they should try to ''beat the system.'' This could actually raise the number of serious accidents. There is also the problem of how to enact the laws. A recent proposal, involving hosts who can be held responsible for allowing drunken guests to leave their parties, has been greeted with a great deal of disapproval. Despite this, many bars are already limiting their ''Happy Hours,'' especially in Connecticut.

Regardless of those who object to a tightening of DWI laws, it seems clear that something has to be done to decrease the number of deaths related to drivers on the roads when they clearly should not be. A series of stiffer laws seems to be the best way to accomplish the saving of lives. It's worked in other countries, and it can work here too.

Evaluation: The topic sentence clearly states the question and the points to be covered. The points include:

Advantages	Disadvantages
saving of lives and property	providing incentive for people to break the law

And the paragraph concludes with the author's point: The advantages far outweigh the disadvantages.

The second paragraph clearly states that the protection of lives is the main advantage of stiffer DWI laws. There are *two* specific examples to back this up:

Candy Lightner, founder of MADD

Result of tighter laws in Scandinavian countries

These are excellent examples because they *specifically* prove the point under discussion.

The third paragraph also has a clear specific example, involving the recent "host law," holding those who let drunken drivers leave their homes responsible for the results. It also discusses the recent change in Connecticut "happy hour" rules. Both these examples serve to make the point.

The conclusion has a sentence that sums up each major point and clearly states the writer's conviction that stiffer DWI laws would help all of us in preventing unnecessary deaths.

This would probably be a 6 paper, because it uses clear specific examples and good organization to make the point. It has a clear voice or tone—the author is obviously very concerned about this issue. The word choice is appropriate, and the grammar and usage are correct.

Here's another essay topic, followed by Sample Essays 4, 5, and 6, which are also evaluated.

Some believe college is a waste of time and money, while others feel it is a valuable tool for happiness and success. Explain some of the advantages and disadvantages of going to college. Be specific.

Sample Essay 4

In today's society it is almost an asset for young Americans to attend at least two years of college.

A person will probably only obtain success through hard work and determination. So if one wants to achieve their life goals it would be recommended that college should be considered as a valuable tool of education. College offers many alternatives in subjects to study, each having advantages and disadvantages.

When the time in life comes for one to decide whether college is worth the time, effort and money they must think about the future and its results. If one decides not to go to college they must begin to think about job opportunities. Even if they are planning to start there own business they must decide whether or not they are qualified to do so and what they will do if the business fails. If the business does fail, what background and qualifications will they have? On the other hand a decision to go to college is a worthwhile experience. Just think, give up 4 years or even 2 and you'll obtain an education that will last a lifetime. A college education is always something in which one will be able to fall back on as a cornerstone in their life.

These are only a few of the many reasons that college is important.

Evaluation: We can see at a glance that the topic paragraph is too short, containing only one sentence. It is also unclear. What is "almost an asset"? Is the author for or against college attendance?

The second paragraph also has serious flaws in logic. The author states that a person "will probably only obtain success through hard work and determination." If this is true, it would seem that college is a waste of time, yet in the next sentence, the writer states that "college would be a valuable tool." Why? Aren't the hard work and determination enough? What purpose does college serve? Then he or she goes off the topic completely, discussing the advantages and disadvantages of the various subjects college offers. What you should study in college was not the question. Rather, the question asked *if* you should go to college at all.

The third paragraph has the same problems with logic. It is very wordy and yet, despite all the language, the point is not clear. Is the writer saying, in the opening to this paragraph, that college is worthwhile or not? By the end of the paragraph, we know that he or she believes that it is, but all the advantages belong in the previous paragraph. There are also some flaws in logic. There's not much sense in saying, as he or she does in his conclusion, that ''a college education is always something in which one will be able to fall back on as a cornerstone in their life.'' What does this mean? What's a ''cornerstone'' in life? What happens if you get a degree and then discover that your training has to be updated or that the job you trained for no longer exists? Then the ''job'' portion of a college degree is not at all valuable.

The conclusion is also incorrect, for it contains only one sentence and that sentence does not serve to conclude the essay. It makes no mention of the disadvantages and none of the specific details we discussed above.

While this paper may appear on a first reading to make the point, it has few specific details and a lot of unnecessary wordiness. It would probably receive a 2–3 grade.

Sample Essay 5

To me, college is not a waste of time. First because its something I have to work for, when I want something bad enough I strive for it. College will help first of all in the long run because it will help in getting jobs and providing for the family. College is only a waste of time and money if you don't put your mind to it; otherwise it is something you can be proud of when you finish, you can be proud that you accomplished something. There are alot of advantages to college because now many places are looking for someone with a background of education if you do not have college it is difficult to find a job. The disadvantage of college might be that a person doesn't want to go but is forced he therefore does not care and money is wasted. Many people think college is a waste of time it is only a waste of time if you make it a waste of time. Alright college takes up alot of time but it is surely worth it and many jobs want people that are qualified if your a quitter than college is not for you.

Evaluation: Is the point made?
The topic sentence clearly states that ''college is not a waste of time.'' Let's see what examples are here to support this statement.

College will cause me to strive for a goal.
College will help me to get a job.
College will help me provide for the family.

There are enough points made to see that the author is on the right track. Does he discuss the *disadvantages* of going to college? Yes, and the disadvantages cited can be paraphrased as follows:

A person who is forced to go to college will waste time and money.

However, the essay's structure and unity can be greatly improved. First of all, there is only one paragraph.

There is also a serious problem with details and examples. The author should discuss *specific jobs* that require college.

There are also some errors in the areas of grammar and usage. ''Alot,'' for example, is two words, spelled ''a lot,'' and the sentence ''The disadvantages of college might be that a person doesn't want to go but is forced therefore he does not care and money is wasted'' is a run-on; two sentences compressed into one, lacking proper punctuation (.:;—) and/or conjunctions (and, or, for). This paper is most seriously lacking in organization and specific details and would probably be between a 2 and 3 on the grading scale.

Now read and evaluate Sample Essay 6.

Sample Essay 6

Attending college is one of the most serious decisions a person has to consider. There are great advantages, including the opportunity to learn fascinating things and meet interesting people, as well as train for a job. Unfortunately, there are grave disadvantages, especially in these times, for college costs a tremendous amount of money, money that could be spent pursuing a career or setting up a business.

There are a lot of interesting things a person can learn at college, things he might otherwise not have a chance to explore. I found music one of the most rewarding for me. Even though it has nothing to do with my job—I'm in sales—I nonetheless found the history of music and musical instruments, especially in the 16th century, wonderfully interesting. I know that I would not have followed this interest on my own. I also met a lot of interesting people, especially people from cultures and countries different from my own. There was an exchange program at my college, and I made friends with a young woman from England. This summer I spent a week at her parents' dairy farm in the southern section of the country, and I found the contrasts between England and America all-absorbing. I never could have had this experience had I not attended college. The final advantage of college, the one most people are interested in, is job training, although college is not a trade school in the sense that it guarantees you training for a specific job. I trained in marketing and retail sales and was lucky enough to find a job with a major department store. College paid off for me, even though I can see there are serious disadvantages.

It costs a tremendous amount to attend college. A state school can cost upwards of $5,000 per year, while the more expensive private colleges and universities charge $18,000 and even more, depending on programs and personal expenses. This money can be applied to setting up a business and my brother did just that. He established his own gas station with the college money my parents had set aside and he is doing very well. One of his friends set up a small electrical supply house; another, a marine supply store. For these people, college would have set back their businesses, as they would not have had the money to begin.

There are both advantages and disadvantages to attending college. It can offer you the chance to explore fascinating areas and meet new people while you train for a job, but it can also cost you a tremendous amount of money that could be used to start a business. You have to balance these considerations when deciding what to do. For me, college was the answer; for my brother, it was not.

Evaluation: This is clearly a 6 essay, as it states the advantages and disadvantages clearly and supports each with specific details and examples. There is a relaxed personal tone to the essay, and each idea is unfolded carefully, in its own place.

Part III
Three PPST Practice Tests

ANSWER SHEET FOR PRACTICE TEST 1

Reading

1. Ⓐ Ⓑ Ⓒ Ⓓ Ⓔ
2. Ⓐ Ⓑ Ⓒ Ⓓ Ⓔ
3. Ⓐ Ⓑ Ⓒ Ⓓ Ⓔ
4. Ⓐ Ⓑ Ⓒ Ⓓ Ⓔ
5. Ⓐ Ⓑ Ⓒ Ⓓ Ⓔ
6. Ⓐ Ⓑ Ⓒ Ⓓ Ⓔ
7. Ⓐ Ⓑ Ⓒ Ⓓ Ⓔ
8. Ⓐ Ⓑ Ⓒ Ⓓ Ⓔ
9. Ⓐ Ⓑ Ⓒ Ⓓ Ⓔ
10. Ⓐ Ⓑ Ⓒ Ⓓ Ⓔ
11. Ⓐ Ⓑ Ⓒ Ⓓ Ⓔ
12. Ⓐ Ⓑ Ⓒ Ⓓ Ⓔ
13. Ⓐ Ⓑ Ⓒ Ⓓ Ⓔ
14. Ⓐ Ⓑ Ⓒ Ⓓ Ⓔ
15. Ⓐ Ⓑ Ⓒ Ⓓ Ⓔ
16. Ⓐ Ⓑ Ⓒ Ⓓ Ⓔ
17. Ⓐ Ⓑ Ⓒ Ⓓ Ⓔ
18. Ⓐ Ⓑ Ⓒ Ⓓ Ⓔ
19. Ⓐ Ⓑ Ⓒ Ⓓ Ⓔ
20. Ⓐ Ⓑ Ⓒ Ⓓ Ⓔ
21. Ⓐ Ⓑ Ⓒ Ⓓ Ⓔ
22. Ⓐ Ⓑ Ⓒ Ⓓ Ⓔ
23. Ⓐ Ⓑ Ⓒ Ⓓ Ⓔ
24. Ⓐ Ⓑ Ⓒ Ⓓ Ⓔ
25. Ⓐ Ⓑ Ⓒ Ⓓ Ⓔ
26. Ⓐ Ⓑ Ⓒ Ⓓ Ⓔ
27. Ⓐ Ⓑ Ⓒ Ⓓ Ⓔ
28. Ⓐ Ⓑ Ⓒ Ⓓ Ⓔ
29. Ⓐ Ⓑ Ⓒ Ⓓ Ⓔ
30. Ⓐ Ⓑ Ⓒ Ⓓ Ⓔ
31. Ⓐ Ⓑ Ⓒ Ⓓ Ⓔ
32. Ⓐ Ⓑ Ⓒ Ⓓ Ⓔ
33. Ⓐ Ⓑ Ⓒ Ⓓ Ⓔ
34. Ⓐ Ⓑ Ⓒ Ⓓ Ⓔ
35. Ⓐ Ⓑ Ⓒ Ⓓ Ⓔ
36. Ⓐ Ⓑ Ⓒ Ⓓ Ⓔ
37. Ⓐ Ⓑ Ⓒ Ⓓ Ⓔ
38. Ⓐ Ⓑ Ⓒ Ⓓ Ⓔ
39. Ⓐ Ⓑ Ⓒ Ⓓ Ⓔ
40. Ⓐ Ⓑ Ⓒ Ⓓ Ⓔ

Mathematics

1. Ⓐ Ⓑ Ⓒ Ⓓ Ⓔ
2. Ⓐ Ⓑ Ⓒ Ⓓ Ⓔ
3. Ⓐ Ⓑ Ⓒ Ⓓ Ⓔ
4. Ⓐ Ⓑ Ⓒ Ⓓ Ⓔ
5. Ⓐ Ⓑ Ⓒ Ⓓ Ⓔ
6. Ⓐ Ⓑ Ⓒ Ⓓ Ⓔ
7. Ⓐ Ⓑ Ⓒ Ⓓ Ⓔ
8. Ⓐ Ⓑ Ⓒ Ⓓ Ⓔ
9. Ⓐ Ⓑ Ⓒ Ⓓ Ⓔ
10. Ⓐ Ⓑ Ⓒ Ⓓ Ⓔ
11. Ⓐ Ⓑ Ⓒ Ⓓ Ⓔ
12. Ⓐ Ⓑ Ⓒ Ⓓ Ⓔ
13. Ⓐ Ⓑ Ⓒ Ⓓ Ⓔ
14. Ⓐ Ⓑ Ⓒ Ⓓ Ⓔ
15. Ⓐ Ⓑ Ⓒ Ⓓ Ⓔ
16. Ⓐ Ⓑ Ⓒ Ⓓ Ⓔ
17. Ⓐ Ⓑ Ⓒ Ⓓ Ⓔ
18. Ⓐ Ⓑ Ⓒ Ⓓ Ⓔ
19. Ⓐ Ⓑ Ⓒ Ⓓ Ⓔ
20. Ⓐ Ⓑ Ⓒ Ⓓ Ⓔ
21. Ⓐ Ⓑ Ⓒ Ⓓ Ⓔ
22. Ⓐ Ⓑ Ⓒ Ⓓ Ⓔ
23. Ⓐ Ⓑ Ⓒ Ⓓ Ⓔ
24. Ⓐ Ⓑ Ⓒ Ⓓ Ⓔ
25. Ⓐ Ⓑ Ⓒ Ⓓ Ⓔ
26. Ⓐ Ⓑ Ⓒ Ⓓ Ⓔ
27. Ⓐ Ⓑ Ⓒ Ⓓ Ⓔ
28. Ⓐ Ⓑ Ⓒ Ⓓ Ⓔ
29. Ⓐ Ⓑ Ⓒ Ⓓ Ⓔ
30. Ⓐ Ⓑ Ⓒ Ⓓ Ⓔ
31. Ⓐ Ⓑ Ⓒ Ⓓ Ⓔ
32. Ⓐ Ⓑ Ⓒ Ⓓ Ⓔ
33. Ⓐ Ⓑ Ⓒ Ⓓ Ⓔ
34. Ⓐ Ⓑ Ⓒ Ⓓ Ⓔ
35. Ⓐ Ⓑ Ⓒ Ⓓ Ⓔ
36. Ⓐ Ⓑ Ⓒ Ⓓ Ⓔ
37. Ⓐ Ⓑ Ⓒ Ⓓ Ⓔ
38. Ⓐ Ⓑ Ⓒ Ⓓ Ⓔ
39. Ⓐ Ⓑ Ⓒ Ⓓ Ⓔ
40. Ⓐ Ⓑ Ⓒ Ⓓ Ⓔ

Writing

1. Ⓐ Ⓑ Ⓒ Ⓓ Ⓔ
2. Ⓐ Ⓑ Ⓒ Ⓓ Ⓔ
3. Ⓐ Ⓑ Ⓒ Ⓓ Ⓔ
4. Ⓐ Ⓑ Ⓒ Ⓓ Ⓔ
5. Ⓐ Ⓑ Ⓒ Ⓓ Ⓔ
6. Ⓐ Ⓑ Ⓒ Ⓓ Ⓔ
7. Ⓐ Ⓑ Ⓒ Ⓓ Ⓔ
8. Ⓐ Ⓑ Ⓒ Ⓓ Ⓔ
9. Ⓐ Ⓑ Ⓒ Ⓓ Ⓔ
10. Ⓐ Ⓑ Ⓒ Ⓓ Ⓔ
11. Ⓐ Ⓑ Ⓒ Ⓓ Ⓔ
12. Ⓐ Ⓑ Ⓒ Ⓓ Ⓔ
13. Ⓐ Ⓑ Ⓒ Ⓓ Ⓔ
14. Ⓐ Ⓑ Ⓒ Ⓓ Ⓔ
15. Ⓐ Ⓑ Ⓒ Ⓓ Ⓔ
16. Ⓐ Ⓑ Ⓒ Ⓓ Ⓔ
17. Ⓐ Ⓑ Ⓒ Ⓓ Ⓔ
18. Ⓐ Ⓑ Ⓒ Ⓓ Ⓔ
19. Ⓐ Ⓑ Ⓒ Ⓓ Ⓔ
20. Ⓐ Ⓑ Ⓒ Ⓓ Ⓔ
21. Ⓐ Ⓑ Ⓒ Ⓓ Ⓔ
22. Ⓐ Ⓑ Ⓒ Ⓓ Ⓔ
23. Ⓐ Ⓑ Ⓒ Ⓓ Ⓔ
24. Ⓐ Ⓑ Ⓒ Ⓓ Ⓔ
25. Ⓐ Ⓑ Ⓒ Ⓓ Ⓔ
26. Ⓐ Ⓑ Ⓒ Ⓓ Ⓔ
27. Ⓐ Ⓑ Ⓒ Ⓓ Ⓔ
28. Ⓐ Ⓑ Ⓒ Ⓓ Ⓔ
29. Ⓐ Ⓑ Ⓒ Ⓓ Ⓔ
30. Ⓐ Ⓑ Ⓒ Ⓓ Ⓔ
31. Ⓐ Ⓑ Ⓒ Ⓓ Ⓔ
32. Ⓐ Ⓑ Ⓒ Ⓓ Ⓔ
33. Ⓐ Ⓑ Ⓒ Ⓓ Ⓔ
34. Ⓐ Ⓑ Ⓒ Ⓓ Ⓔ
35. Ⓐ Ⓑ Ⓒ Ⓓ Ⓔ
36. Ⓐ Ⓑ Ⓒ Ⓓ Ⓔ
37. Ⓐ Ⓑ Ⓒ Ⓓ Ⓔ
38. Ⓐ Ⓑ Ⓒ Ⓓ Ⓔ
39. Ⓐ Ⓑ Ⓒ Ⓓ Ⓔ
40. Ⓐ Ⓑ Ⓒ Ⓓ Ⓔ
41. Ⓐ Ⓑ Ⓒ Ⓓ Ⓔ
42. Ⓐ Ⓑ Ⓒ Ⓓ Ⓔ
43. Ⓐ Ⓑ Ⓒ Ⓓ Ⓔ
44. Ⓐ Ⓑ Ⓒ Ⓓ Ⓔ
45. Ⓐ Ⓑ Ⓒ Ⓓ Ⓔ

PPST PRACTICE TEST 1

READING

60 Minutes—40 Questions

Directions: Each passage in this test is followed by a question or questions based on its content. Read each passage and answer the accompanying questions by choosing the best answer from among the five choices given. Base your answers on what is *stated* or *implied* in the passage.

Questions 1–3

A legendary island in the Atlantic Ocean beyond the Pillars of Hercules was first mentioned by Plato in the *Timaeus*. Atlantis was a fabulously beautiful and prosperous land, the seat of an empire nine thousand years before Solon. Its inhabitants overran part of Europe and Africa, Athens alone being able to defy them. Because of the impiety of its people, the island was destroyed by an earthquake and inundation. The legend may have existed before Plato and may have sprung from the concept of Homer's Elysium. The possibility that such an island once existed has caused much speculation, resulting in a theory that pre-Columbian civilizations in America were established by colonists from the lost island.

1. The title below that best expresses the ideas of this passage is

    (A) A Persistent Myth
    (B) Geography According to Plato
    (C) The First Discoverers of America
    (D) Buried Civilizations
    (E) A Labor of Hercules

2. According to the passage, we may safely conclude that the inhabitants of Atlantis

    (A) were known personally to Homer
    (B) were ruled by Plato
    (C) were a religious and superstitious people
    (D) used the name Columbus for America
    (E) left no recorded evidence of their civilization

3. According to the legend, Atlantis was destroyed because the inhabitants

    (A) failed to obtain an adequate food supply
    (B) failed to conquer Greece
    (C) failed to respect their gods
    (D) believed in Homer's Elysium
    (E) had become too prosperous

4. The 1950s were a time of happiness and growth for America. Although it is argued that times were dull, the economy was doing well, unemployment was low, and America ruled the world.

    Which of the following sentences would provide the most logical continuation of the paragraph?

    (A) In addition, the Russians launched Sputnik in the 1950s.
    (B) In these more turbulent times, many people would accept some dullness if accompanied by peace, power, and prosperity.
    (C) The New York Yankees won the pennant 8 of the 10 years that decade.
    (D) The 1850s was not so prosperous a decade.
    (E) Who knows what the next decade will bring?

5. Life is very complicated, and it is art's business to simplify it. The artist must find the common denominator, that which is similar among all of us, and draw upon that to produce a work that not only unites us but also separates us. Each of us must be able to see something different in the work, although the underlying thing we grasp in it is the same.

    With which of the following statements is the author most likely to agree?

    (A) All art imitates nature.
    (B) Every man is an artist.

(C) Because we cannot see it, music is not art.

(D) The artist must simplify and then complicate.

(E) No great art was ever created without tears.

Questions 6–10

There should be no mystery about nuclear power: it is simply a source of heat generated by a machine we call a nuclear reactor. The core of this reactor serves as a fiery-hot but flameless (and therefore smokeless) substitute for the firebox of a conventional coal-steam (or oil-burning) plant. In the core, water under pressure of 2,250 pounds per square inch is heated to above the boiling point—to more than 600 degrees Fahrenheit. This superheated water is piped through the coils of a heat exchanger where it gives up its heat to a water boiler, producing steam, and is then pumped back to the reactor core to be heated again. The steam is pumped around in another closed loop so that it hits the blades of a turbine, spinning it at high speed. The turbine is coupled to the drive shaft of a generator—and electricity is thereby produced just as in a conventional power plant. The steam is then led off to a condenser, where it is cooled and turned back to water—which is pumped back to the heat exchanger to become steam once again, and so on. In two thirds of the 100 nuclear power plants built or being constructed, the cooling at the condenser is done by still another stream of water—a "once-through" stream—drawn from an adjacent river, lake, or estuary, used and discharged back into its original source.

6. The best title for this passage would be

   (A) The Economic Advantages of Nuclear Power
   (B) How Nuclear Power Plants Work
   (C) Nuclear Power's Effect on River Ecological Systems
   (D) Theories of Nuclear Physics
   (E) Nuclear Power Safety

7. From this passage it may be inferred that

   (A) nuclear power is cheaper than coal power
   (B) the smoke from a nuclear plant is unsafe
   (C) in a third of the nuclear power plants being constructed, the coolant is helium sulfate
   (D) steam may be a by-product of a nuclear reaction
   (E) none of the above is true

8. In the nuclear power plant described in this passage, the turbine is driven by

   (A) superheated water
   (B) electricity
   (C) the generator
   (D) the closed loop
   (E) steam

9. It can be inferred from this passage that the temperature of the core of an active nuclear reactor is

   (A) about the same as that of a conventional firebox
   (B) not measurable with conventional instruments
   (C) 2,250 pounds per square inch
   (D) the same as that in the closed loop
   (E) more than 6,000 degrees Fahrenheit

10. According to the passage, after the steam has produced electricity in a nuclear power plant it is

    (A) pumped around in another closed loop
    (B) superheated to form superheated water
    (C) discharged back to its original source
    (D) condensed
    (E) evaporated

11. Through advertising, manufacturers exercise a high degree of control over consumers' desires. However, the manufacturer assumes enormous risks in attempting to predict what consumers will want and in producing goods in quantity and distributing them in advance of final selection by the consumers.

    The paragraph best supports the statement that manufacturers

    (A) can eliminate the risk of overproduction by advertising
    (B) distribute goods directly to the consumers
    (C) must depend on the final consumers for the success of their undertakings
    (D) can predict with great accuracy the success of any product they put on the market
    (E) are more concerned with advertising than with the production of goods

Questions 12–13

In most Asian countries, rice is the principal food crop. Increased cultivation has barely met the demands of the growing populations. In the Philippines, while food production has increased slightly faster than the size of the population, even greater increases in per capitia food demand have created new shortfalls. Indonesia, once an important rice exporter, has been dependent upon imported rice for several years. Most countries are just keeping up with their current needs, and gross shortages can be anticipated.

The intensified agricultural production required in these countries has potential adverse side effects on other resources. The disruptive effects of absent reservoirs are self-evident. Some other problems include waterlogging, soil erosion, increased population of pests, and agricultural pollution.

12. According to the passage, in the Philippines

(A) rice is being replaced by other grains
(B) gross shortages are a thing of the past
(C) there has been a dependence upon rice for trade
(D) a greater demand for food outweighs greater production
(E) there is a grain surplus problem

13. The author states that more food production in these countries could lead to

(A) a decrease in reservoir use
(B) soil erosion
(C) a decline in pest populations
(D) a gross abuse of insecticides
(E) a shortage of workers in the industrial areas

14. For a society to function properly, everyone must function with everyone else. Individual effort is great—for the individual. Social scientists should devote less time to figuring out how and why the individual does what he or she does and should spend more time figuring out how to get people to do more of what everybody should do—cooperate.

The author of this statement would probably approve most of

(A) a psychological study of the determinants of behavior
(B) a sociologic study of why people go to war
(C) an historical study of the communes that have failed
(D) an increased number of social scientists
(E) a psychologic study of what makes people cooperative or antisocial

15. Statistics tell us that heart disease kills more people than any other illness, and the death rate continues to rise. People over 30 have a fifty-fifty chance of escaping, for heart disease is chiefly an illness of people in late middle age and advanced years. Because there are more people in this age group living today than there were some years ago, heart disease is able to find more victims.

This paragraph best supports the statement that

(A) half of the people over 30 years of age have heart disease today
(B) more people die of heart disease than of all other causes
(C) older people are the chief victims of heart disease
(D) the rising birth rate has increased the possibility that the average person will die of heart disease
(E) the stresses of modern living increase the risk of heart disease

Questions 16–20

Educators are seriously concerned about the high rate of dropouts among the doctor of philosophy candidates and the consequent loss of talent to a nation in need of Ph.D.'s. Last week a well-rounded study was published. The dropout rate was found to be 31 percent, and in most cases the dropouts, while not completing the Ph.D. requirements, went on to productive work.

They are not only doing well financially, but, according to the report, are not far below the income levels of those who went on to complete their doctorates.

The study was conducted by Dr. Allan Tucker. Discussing the study last week, Dr. Tucker said the project was initiated "because of the concerns frequently expressed by graduate faculties and administrators that some of the individuals who dropped out of Ph.D. programs were capable of completing the requirements for the degree. Some people expressed the opinion that the shortage of highly trained specialists and college teachers could be reduced by persuading the dropouts to return to graduate school to complete the Ph.D. program."

"The results of our research," Dr. Tucker concluded, "did not support these opinions."

The study found that:

(1) lack of motivation was the principal reason for dropping out.

(2) most dropouts went as far in their doctoral programs as was consistent with their levels of ability or their specialties.

(3) most dropouts are now engaged in work consistent with their education and motivation.

(4) the dropout rate was highest in the humanities (50%) and lowest in the natural sciences (29%)—and is higher in lower-quality graduate schools.

Nearly 75 percent of the dropouts said there was no academic reason for their decision, but those who mentioned academic reasons cited failure to pass qualifying examinations, uncompleted research, and failure to pass language exams.

"Among the single most important personal reasons identified by dropouts for noncompletion of their Ph.D. program," the study found, "lack of finances was marked by 19 percent."

As an indication of how well the dropouts were doing, a chart showed that 2 percent whose studies were in the humanities were receiving $20,000 and more annually, while none of the Ph.D.'s with that background reached this figure. In the social sciences 5 percent of the Ph.D.'s reached the $20,000 plus figure as against 3 percent of the dropouts, but in the physical sciences they were neck-and-neck with 5 percent each.

As to the possibility of getting dropouts back on campus, the outlook was glum.

"The main conditions which would have to prevail for at least 25 percent of the dropouts who might consider returning to graduate school would be to guarantee that they would retain their present level of income and in some cases their present job."

16. The author states that many educators feel that

(A) steps should be taken to get the dropouts back to school particularly in certain disciplines

(B) since the dropout does just about as well financially as the Ph.D. holder, there is no justifiable reason for the former to return to his studies

(C) the high dropout rate is largely attributable to the lack of stimulation on the part of faculty members

(D) the dropout should return to a lower-quality school to continue his studies

(E) the Ph.D. holder is generally a better-adjusted person than the dropout

17. Research has shown that

(A) dropouts are substantially below Ph.D.'s in financial attainment

(B) the incentive factor is a minor one in regard to pursuing Ph.D. studies

(C) the Ph.D. candidate is likely to change his field of specialization if he drops out

(D) about one third of those who start Ph.D. work do not complete the work to earn the degree

(E) there are comparatively few dropouts in the Ph.D. humanities disciplines

18. Meeting foreign language requirements for the Ph.D.

(A) is the most frequent reason for dropping out

(B) is more difficult for the science candidate than for the humanities candidate

(C) is considered part of the so-called "qualification" examination

(D) is an essential part of many Ph.D. programs

(E) does not vary in difficulty among universities

19. Dr. Tucker felt that

(A) a primary purpose of his research project was to arrive at a more efficient method for dropping incapable Ph.D. applicants

(B) a serious aspect of the dropout situation was the deplorable waste of productive talent

(C) one happy feature about the dropout situation was that the dropouts went into college teaching rather than into research

(D) his project should be free of outside interference and so he rejected outside financial assistance for the project

(E) it was important to determine how well Ph.D. dropouts did in comparison to those who completed their program

20. After reading the article, one would refrain from concluding that

(A) colleges and universitites employ a substantial number of Ph.D. dropouts

(B) Ph.D.'s are not earning what they deserve in nonacademic positions

(C) the study was conducted with efficiency and validity

(D) a Ph.D. dropout, by and large, does not have what it takes to earn the degree

(E) optimism reigns in regard to getting Ph.D. dropouts to return to their pursuit of the degree

21. As one of the most common serious infectious diseases of mankind, malaria presents a considerable challenge to public health workers. The challenge is the more irresistible because of the complicated mode of transmission of the disease. Humans can only get infected from the bite of an infected mosquito, which is itself infected by biting an infected human. Interrupting the mosquito link in the chain is an ecologically sound, though expensive, way to clear large regions of the world of this scourge. More money should be spent on solving this problem right now.

One of the author's assumptions is that

(A) mosquitoes are a necessary environmental evil

(B) the means to eliminate mosquito populations are currently known and available

(C) enough money is now being spent on cancer research

(D) malaria is sometimes fatal

(E) only public health workers should fight malaria

22. "This little car is the best, the greatest, the most fantastic economy car on the market. I cannot begin to describe to you the praise, the cries of delight, the veritable enthusiasm that its buyers have expressed to me," the salesman spluttered.

"Try more information and less pitch next time, fella," the woman said and walked away.

The customer criticizes the salesman because his remarks are too

(A) detailed and circumstantial
(B) exact and specific
(C) inflated and unspecific
(D) general and philosophical
(E) impolite and disrespectful

23. For the United States, Canada has become the most important country in the world, yet there are few countries about which Americans know less. Canada is the third largest country in the world; only Russia and China are larger. The area of Canada is more than a quarter of the whole British Commonwealth.

The paragraph best supports the statement that

(A) the British Commonwealth is smaller than Russia or China
(B) the territory of China is greater than that of Canada
(C) Americans know more about Canada than about China or Russia
(D) the United States is the most important nation in the world as far as Canada is concerned
(E) Americans know less about Canada than about China or Russia

24. During the past decade we have doubled our real expenditures on health, yet our life span has not increased at all. It seems clear that the country therefore needs fewer, not more, doctors, and that people should visit their doctors less frequently and have fewer tests performed on themselves.

Which of the following statements represents an implication or assumption of the author?

I. Better health can lead to increased life span.

II. Decreasing the number of doctors would not lead to an increase in the average doctor's fee.

III. Laboratory tests are unreasonably expensive.

(A) I
(B) III
(C) I and II
(D) II and III
(E) I, II, and III

Questions 25–26

Monseigneur, one of the great lords in power at the court, held his fortnightly reception in his grand hotel in Paris. Monseigneur was in his inner room, his sanctuary of sanctuaries, the Holiest of Holiests to the crowd of worshippers in the suite of rooms without. Monseigneur took his royal chocolate at this time. Monseigneur could swallow a great many things with ease, and was by some few sullen minds supposed to be rather rapidly swallowing France.

25. The locale of this passage is

(A) the opera
(B) a sweet shop
(C) the field of battle
(D) an apartment
(E) a church

26. The tone of the selection is

(A) sarcastic
(B) inquiring
(C) objective
(D) informative
(E) serious

27. According to Congressman X, "Too much of our taxpayers' money is spent on the rehabilitation of drug addicts. This is no way to solve the problem. Most of the people who spend time in rehabilitation centers go right back to taking narcotics after they leave. Instead of wasting money on rehabilitation, we should be using it to get rid of the drug peddlers who profit from growing and selling the drugs."

The paragraph best supports the statement that Congressman X implies that the way to solve the problem of drug addiction is to

(A) create more rehabilitation centers

(B) do away with rehabilitation centers
(C) put drug addicts in jail
(D) tax drug peddlers
(E) eliminate the source of the drugs

Questions 28–32

Whether the search for extraterrestrial intelligence succeeds or fails, its consequences will be extraordinary. If we make a long dedicated search that fails, we will not have wasted our time. We will have developed important technology, with applications to many other aspects of our own civilization. We will surely have added greatly to our knowledge of the physical Universe.

We will have strengthened belief in the near uniqueness of our species, our civilization, and our planet. Lacking any detection, the conviction of our uniqueness would hardly ever reach certainty; it would form over a long time, less into sharp conclusions than into a kind of substructure of human thought, a ruling consensus of attitudes. If intelligent, technological life is rare or absent elsewhere, we will have learned how precious is our human culture, how unique our biological patrimony, painstakingly evolved over three or four thousand million years of tortuous evolutionary history. Even a growing possibility of such a finding will stress, as perhaps nothing else can, our lonely responsibilities to the human dangers of our time.

On the other hand, were we to locate but a single extraterrestrial signal, we would know immediately one great truth: that it is possible for a civilization to maintain an advanced technological state and *not* destroy itself. The sharpness of the impact of simple detection will depend on the circumstances of discovery. If we were to find real signals after only a few years of a modest search, there is little doubt the news would be sensational. If, on the other hand, signals were detected only after a protracted effort over generations with a large search system, the result might be less conspicuous.

Note well that it is likely that the early announcements of the detection of deliberate signals may turn out to be mistaken, not verified by further study and observation. They may be natural phenomena of a new kind, or some terrestrial signal, or even a hoax. Press and public must use caution because we hold that even a single genuine detection would in and of itself have enormous importance.

Of course it is very difficult to foresee the content of a signal except in the most general way. A signal could be a beacon—a deliberate transmission specifically for the purpose of attracting the attention of an emerging civilization like ourselves. Alternately, it could be a leakage signal similar to our own television broadcasts or radars, not intended for our detection.

28. The author would probably agree with which of the following statements?

(A) A hoax could be a constructive experience.
(B) An authentic detection of an extraterrestrial signal would have staggering implications.
(C) It is important that the search for life on other planets be successful.
(D) Interest in radio-astronomy is nonexistent.
(E) Signals from intelligent extraterrestrials have been detected more than once.

29. The primary purpose of the passage is to

(A) convince people that life exists on other planets
(B) demonstrate how projects can waste time
(C) raise funds for a radio telescope
(D) show the benefits of searching for extraterrestrial life
(E) make an early announcement of discovery

30. The author states that the one thing we would immediately know if an extraterrestrial signal were detected is that

(A) life dominates the universe
(B) advanced technology could return the signal
(C) an advanced civilization could survive
(D) the television would be a good medium of communication
(E) it would be counterproductive to tell the press

31. The author states that all of the following would be gained from a failed search *except*

(A) a sense of frustration due to a failed endeavor
(B) an increased sense of the importance of the human culture
(C) a sense of how unique our species is
(D) the use of advanced technologies
(E) a strong sense of the responsibility to correct current human problems

32. The sharpness of the impact of the discovery of extraterrestrial signals would depend on

(A) how strong the signal was
(B) how many years it takes to detect the signal

(C) the human condition at the time

(D) whether it was a beacon signal or television leakage

(E) the contents of the message

33. The labor required to produce a bushel of wheat in 1830 was three hours. Today it takes less than ten minutes. Further, it has been estimated that fifty people, employing modern farm machinery and agricultural methods, can do the work of five hundred peasants toiling under the conditions of the eighteenth century.

The paragraph best supports the conclusion that

(A) the increase of efficiency in agriculture is almost as great as that in manufacturing

(B) modern farm machinery has resulted in serious unemployment among farmers

(C) more than 18 times as much wheat is produced today as in 1830

(D) a bushel of wheat today is more valuable than it was in the eighteenth century

(E) modern farm machinery is labor-saving

34. Should the people who decide on our transportation priorities continue to ignore the fact that the last thing we want or need or will tolerate is more expressways?

The rhetorical technique most similar to the one used in the passage above is the one used in which of the following examples?

(A) Should those who decide our environmental policy decide that the last thing we need is expensive pollution-control equipment?

(B) Do those who decide on our war strategy believe that what we need most is a quick victory?

(C) Should those who direct our health care policies close their eyes to the fact that the last thing we need is more specialists?

(D) When will those who choose our foreign policy accept the fact that the last thing we will tolerate is more imperialistic adventurism?

(E) When will those who fix our military policy see that the infantryman is the backbone of our army?

Questions 35–38

On May 8, 1939 folk song collector and scholar Herbert Halpert arrived in Mississippi to document folk-lore and folk music during a recording tour of the South sponsored by the Joint Committee on the Arts of the Works Progress Administration (WPA). He drove into the state in an old ambulance outfitted with cabinets, a small cot, food, and clothes. The ambulance also had specially built shelves for the latest in recording equipment—an acetate disc recorder lent by the Archive of American Folk Song at the Library of Congress.

To take full advantage of Halpert's short visit, local WPA workers acted as intermediaries, preceding the recording truck to make arrangements with the folk musicians he would visit and grouping artists in convenient places to minimize travel and maximize recording time. Following their schedule, with a few side trips to pursue a couple of leads of his own, Halpert cut 168 records between May 8 and June 11, 1939. Abbot Ferriss, a Mississippi native, assisted him.

In addition to helping with the actual recording, Ferriss kept fieldnotes on the trip and took photographs of the musicians, their families, homes, and surroundings. At the project's conclusion the recordings became part of the folk music collections at the Library of Congress. The photographs and much of the manuscript material related to the project remained in Mississippi.

35. According to the passage, what was the purpose of Halpert's journey to Mississippi?

(A) to make arrangements for the writing of folk songs

(B) to consult with a local native

(C) to record the folk music of Mississippi performers

(D) to photograph the Mississippi landscape

(E) to promote local use of the Library of Congress

36. Which of the following is NOT stated in the passage?

(A) The WPA sponsored a recording project in the South.

(B) Local workers helped Halpert by searching for musicians.

(C) The local workers sought to minimize Halpert's travel time.

(D) The photographs were sent to the Library of Congress.

(E) Halpert had the most modern sound equipment available.

37. Which of the following can be reasonably inferred about the WPA?

    (A) It was only interested in folk music.
    (B) It took full advantage of short visits to the Library of Congress.
    (C) It was a national organization with local offices.
    (D) It was sponsored by the Joint Committee on the Arts.
    (E) It never again sponsored a similar project.

38. According to the passage, Ferriss did which of the following:

    I. took photographs
    II. helped with the recording
    III. took notes

    (A) I only
    (B) II only
    (C) III only
    (D) I and III only
    (E) I, II, and III

39. Every action has an equal and opposite reaction. When a ball is dropped, it exerts a force upon the earth. The earth simultaneously exerts an equal force upon the ball in the opposite direction.

    Which of the following sentences would provide the most logical continuation of this paragraph?

    (A) Because the ball is so much lighter than the earth, you see it bounce, but you do not see the earth move.
    (B) The people on the other side of the earth do not feel the ball drop.
    (C) A solid rubber ball bounces higher than a hollow rubber ball.
    (D) Newton, who discovered this law of action-reaction, was one of the greatest geniuses of all time.
    (E) This is why a gun has recoil when fired.

40. Since the government can spend only what it obtains from the people and this amount is ultimately limited by their capacity and willingness to pay taxes, it is very important that the people be given full information about the work of the government.

    The paragraph best supports the statement that

    (A) governmental employees should be trained not only in their own work, but also in how to perform the duties of other employees in their agency
    (B) taxation by the government rests on the consent of the people
    (C) the release of full information on the work of the government will increase the efficiency of governmental operations
    (D) the work of the government, in recent years, has been restricted because of reduced tax collections
    (E) the foundation of our government is abhorrence of the principle of taxation without representation

MATHEMATICS

60 minutes—40 questions

Directions: Each of the questions or statements below is followed by five suggested answers. Choose the one that is best in each case.

1. Two angles of a triangle measure 30° and 50°. The number of degrees in the third angle is

   (A) 10
   (B) 40
   (C) 50
   (D) 90
   (E) 100

2. If a recipe for a cake calls for $2\frac{1}{2}$ cups of flour, and Mary wishes to make three such cakes, the number of cups of flour she must use is

   (A) 5
   (B) $6\frac{1}{2}$
   (C) $7\frac{1}{2}$
   (D) 9
   (E) $9\frac{1}{2}$

3. An appliance store gives a 15% discount off the list price of all of its merchandise. An additional 30% reduction of the store price is made for the purchase of a floor model. A television set that has a list price of $300 and is a floor model sells for

   (A) $210.00
   (B) $228.50
   (C) $178.50
   (D) $165.00
   (E) $135.00

Questions 4 and 5 refer to the following graph.

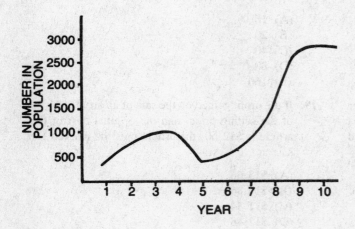

4. During which years did the population increase at the fastest rate?

   (A) years 5–7
   (B) years 1–3
   (C) years 4–5
   (D) years 7–9
   (E) years 9–10

5. During which years did the size of the population decrease the most?

   (A) years 4–5
   (B) years 3–4
   (C) years 9–10
   (D) years 1–2
   (E) years 4–6

6. Which quantity is NOT equal to 75 (32 + 88)?

   (A) $75 \cdot 32 + 75 \cdot 88$
   (B) $(75 \cdot 32) + 88$
   (C) $75 (88 + 32)$
   (D) $(88 + 32) \cdot 75$
   (E) $88 \cdot 75 + 32 \cdot 75$

7. If 1 ounce is approximately equal to 28 grams, then 1 pound is approximately equal to

   (A) 250 grams
   (B) 350 grams
   (C) 450 grams
   (D) 550 grams
   (E) 650 grams

8. If $x (p + 1) = m$, then $p =$

   (A) $m - 1$
   (B) m
   (C) $\dfrac{m - 1}{x}$
   (D) $m - x - 1$
   (E) $\dfrac{m}{x} - 1$

9 Which of the following is equal to 3.14×10^6?

   (A) 314
   (B) 3,140
   (C) 31,400
   (D) 314,000
   (E) 3,140,000

10. On a house plan on which 2 inches represents 5 feet, the length of a room measures $7\frac{1}{2}$ inches. The actual length of the room is

(A) $12\frac{1}{2}$ feet

(B) $15\frac{3}{4}$ feet

(C) $17\frac{1}{2}$ feet

(D) $18\frac{3}{4}$ feet

(E) $13\frac{3}{4}$ feet

11. Which of the following is the graph of $x > = -2$ and $x < = 3$?

(A)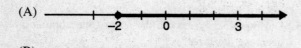

(B)

(C)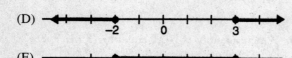

(D)

(E)

12. A road runs 1200 feet from A to B, and then makes a right angle going to C, a distance of 500 feet. A new road is being built directly from A to C. How much shorter will the new road be?

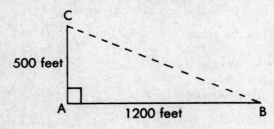

(A) 400 feet

(B) 609 feet

(C) 850 feet

(D) 1300 feet

(E) 1500 feet

13. A man travels a certain distance at 60 miles per hour and returns over the same road at 40 miles per hour. What is his average rate for the round trip in miles per hour?

(A) 42

(B) 44

(C) 46

(D) 48

(E) 50

14. The winner of a race received $\frac{1}{3}$ of the total purse. The third-place finisher received one third of the winner's share. If the winner's share was $2,700, what was the total purse?

(A) $2,700

(B) $8,100

(C) $900

(D) $1,800

(E) $1,400

15. What will it cost to carpet a room 12 feet wide and 15 feet long if carpeting costs $20.80 per square yard?

(A) $334.60

(B) $374.40

(C) $416.00

(D) $504.60

(E) $560.00

16. Which of the following fractions is more than $\frac{3}{4}$?

(A) $\frac{35}{71}$

(B) $\frac{13}{20}$

(C) $\frac{71}{101}$

(D) $\frac{19}{24}$

(E) $\frac{15}{20}$

17. John is three times his son's age. If the difference between their ages is 30, how old is the son?

(A) 5

(B) 10

(C) 15

(D) 20

(E) 25

18. How many ice cubes, measuring 2 inches on an edge, can be held in a container measuring 8 inches deep, 5 inches high, and 4 inches wide?

(A) 16

(B) 20

(C) 40

(D) 80

(E) 160

19. If the profit gained on the sale of an article is 10% of the selling price, and the original cost of the article is $12.60, the article must be marked for sale at

(A) $13.66

(B) $13.86

(C) $11.34

(D) $12.48

(E) $14.00

20. If $7M = 3M - 20$, then $M + 7 =$

    (A) 0
    (B) 2
    (C) 5
    (D) 12
    (E) 17

21. If all P are S and no S are Q, it necessarily follows that

    (A) all Q are S
    (B) all Q are P
    (C) no P are Q
    (D) no S are P
    (E) some Q are P

22. The toll on the Islands Bridge is $1.00 for car and driver and $.75 for each additional passenger. How many people were riding in a car for which the toll was $3.25?

    (A) 2
    (B) 3
    (C) 4
    (D) 5
    (E) 6

23. A recent survey shows that .25% of smokers find it easy to stop. Which of the following fractions is equal to .25%?

    (A) $\frac{1}{400}$
    (B) $\frac{1}{40}$
    (C) $\frac{1}{4}$
    (D) $\frac{5}{2}$
    (E) $\frac{50}{2}$

24. If fencing costs $9.00 per yard, what would be the total cost of the fencing needed to enclose a rectangular area measuring 46 feet by 34 feet?

    (A) $34
    (B) $46
    (C) $160
    (D) $480
    (E) $640

25. The number of grams in one kilogram is

    (A) .001
    (B) .01
    (C) .1
    (D) 10
    (E) 1000

26. A man spent exactly one dollar in the purchase of 3-cent stamps and 5-cent stamps. The number of 5-cent stamps that he could NOT have purchased under the circumstances is

    (A) 5
    (B) 8
    (C) 9
    (D) 11
    (E) 14

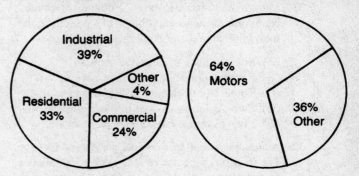

Questions 27 and 28 pertain to the pie charts above, which show how much oil and electricity is consumed in the United States.

27. If nine million barrels of oil daily are required to produce electricity in the United States, how many barrels are required to meet commercial and industrial needs?

    (A) 4,750,000
    (B) 7,400,000
    (C) 5,670,000
    (D) 3,420,000
    (E) 2,840,000

28. 64% of the electricity is used to run motors of different kinds. About how many barrels of oil are required to run residential motors?

    (A) 2.4 million
    (B) .8 million
    (C) 3.3 million
    (D) 1.9 million
    (E) 1.1 million

29. Susan got up one morning at 7:42 A.M. and went to bed that evening at 10:10 P.M. How much time elapsed between her getting up and going to bed that day?

    (A) 18 hrs. 2 min.
    (B) 14 hrs. 18 min.
    (C) 15 hrs. 18 min.
    (D) 9 hrs. 22 min.
    (E) 14 hrs. 28 min.

30. Roger receives a basic weekly salary of $80 plus a 5% commission. In a week in which his sales amounted to $800, the ratio of his basic salary to his commission was

(A) 2:1
(B) 1:2
(C) 2:3
(D) 3:2
(E) 3:1

31. Mrs. Jones wishes to buy 72 ounces of canned beans for the least possible cost. Which of the following should she buy?

(A) Six 12-ounce cans at 39¢ per can
(B) Seven 10-ounce cans at 34¢ per can
(C) Three 24-ounce cans at 79¢ per can
(D) Two 25-ounce cans at 62¢ per can
(E) Five 13-ounce cans at 37¢ per can

32. A class punchball team won 2 games and lost 10. The fraction of the games won to the total number of games played is

(A) $\frac{1}{6}$
(B) $\frac{1}{2}$
(C) $\frac{4}{5}$
(D) $\frac{5}{6}$
(E) $\frac{1}{10}$

33. In triangle ABC, $\overline{AB} = \overline{BC}$ and $\overline{AC}$ is extended to D. If angle BCD contains $100°$, find the number of degrees in angle B.

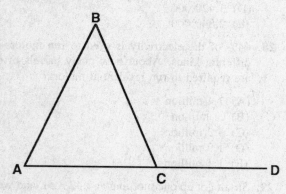

(A) 50
(B) 80
(C) 60
(D) 40
(E) 20

34. A boy buys oranges at 3 for 30¢ and sells them at 5 for 60¢. How many oranges must he sell in order to make a profit of 50¢?

(A) 12
(B) 25
(C) 50
(D) 75
(E) 100

35. The average of two numbers is A. If one of the numbers is x, the other number is

(A) $A - x$

(B) $\frac{A}{2} - x$

(C) $2A - x$

(D) $\frac{A + x}{2}$

(E) $x - A$

36. Six tractors can plow a field in 8 hours if they all work together. How many hours will it take 4 tractors to do the job?

(A) 9
(B) 10
(C) 11
(D) 12
(E) 14

37. The figure below is composed of 5 equal squares. If the area of the figure is 125, find its perimeter.

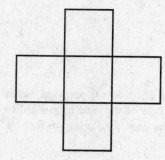

(A) 60
(B) 100
(C) 80
(D) 75
(E) 20

38. If $x < 0$ and $y < 0$, then

(A) $x + y > 0$
(B) $x = -y$
(C) $x > y$
(D) $xy > 0$
(E) $xy < 0$

39. If the perimeter of a rectangular swimming pool is 68 yards and the width is 48 feet, the length is

(A) 10 yards
(B) 18 yards
(C) 20 feet
(D) 56 feet
(E) 60 feet

40. One tenth is what part of three fourths?

(A) $\frac{40}{3}$
(B) $\frac{3}{40}$
(C) $\frac{15}{2}$
(D) $\frac{1}{8}$
(E) $\frac{2}{15}$

WRITING: SECTION 1

30 Minutes—45 Questions

Part A

25 Questions: Suggested time—10 Minutes

Directions: The sentences below may contain errors in punctuation, capitalization, grammar, usage, word choice, and idiom. Parts of each sentence are underlined and lettered. Decide which underlined part contains the error and choose its corresponding letter as your answer choice. If the sentence is correct as it stands, choose E. No sentence contains more than one error.

1. These oranges taste <u>more sweetly</u> <u>than</u> any oth-
   <u>A</u>   <u>B</u>
   ers <u>I've ever tried.</u> <u>No error</u>
       <u>C</u>   <u>D</u>   <u>E</u>

2. The gentleman <u>who's</u> wallet I found <u>on the</u>
                  <u>A</u>
   <u>train</u> <u>came</u> to the lost-and-found window to
   <u>B</u>   <u>C</u>
   <u>claim it.</u> <u>No error</u>
   <u>D</u>   <u>E</u>

3. <u>To impress</u> a prospective employer, <u>one should</u>
   <u>A</u>   <u>B</u>
   dress neatly, <u>be prompt,</u> and <u>displaying</u> interest
                 <u>C</u>   <u>D</u>
   in the job. <u>No error</u>
               <u>E</u>

4. A <u>craze</u> for tobacco <u>swept</u> the <u>English court</u>
     <u>A</u>   <u>B</u>   <u>C</u>
   when the plant was <u>first imported</u> by early ex-
                      <u>D</u>
   plorers of the American continent. <u>No error</u>
                                      <u>E</u>

5. The influence of radio <u>on</u> American life <u>during</u>
                          <u>A</u>   <u>B</u>
   the Depression years <u>were</u> <u>profound.</u> <u>No error</u>
                        <u>C</u>   <u>D</u>   <u>E</u>

6. <u>All of</u> the children in the family receive a
   <u>A</u>   <u>B</u>
   <u>check-up</u> <u>annually each year.</u> <u>No error</u>
   <u>C</u>   <u>D</u>   <u>E</u>

7. <u>Although</u> Dolores <u>is</u> in this country since she
   <u>A</u>   <u>B</u>
   was a little girl<u>,</u> she still thinks of <u>Colombia</u> as
                    <u>C</u>   <u>D</u>
   home. <u>No error</u>
         <u>E</u>

8. <u>According to</u> Thoreau, Walden was the <u>deepest</u>
   <u>A</u>   <u>B</u>
   pond in the area and the last <u>to freeze</u> every
                                 <u>C</u>
   winter. <u>No error</u>
   <u>D</u>   <u>E</u>

9. If you <u>exceed</u> to their <u>unreasonable</u> demands
          <u>A</u>   <u>B</u>
   this time, they will not <u>hesitate</u> <u>to impose on</u>
                            <u>C</u>   <u>D</u>
   you again. <u>No error</u>
              <u>E</u>

10. In the four years since the course <u>was instituted,</u>
                                       <u>A</u>
    no more <u>than</u> ten students <u>has signed up</u> for it
            <u>B</u>   <u>C</u>
    in <u>any one</u> semester. <u>No error</u>
       <u>D</u>   <u>E</u>

11. <u>There's scarcely</u> <u>no</u> time to write one essay be-
    <u>A</u>   <u>B</u>
    fore the next is <u>due.</u> <u>No error</u>
    <u>C</u>   <u>D</u>   <u>E</u>

12. The unique *Beowulf* manuscript <u>has survived</u>
                                    <u>A</u>
    the centuries only through a series of lucky cir-
    cumstances<u>,</u> no one knows <u>how much</u> litera-
               <u>B</u>   <u>C</u>
    ture of equal stature has been irrevocably <u>lost to</u>
                                               <u>D</u>
    us. <u>No error</u>
    <u>D</u> <u>E</u>

13. Over several thousand years of cultivation<u>,</u>
                                               <u>A</u>
    white rice <u>has been modified</u> genetically to
               <u>B</u>
    yield a much higher quantity of grain <u>per acre</u>
                                          <u>C</u>
    as wild rice. <u>No error</u>
    <u>D</u>   <u>E</u>

14. If the game <u>went</u> <u>into</u> extra innings, the <u>relief</u>
                <u>A</u>   <u>B</u>
    <u>pitcher</u> would have won <u>it</u> for the visiting
    <u>C</u>   <u>D</u>
    team. <u>No error</u>
          <u>E</u>

15. <u>Of</u> biology and psychology, I believe biology
    <u>A</u>
    to be the <u>more exact</u> <u>science.</u> <u>No error</u>
    <u>B</u>   <u>C</u>   <u>D</u>   <u>E</u>

16. If she were as old as us, she might behave
         A   B   C
more responsibly. No error
       D   E

17. Because the moon rotates on its axis at the
                                A
same rate as revolving around the earth,
     B   C
only one side of the lunar surface
is ever visible to us. No error
       D   E

18. As a documentary photographer for the Farm
          A
Security Administration during the Depression,
                                  B
Dorothea Lange recorded the hardships and des-
                 C
peration of America's dispossessed. No error
                       D   E

19. The paper attempted to magnify the importance
                          A
of Defoe's novel's by belittling the achieve-
          B   C
ments of his predecessors. No error
              D   E

20. The Piltdown man, one of the most extraordinary scientific hoax of all time, was accepted
                A   B
by anthropologists as the "missing link" be-
   C   D
tween man and the apes. No error
                        E

21. Although the suspect was arrested early this
    A
morning, he has not yet been formerly
       B   C   D
charged. No error
         E

22. Georgette's game has improved considerable
                    A   B
since she started training with her new coach.
  C   D
No error
  E

23. Each successive appeal for donations have elic-
         A   B   C
ited a wider and more enthusiastic response. No
                D
error
  E

24. At the heart of the New England town was the
    A   B
common, a public pasture for the citizens'
       C   D
sheep and cattle. No error
                  E

25. The Sudan, the largest country in africa, con-
         A   B
tains almost one million square miles of desert,
      C   D
savanna, and papyrus swamp. No error
                            E

Part B

20 Questions: Suggested time—20 Minutes

Directions: The sentences below may contain errors in grammar, sentence construction, word choice, and punctuation. Part or all of each sentence is underlined. Select the lettered answer that contains the best version of the underlined section. Answer A always repeats the original underlined section exactly. If the sentence is correct as it stands, select A.

26. Despite the danger that the roof might collapse, the fireman entered the building.

   (A) Despite
   (B) Irrespective of
   (C) Disregarding of
   (D) Irregardless of
   (E) However

27. Anatomical abnormalities in the brain often accompany chronic schizophrenia, but no one knows if as a cause or effect of the illness.

   (A) if as a cause or effect
   (B) are they a cause or an effect

   (C) do they cause, or are they an effect,
   (D) if they cause it, or as an effect
   (E) whether they are a cause or an effect

28. Unlike football, baseball fields can vary somewhat in size and shape.

   (A) Unlike football
   (B) Not like in footballs
   (C) Contrary to football fields
   (D) Unlike football fields
   (E) Contrary to football

29. By means of utilizing a public relations campaign, the company sought to improve its·image.

    (A) By means of utilizing a public relations campaign
    (B) By means of using a public relations campaign
    (C) By means of a public relations campaign
    (D) By a public relations campaign for its means
    (E) Utilizing a public relations campaign as the means

30. Legal discrimination being against Catholics in eighteenth-century England, the great poet and scholar Alexander Pope never attended a university.

    (A) Legal discrimination being against Catholics
    (B) Because of legal discrimination against Catholics
    (C) Catholics having to be discriminated against legally
    (D) Catholics against whom there existed legal discrimination
    (E) Due to the reason of legal discrimination against Catholics

31. Sunshine, good soil, and caring continually will almost always result in beautiful houseplants.

    (A) and caring continually
    (B) and caring on a continual basis
    (C) and continual care
    (D) and care that is continuing
    (E) and care which can be continuous

32. Information recorded by the Voyager I spacecraft indicated that Jupiter has an aurora borealis similar to earth's and a surface covered with swirling gases.

    (A) an aurora borealis similar to earth's and a surface
    (B) an aurora borealis similar to earth and a surface
    (C) an aurora borealis similar to earth's and it's surface
    (D) an aurora borealis similarly to earth's and a surface
    (E) an aurora borealis which is like to earth's and a surface

33. Because it is now punishable by heavy fines and jail terms, the survival of caribou in Maine is not considered as threatened by poaching any longer.

    (A) the survival of caribou in Maine is not considered as threatened by poaching any longer
    (B) the survival of caribou in Maine is considered not threatened longer by poaching
    (C) that caribou in Maine survive isn't considered as threatened by poaching no longer
    (D) poaching is no longer considered a threat to the survival of caribou in Maine
    (E) poaching is not considered to threaten the survival of caribou in Maine any longer

34. The ancient Egyptians built structures that still stand after 2,500 years, their accomplishments are a marvel to behold.

    (A) years, their accomplishments are a marvel to behold
    (B) years, their accomplishing marvels that are to be beheld
    (C) years; and they have accomplished marvelous beholdings
    (D) years; their accomplishments are a marvel to behold
    (E) years, beholding their accomplishments is a marvel

35. The practice of denying people mortgage and home-improvement loans on the basis of your neighborhood is known as ''redlining.''

    (A) on the basis of your neighborhood
    (B) because of where you live
    (C) on the basis of your neighborhood
    (D) on the reason of your neighborhood
    (E) on the basis of their neighborhoods

36. With the nation's highway traffic expected to double over the next 30 years, to increase the use of computerized traffic control systems seems inevitable.

    (A) to increase the use of computerized traffic control systems seems inevitable
    (B) the increasing use of computerized traffic control systems seems inevitable
    (C) the increasing usage of computerized traffic control systems seems inevitable
    (D) it seems inevitable for increased use of computerized traffic control systems
    (E) increased usage of computerized traffic control systems seem inevitable

37. William Faulkner, now considered the great American novelist of the 1930s, did not receive hardly any recognition until after World War II.

    (A) did not receive hardly
    (B) didn't receive hardly
    (C) received not hardly
    (D) hardly did receive
    (E) received hardly

38. I love both sports equally as well.

    (A) equally as well
    (B) as well
    (C) equally
    (D) well and equally
    (E) equally as well as the other

39. Paper was in use in England in the early part of the fourteenth century, but it was not until the late fifteenth century that the first English paper mill was established.

    (A) it was not until the late fifteenth century that the first English paper mill was
    (B) not until the late fifteenth century when the first English paper mill was
    (C) it was the late fifteenth century until the first English paper mill was
    (D) it was not until the late fifteenth century that the first English paper mill had been
    (E) not until the late fifteenth century was when the first English paper mill had been

40. It is important that adults and children be familiar with the Heimlich Maneuver, that is a technique for helping people who are choking on an object.

    (A) that is a technique for helping people who are choking on an object
    (B) that is a way to help people when they are choking on an object
    (C) a technique used to help people who are choking on an object
    (D) a technique used to help people who are being choked by an object
    (E) this is used when choking someone on an object

41. The climate of Israel is somewhat like California.

    (A) like California
    (B) like California's
    (C) as California

    (D) as California's
    (E) similar to California

42. The planet Mercury was thought to have an iron-rich core with a diameter 80 percent of the diameter of the planet itself, thus making Mercury the most iron rich of all the planets.

    (A) was thought to have
    (B) was thought that it had
    (C) was thought it had
    (D) it thought was to have
    (E) that was thought to have

43. The woman known as being Mother Hale has earned the gratitude of her community's because of the care she provides to infants born addicted to drugs.

    (A) as being Mother Hale has earned the gratitude of her community's
    (B) as Mother Hale has earned the gratitude of her community
    (C) to be called Mother Hale has earned the gratitude of her community's
    (D) as Mother Hale having earned the gratitude of her community's
    (E) to be Mother Hale having earned the gratitude of her community

44. New technologies entering the classroom, those like computers and interactive video, will enable educators to overhaul teaching so that students need never be passive receptors of knowledge.

    (A) New technologies entering the classroom, those like computers and interactive video,
    (B) New technologies, as for instance computers and interactive video, in their entering the classroom
    (C) To enter new technologies such as computers and interactive video into the classroom
    (D) The entrance into the classroom of new technologies such as computers and interactive video
    (E) That the entrance of new technologies into the classroom, like computers and interactive video,

45. His music never has and never will be widely appreciated.

    (A) has and never will be
    (B) has and never will have been
    (C) has been and never will be
    (D) has been nor will be
    (E) has been and will be

WRITING: SECTION 2

Essay

Time—30 Minutes

Directions: You will have thirty minutes to plan and write an essay on the topic given below. Read the topic carefully, and organize your ideas before you start writing. Remember to use specific examples and details where appropriate.

Some educators feel that students should be allowed to drop out of school after the 7th grade, age 12. Do you think this is good or bad? State your opinion and give your reasons for holding it.

The space below is for any notes you may wish to make. Begin your essay on a separate sheet of paper.

ANSWER KEY FOR PRACTICE TEST 1

Reading		Mathematics		Writing	
1. A	21. B	1. E	21. C	1. A	24. E
2. E	22. C	2. C	22. C	2. A	25. B
3. C	23. B	3. C	23. A	3. D	26. A
4. B	24. A	4. D	24. D	4. E	27. E
5. D	25. D	5. A	25. E	5. C	28. D
6. B	26. A	6. B	26. C	6. D	29. C
7. D	27. E	7. C	27. C	7. B	30. B
8. E	28. B	8. E	28. D	8. E	31. C
9. A	29. D	9. E	29. E	9. A	32. A
10. D	30. C	10. D	30. A	10. C	33. D
11. C	31. A	11. E	31. A	11. B	34. D
12. D	32. B	12. A	32. A	12. B	35. E
13. B	33. E	13. D	33. E	13. D	36. B
14. E	34. C	14. B	34. B	14. A	37. E
15. C	35. C	15. C	35. C	15. E	38. C
16. A	36. D	16. D	36. D	16. C	39. A
17. D	37. C	17. C	37. A	17. C	40. C
18. D	38. E	18. A	38. D	18. E	41. B
19. E	39. A	19. E	39. B	19. A	42. A
20. E	40. B	20. B	40. E	20. A	43. B
				21. D	44. D
				22. B	45. C
				23. C	

EXPLANATORY ANSWERS FOR PRACTICE TEST 1

Reading

1. (A) The passage stresses the endurance of the legend of Atlantis, an island first mentioned in Plato's *Timaeus*. Although (B) mentions Plato, geography is not relevant. Choice (C) also has some relation to the speculations about Atlantis, but only (A) covers the broadest possibilities.

2. (E) Since the main thrust of the passage indicates that Atlantis is a legendary island, no recorded evidence by its inhabitants could have been left. Thus, (E) is the only choice that could be derived.

3. (C) The passage states that the island was destroyed because of the "impiety of its people." There is no other cause mentioned.

4. (B) The tenor of the passage is that things were pretty good in the 50s. The mention of the criticism that the times were dull is most logically followed by a rebuttal of that criticism, which (B) does. The other choices digress substantially from the theme.

5. (D) The passage begins by saying that the artist must simplify and find the common denominator. It then says that the artist must draw upon the common denominator to produce something that separates us. This act of separation presumably involves adding to the common denominator, and thus may be considered as a complicating act. (A), (B), and (E) have no relation to the passage. (C) is presumably derived from the statement that "each of us must be able to *see* something different in the work." That statement uses *see* in a broader sense than mere visual perception.

6. (B) The passage is a generalized description of the operations of a typical power plant, so (B) is the only pertinent choice. (C) deals only with a subtopic; (A) is unsuitable because only one sentence, the second, even hints at "advantages." (D) and (E) are not treated by the passage.

7. (D) The author makes no value judgments such as (A) or (B), and he does not specify which coolant is used in the third of power plants not using water (C). But he does say that the process is "producing steam," which validates (D) and invalidates (E).

8. (E) The author says, "The steam . . . hits the blades of a turbine, spinning it" (that is, the turbine is "driven by steam").

9. (A) The author says that the "core of this reactor serves as a . . . substitute for the firebox of a conventional . . . plant."

10. (D) The author describes how, after electricity is produced, "The steam is then led off to a condenser" where it is "condensed" (D).

11. (C) The correct answer (C) is supported by the paragraph's statement that although advertising gives manufacturers considerable control over the consumers' demand for their products, there are still big risks involved in producing and distributing their goods in advance of the consumers' final selection, which implies that manufacturers' ultimate success depends on the consumers. The statement that there are such risks, in spite of advertising, contradicts (A) and (D). There is no support for the statements that manufacturers distribute goods *directly* to consumers (B) or that they are *more* concerned with advertising than production (E).

12. (D) The third sentence in the first paragraph makes this clear.

13. (B) Soil erosion is one of the side effects that is listed in the second paragraph.

14. (E) Answer (E) suggests what the author is most in favor of—finding out how to make people cooperate. Clearly, finding out why people are cooperative or antisocial is a crucial part of this research undertaking. The other choices do not come as close to achieving this goal.

15. (C) The second sentence tells us that heart disease is an illness of late middle age and old age. Choice (A) is a misinterpretation. Choice (B) says that more people die of heart disease than all other *causes*, discounting suicide and accidents, which may be true, but the paragraph tells us that heart disease kills more people than any other *illness*. Choices (D) and (E) are not supported by the paragraph.

16. (A) Answer (B) is not correct because it is so farfetched. There is a lack of sufficient evidence to support answers (C), (D), and (E). Response (A) is the correct choice to this question and is one of the central ideas of the author's thesis.

17. (D) Answer (A) is inaccurate because the passage states that dropouts from the humanities were earning more than Ph.D.'s. Choice (B) is wrong, as incentive is a major reason for dropping out. The research shows that most dropouts work within fields consistent with their education; thus, choice (C) is not correct. Response (E) is in direct contradiction to the study's findings. Answer (D) is the correct response and is supported by the article's statement that the dropout rate was 31 percent.

18. (D) It can be inferred from the author's statement regarding failure to pass language exams that languages are an important part of Ph.D. programs. There is not sufficient data to confirm answers (A), (B), (C), or (E). The correct choice is (D).

19. (E) Answer (A) is not correct, as it was not the purpose of his research. Answers (B) and (C) are false statements. There is no evidence to support choice (D). Answer (E) is the correct answer and reflects the purpose of the study.

20. (E) As lack of motivation was the primary reason for dropping out, it can be inferred that it would be the primary focus for getting the candidates to return to the program. This is best expressed by choice (E).

21. (B) The third sentence of the passage indicates that the author is confident that the disease's mode of transmission is completely understood, and can, by limiting the mosquito population, be controlled. None of the other statements is implicit in the passage.

22. (C) The salesman uses exaggerated language in describing the car, but provides no useful information about the car's features. A customer might reasonably want to know, for instance, about a car's mileage, safety record, and durability, but the salesman's remarks address no specific points.

23. (B) The paragraph states that Russia and China are larger than Canada. No other answer to this question is correct. Choices (C) and (D) make statements in direct contradiction to the paragraph. Choice (A) is wrong because the paragraph compares the size of *Canada* with that of Russia and China, not the size of the *British Commonwealth* with Russia and China. It is entirely possible that Americans do know less about Canada than about China or Russia, but choice (E) is not directly supported by the paragraph.

24. (A) The author equates the lack of increase in the life span with lack of improvement in health in general. The question of fees is not discussed, although it might be thought that the author feels that *total* expenditures on health would go down with fewer doctor's visits. It may not be inferred that he or she feels that the average doctor's fee would change or not change as the number of doctors is decreased. The author does not imply that laboratory tests are unreasonably ex-

pensive, but he or she does imply that too many of them are performed.

25. (D) The first line states that Monseigneur is in his "grand hotel" in Paris.

26. (A) "Sarcasm" is a taunting or caustic tone that is generally ironical. The last line of the paragraph most fully expresses this attitude.

27. (E) When Congressman X suggests that money be spent to "get rid of the drug peddlers," he is suggesting eliminating the source of the drugs.

28. (B) The author states that even a single detection would have staggering implications.

29. (D) The author maintains that there will be benefits whether the project is successful or not.

30. (C) The author states that it would be the one great truth that we could immediately ascertain.

31. (A) The author never broaches the possibility that there could be any negative results from this search.

32. (B) This is stated in the second paragraph.

33. (E) Choice (E) offers an irrefutable conclusion. Choice (B) goes beyond the scope of the paragraph. Farmers might well be doing other types of jobs on the farm. Choice (C) also cannot be concluded on the basis of the paragraph. The amount of wheat produced depends on the amount of land devoted to its production, not on the speed of labor. Choice (D) is both ridiculous and unsupported.

34. (C) Answer (C) is the only one that, like the stem question, poses a question to which either an affirmative or a negative answer constitutes an admission of the truth of the questioner's actual point. (A) and (B) are incorrect because they can be answered without conceding the questioner's argument. (D) and (E) are incorrect because they cannot be answered "Yes" or "No" and are merely rhetorical phrasings rather than logical traps.

35. (C) The first sentence states the purpose of the visit.

36. (D) The last sentence states that the photographs remained in Mississippi.

37. (C) Halpert was on a tour of the South, and the results would be kept in the Library of Congress, indicating some kind of national scope. The second paragraph refers to *local workers*.

38. (E) All three are clearly stated.

39. (A) Choice (A) presents a reasonable extension

of the train of thought. (B) is eccentric. (C) starts a new thought. (D) is part of the general topic, but it has no place in the middle of a discussion of the action-reaction law. (E) is an inferior answer to (A) because it changes the example from ball-earth to gun-recoil without proper transition.

40. (B) According to the paragraph, the government can spend only what it obtains from the people. The government obtains money from the people by taxation. If the people are unwilling to pay taxes, the government has no source of funds.

Mathematics

1. (E) The sum of the angles of a triangle is 180°. The two given angles total 80°.

$$180° - 80° = 100°$$

The third angle is 100°.

2. (C) $2\frac{1}{2} \cdot 3 = \frac{5}{2} \cdot 3$

$$= \frac{15}{2}$$

$$= 7\frac{1}{2}$$

3. (C) The price after the 15% discount is

$$85\% \text{ of } \$300 = .85(\$300)$$
$$= \$255$$

The price after the 30% discount is

$$70\% \text{ of } \$255 = .70(\$255)$$
$$= \$178.50$$

4. (D) The graph is steepest between years 7 and 9. The population was approximately 1,000 in year 7, and increased to over 2,500 by year 9.

5. (A) The size of the population was quite constant from year 3 to 4, and decreased from year 4 to 5, almost 1,000 to 500. Notice the population was the same in year 3 as in year 7.

6. (B) Choices (A), (C), (D), and (E) are all examples of the commutative and distributive properties. The quantity in choice (B) is not equal to 75 (32 + 88).

7. (C) 1 pound = 16 ounces
$$(16)(28) = 448$$

8. (E) $x(p + 1) = m$. Divide both sides by x.

$$p + 1 = \frac{m}{x}$$

$$\text{or } p = \frac{m}{x} - 1$$

9. (E) $3.14 \times 10^6 = 3.14 \times 1,000,000$
$$= 3,140,000$$

10. (D) This is a proportion:

$$\frac{2 \text{ inches}}{7\frac{1}{2} \text{ inches}} = \frac{5 \text{ ft.}}{x \text{ ft.}}$$

$$x = 18\frac{3}{4} \text{ feet.}$$

11. (E) It can be helpful to graph each of the inequalities and then put the two graphs together to find the overlapping area.

12. (A) The new road is the hypotenuse of a right triangle whose legs are the old road.

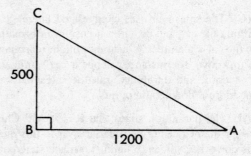

$$(AC)^2 = 500^2 + 1200^2$$
$$= 250000 + 1440000$$
$$= 1690000$$
$$AC = \sqrt{1690000}$$
$$= \sqrt{169} \cdot \sqrt{10000}$$
$$= 13 \cdot 100$$
$$= 1300$$

If you remember the 5-12-13 right triangle, you can see right away that the new road will be 1300 feet.

Old road = 500 ft + 1200 ft
  = 1700 ft
New road = 1300 ft
Difference = 400 ft

13. (D) Let the number of miles traveled each way = M

The time going = $\dfrac{distance}{rate} = \dfrac{M}{60}$

The time coming = $\dfrac{M}{40}$

Total time for round trip = $\dfrac{M}{60} + \dfrac{M}{40}$

$= \dfrac{2M + 3M}{120} = \dfrac{5M}{120} = \dfrac{M}{24}$

Average rate =

$\dfrac{total\ distance}{total\ time} = \dfrac{2M}{\dfrac{M}{24}} = 48$ miles per hour

14. (B) You have to read only the first and third sentences of the problem. The information in the second sentence contains information not relevant to the problem. The winner received $\frac{1}{3}$ of the total, or $2,700. Thus, the total purse was $2,700 × 3 = $8,100.

15. (C)
$$12 \text{ feet} = 4 \text{ yards}$$
$$15 \text{ feet} = 5 \text{ yards}$$
$$4 \text{ yards} \cdot 5 \text{ yards} = 20 \text{ square yards}$$

$$\begin{array}{r} \$20.80 \quad \text{per square yard} \\ \times \quad\quad 20 \quad \text{square yards} \\ \hline \$416.00 \end{array}$$

16. (D) $\frac{3}{4} = .75$

$\dfrac{35}{71}$ is slightly less than $\dfrac{35}{70} = .5$

$\dfrac{13}{20} = \dfrac{13 \times 5}{20 \times 5} = \dfrac{65}{100} = .65$

$\dfrac{71}{101}$ is very close to $\dfrac{7}{10}$ or .7

$\dfrac{15}{20} = \dfrac{15 \times 5 = 75}{20 \times 5\ 100} = .75$

$\dfrac{19}{24} = \begin{array}{r} .79 \text{ which is more than } \frac{3}{4} \\ 24\overline{)19.00} \\ 168 \\ \hline 220 \\ 216 \end{array}$

17. (C) Let n = the son's age. Then $3n$ = the father's age. The difference of the numbers is 30.

$$3n - n = 30$$
$$\dfrac{2n}{2} = \dfrac{30}{2}$$
$$n = 15$$

18. (A) Since the ice cubes are 2 inches on an edge, there can be only 2 layers of 8 cubes each or a total of 16 cubes.

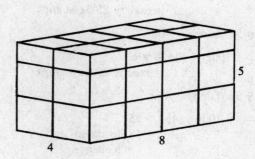

19. (E) If the gain was 10% of the selling price, then $12.60 was 90%, so 100% was equal to $14.00.

20. (B)
$$7M = 3M - 20$$
$$4M = -20$$
$$M = -5$$
$$M + 7 = -5 + 7 = 2$$

21. (C) Analyze this by means of the diagram below

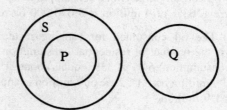

From the figure, we readily see that no P are Q.

22. (C) Basic toll $1.00
Extra toll $2.25, which is 3($.75).
Therefore the car holds a driver and 3 extra passengers for a total of 4 persons.

23. (A) .25% = .0025

$= \dfrac{25}{10000}$

$= \dfrac{1}{400}$

24. (D) The perimeter is twice the width plus twice the length, or $(2 \times 46) + (2 \times 34) = 160$ feet. If the cost is $9.00 per yard, it would be $\frac{9}{3}$ or $3.00 per foot (1 yard is 3 feet). The total cost is 160 ft × $3/ft = $480.

25. (E) 1 kilogram = 1000 grams

26. (C) Try each choice:

(A) 5 5¢ stamps = 25¢

$$100¢ - 25¢ = 75¢$$
$$= \text{exactly } 25 \text{ 3¢ stamps}$$

(B) 8 5¢ stamps = 40¢

$$100¢ - 40¢ = 60¢$$
$$= \text{exactly } 20 \text{ 3¢ stamps}$$

(C) 9 5¢ stamps = 45¢

$$100¢ - 45¢ = 55¢$$
$$= 18 \text{ 3¢ stamps and}$$
$$1¢ \text{ change}$$

(D) 11 5¢ stamps = 55¢

$$100¢ - 55¢ = 45¢$$
$$= \text{exactly } 15 \text{ 3¢ stamps}$$

(E) 14 5¢ stamps = 70¢

$$100¢ - 70¢ = 30¢$$
$$= \text{exactly } 10 \text{ 3¢ stamps}$$

In choice (C), exactly $1.00 cannot be spent.

27. (C) Commercial and industrial needs total 63% of daily oil consumption. Since consumption is 9 million barrels, 63% of 9 million is 5,670,000 barrels.

28. (D) The oil consumed for running residential motors is the product of residential consumption and motor consumption. 64% of 33% equals about 21% of the total 9 million barrels. 21% of 9 million is approximately 1.9 million.

29. (E) Figure the time elapsed on either side of 12 noon. From 7:42 A.M. to 12 noon is 4 hrs. 18 min. From 12 noon to 10:10 P.M. is 10 hrs. 10 min. The sum of the two is 14 hrs. 28 min.

30. (A) .05(800) = $40 commission
$$80:40 = 2:1$$

31. (A) Only choices (A) and (C) represent 72 ounces.

Choice (A): 6($.39) = $2.34
Choice (C): 3($.79) = $2.37

32. (A) Out of 12 total games, two were won. Thus, the fraction is $\frac{2}{12}$, or $\frac{1}{6}$.

33. (E) Angle BCA = Angle BAC = 80°
There are 20° left for angle B.

34. (B) The boy buys oranges for 10¢ each (30¢ ÷ 3). He sells them for 12¢ each (60¢ ÷ 5). Therefore his profit is 2¢ per orange. He must sell 50¢ ÷ 2¢ = 25 oranges for a 50¢ profit.

35. (C)
$$\frac{x+y}{2} = A$$
$$x + y = 2A$$
$$y = 2A - x$$

36. (D) This is an inverse proportion.
$$\frac{6}{4} = \frac{x}{8}$$
$$4x = 48$$
$$x = 12$$

37. (A) Area of each square = $\frac{1}{5} \cdot 125 = 25$
Side of each square = 5
Perimeter is made up of 12 sides.
$$12(5) = 60$$

38. (D) When two negative numbers are multiplied, their product is positive (greater than zero).

39. (B)
$$68 = 2\ell + 2(16)$$
$$68 = 2\ell + 32$$
$$68 - 32 = 2\ell$$
$$36 = 2\ell$$
$$18 = 1$$

40. (E) $\frac{1}{10} = x \cdot \frac{3}{4} = \frac{3x}{4}$
Cross-multiplying, we obtain
$$30x = 4$$
$$x = \frac{2}{15}$$

Writing

1. (A) Here, *taste* is a linking (copulative) verb that should be modified *not* by an adverb (*more sweetly*) but by an adjective (*sweeter*). Think of such linking verbs as replacing *to be*. Thus, in the sentence, "These oranges taste sweeter," *taste* has replaced *are*: "These oranges are sweeter."

2. (A) *Who's* is a contraction for *who is*, not to be confused with the possessive form *whose*.

3. (D) The writer has started a parallel structure, *dress neatly, be prompt, and,* and then violated it: *displaying interest*. The third item, like the first two, should be cast as an infinitive without *to: display* interest.

4. (E) There is no error here.

5. (C) The writer has assumed that the subject is

years, which takes a plural verb: *were*. But the subject is *influence,* which takes the singular: *was*. All the words between *influence* and *was* are modifiers of *influence,* and they do not change the singular nature of the word.

6. (D) In this sentence, "annually" and "each year" convey the same meaning, creating a redundancy. Either the word "annually" or the phrase "each year" should be deleted.

7. (B) The context requires the present perfect for action (or state of being) that began at a point in the past and has continued to the present: "Dolores *has been* in this country since . . . ."

8. (E) Some writers might argue that "in the winter" would make for better style, but there is nothing wrong in the spelling, grammar, usage, word choice, or idiom.

9. (A) The writer has confused *exceed,* meaning surpass, with *accede,* meaning yield.

10. (C) *Students* is plural and takes a plural verb: hence, ". . . ten students *have signed up.*"

11. (B) The word *scarcely* is already a negative word; *no* makes a double negative, which is incorrect in English.

12. (B) A comma cannot be used to separate two independent clauses. The comma at (B) should be replaced by a semicolon.

13. (D) The correct idiom for the kind of comparison expressed by the sentence requires the word "than," not "as."

14. (A) The sentence deals with an *IF,* a condition contrary to fact. This requires the subjunctive and conditional moods of verbs. The first clause suggests the *IF* is meant to occur in the present tense, because *went* is a present subjunctive form. The second clause suggests past tense, because *would have won* is the past conditional. But both verbs should be in the same tense. Which one is wrong? *Would have won* is not underlined, so you assume it to be correct and not subject to change. *Went* is underlined and thus must be the tense out of line. It should be changed to past subjunctive. "If the game *had gone* into extra innings. . . ."

15. (E) Correct. *Of* is a correct preposition here, because the meaning is "the more exact science of [these two] biology and psychology." *To be* is correct; this is the subjunctive mood after *believe. More exact* is correct because only two things are being compared.

16. (C) You can remember the correct case (*us? we? me? I?*) by always expanding the elliptical clause to its full (understood) meaning. For example, "If she were as old as *we* (are)" or "He is not so old as *I* (am.)"

17. (C) The idea calls for parallel structure: "Because the moon rotates on its axis at the same rate as *it revolves* around the earth. . . ."

18. (E) This sentence is correct.

19. (B) The apostrophe signifies that the plural noun "novels" is in the possessive case; however, since no attributes of the novels are named, the possessive is incorrect. The sense of the sentence requires "novels" to appear in the objective case; the apostrophe should thus be deleted.

20. (A) The plural of *hoax* is *hoaxes.*

21. (D) The writer has confused *formerly,* meaning previously, with *formally,* meaning officially, or with due regard to *form.*

22. (B) The underlined word is intended to modify the verb *has improved*. Therefore it must be in adverbial form: *considerably.*

23. (C) The subject is singular: *appeal*. Therefore the verb is singular: *has* elicited.

24. (E) The sentence is correct.

25. (B) Because "Africa" is a proper noun—the name of a continent—the first letter should be capitalized.

26. (A) The original sentence is correct.

27. (E) Sentences (A) and (D) both use *if* instead of *whether;* (D) additionally lacks a necessary verb. (B) and (C) use the structure of direct questions, but since the sentence is not punctuated as a question, they are run-ons. The idea of the underlined part must be presented in a clause that uses a conjunction (in this case, *whether*) to introduce an indirect question in normal word order. Only (E) does this correctly.

28. (D) Sentences (A), (B), and (E) improperly contrast an entire sport (*football*) with one aspect of another sport (*baseball fields*). (B), (C), and (E) are also unidiomatic. Only (D) corrects the sentence logically and idiomatically.

29. (C) *By means of* signifies *with the use of*. Therefore, sentences (A), (B), and (E) contain redundancies. Sentence (D) is clumsy and unidiomatic. Only (C) is correct.

30. (B) The use of *being* to indicate a cause is nonstandard.

31. (C) Maintain parallelism; the third ingredient must also be a noun.

32. (A) The original sentence is correct.

33. (D) Sentences (A), (B), and (C) all contain dangling modifiers. Since poaching is the referent of the pronoun *it* and the subject described by the modifying clause that begins the sentence, *poaching* should immediately follow the comma. The phrase *considered to threaten* in (E) is unidiomatic, so only (D) is correct.

34. (D) This sentence contains two independent clauses. If there is not a connective, then the first clause must be followed by a semicolon.

35. (E) Do not switch from the third person *(people)* to the second person *(your)* in the middle of a sentence.

36. (B) Sentence (B) is best. Sentences (C) and (E) incorrectly pair a plural verb *(seem)* with a singular noun, and *usage* is unnecessarily wordy and inflated in tone. The use of an infinitive phrase *(to increase the use)* rather than a noun phrase *(the increasing use)* in sentence (A) is an error because the sentence as a whole lacks a grammatical subject. (D) is ungrammatical and unidiomatic; the phrase introduced by *for* should be replaced by a "that" clause that includes a conjugated verb.

37. (E) The original (A) is wrong because it contains a double negative—*not* and *hardly*. (B) and (C) are simply variants of the same error. Of the two correct versions, (D) and (E), the latter is the more graceful.

38. (C) The writer has confused the language for three different ideas. The adverb *equally* suffices to make his point that he loves sport A *as much as* he loves sport B. That indicates the degree of his love. If he wanted to compare only his ability to love them, he would say, "I love both sports equally well." If he wanted to say that he loved B *in addition to* A, he would say, "I love A. I love B as well." Of these three ideas, only the first *(equally)* is offered as a choice (C).

39. (A) The original sentence is correct.

40. (C) *That is* is not necessary for the thought to be complete.

41. (B) Of the choices, (B) is best. A completely parallel comparison would be "Israel's climate is somewhat like California's climate" or "The climate of Israel is somewhat like the climate of California."

42. (A) The original sentence is correct.

43. (B) The phrases *known as being, known to be called,* and *known to be* in sentences (A), (C), and (E) are wordy, and the use of the possessive form of community *(community's)* is redundant and incorrect. Since *of her* already indicates the possessive. In addition, the lack of a conjugated verb form in (D) and (E) makes those choices ungrammatical.

44. (D) Sentence (D) is the best answer. Sentences (A) and (B) are awkward and wordy. The structure of the sentence requires that the subject be a noun phrase, such as is found in (D). In (C), the position of the subject is occupied not by a noun phrase but by an infinitive phrase, and in (E) the position of the subject is occupied by a "that" clause. These sentences are unidiomatic and ungrammatical.

45. (C) You may use two tenses with a common complement (here, the predicate adjective *appreciated*), but you must check that both tenses are complete. (A) omits the *been* after *has*. (B) and (E) would change the meaning. (D) lacks the parallelism of *never*. Only (C) completes the verbs and preserves the parallelism.

ANSWER SHEET FOR PRACTICE TEST 2

Reading	Mathematics	Writing

Reading

1 Ⓐ Ⓑ Ⓒ Ⓓ Ⓔ
2 Ⓐ Ⓑ Ⓒ Ⓓ Ⓔ
3 Ⓐ Ⓑ Ⓒ Ⓓ Ⓔ
4 Ⓐ Ⓑ Ⓒ Ⓓ Ⓔ
5 Ⓐ Ⓑ Ⓒ Ⓓ Ⓔ
6 Ⓐ Ⓑ Ⓒ Ⓓ Ⓔ
7 Ⓐ Ⓑ Ⓒ Ⓓ Ⓔ
8 Ⓐ Ⓑ Ⓒ Ⓓ Ⓔ
9 Ⓐ Ⓑ Ⓒ Ⓓ Ⓔ
10 Ⓐ Ⓑ Ⓒ Ⓓ Ⓔ
11 Ⓐ Ⓑ Ⓒ Ⓓ Ⓔ
12 Ⓐ Ⓑ Ⓒ Ⓓ Ⓔ
13 Ⓐ Ⓑ Ⓒ Ⓓ Ⓔ
14 Ⓐ Ⓑ Ⓒ Ⓓ Ⓔ
15 Ⓐ Ⓑ Ⓒ Ⓓ Ⓔ
16 Ⓐ Ⓑ Ⓒ Ⓓ Ⓔ
17 Ⓐ Ⓑ Ⓒ Ⓓ Ⓔ
18 Ⓐ Ⓑ Ⓒ Ⓓ Ⓔ
19 Ⓐ Ⓑ Ⓒ Ⓓ Ⓔ
20 Ⓐ Ⓑ Ⓒ Ⓓ Ⓔ
21 Ⓐ Ⓑ Ⓒ Ⓓ Ⓔ
22 Ⓐ Ⓑ Ⓒ Ⓓ Ⓔ
23 Ⓐ Ⓑ Ⓒ Ⓓ Ⓔ
24 Ⓐ Ⓑ Ⓒ Ⓓ Ⓔ
25 Ⓐ Ⓑ Ⓒ Ⓓ Ⓔ
26 Ⓐ Ⓑ Ⓒ Ⓓ Ⓔ
27 Ⓐ Ⓑ Ⓒ Ⓓ Ⓔ
28 Ⓐ Ⓑ Ⓒ Ⓓ Ⓔ
29 Ⓐ Ⓑ Ⓒ Ⓓ Ⓔ
30 Ⓐ Ⓑ Ⓒ Ⓓ Ⓔ
31 Ⓐ Ⓑ Ⓒ Ⓓ Ⓔ
32 Ⓐ Ⓑ Ⓒ Ⓓ Ⓔ
33 Ⓐ Ⓑ Ⓒ Ⓓ Ⓔ
34 Ⓐ Ⓑ Ⓒ Ⓓ Ⓔ
35 Ⓐ Ⓑ Ⓒ Ⓓ Ⓔ
36 Ⓐ Ⓑ Ⓒ Ⓓ Ⓔ
37 Ⓐ Ⓑ Ⓒ Ⓓ Ⓔ
38 Ⓐ Ⓑ Ⓒ Ⓓ Ⓔ
39 Ⓐ Ⓑ Ⓒ Ⓓ Ⓔ
40 Ⓐ Ⓑ Ⓒ Ⓓ Ⓔ

Mathematics

1 Ⓐ Ⓑ Ⓒ Ⓓ Ⓔ
2 Ⓐ Ⓑ Ⓒ Ⓓ Ⓔ
3 Ⓐ Ⓑ Ⓒ Ⓓ Ⓔ
4 Ⓐ Ⓑ Ⓒ Ⓓ Ⓔ
5 Ⓐ Ⓑ Ⓒ Ⓓ Ⓔ
6 Ⓐ Ⓑ Ⓒ Ⓓ Ⓔ
7 Ⓐ Ⓑ Ⓒ Ⓓ Ⓔ
8 Ⓐ Ⓑ Ⓒ Ⓓ Ⓔ
9 Ⓐ Ⓑ Ⓒ Ⓓ Ⓔ
10 Ⓐ Ⓑ Ⓒ Ⓓ Ⓔ
11 Ⓐ Ⓑ Ⓒ Ⓓ Ⓔ
12 Ⓐ Ⓑ Ⓒ Ⓓ Ⓔ
13 Ⓐ Ⓑ Ⓒ Ⓓ Ⓔ
14 Ⓐ Ⓑ Ⓒ Ⓓ Ⓔ
15 Ⓐ Ⓑ Ⓒ Ⓓ Ⓔ
16 Ⓐ Ⓑ Ⓒ Ⓓ Ⓔ
17 Ⓐ Ⓑ Ⓒ Ⓓ Ⓔ
18 Ⓐ Ⓑ Ⓒ Ⓓ Ⓔ
19 Ⓐ Ⓑ Ⓒ Ⓓ Ⓔ
20 Ⓐ Ⓑ Ⓒ Ⓓ Ⓔ
21 Ⓐ Ⓑ Ⓒ Ⓓ Ⓔ
22 Ⓐ Ⓑ Ⓒ Ⓓ Ⓔ
23 Ⓐ Ⓑ Ⓒ Ⓓ Ⓔ
24 Ⓐ Ⓑ Ⓒ Ⓓ Ⓔ
25 Ⓐ Ⓑ Ⓒ Ⓓ Ⓔ
26 Ⓐ Ⓑ Ⓒ Ⓓ Ⓔ
27 Ⓐ Ⓑ Ⓒ Ⓓ Ⓔ
28 Ⓐ Ⓑ Ⓒ Ⓓ Ⓔ
29 Ⓐ Ⓑ Ⓒ Ⓓ Ⓔ
30 Ⓐ Ⓑ Ⓒ Ⓓ Ⓔ
31 Ⓐ Ⓑ Ⓒ Ⓓ Ⓔ
32 Ⓐ Ⓑ Ⓒ Ⓓ Ⓔ
33 Ⓐ Ⓑ Ⓒ Ⓓ Ⓔ
34 Ⓐ Ⓑ Ⓒ Ⓓ Ⓔ
35 Ⓐ Ⓑ Ⓒ Ⓓ Ⓔ
36 Ⓐ Ⓑ Ⓒ Ⓓ Ⓔ
37 Ⓐ Ⓑ Ⓒ Ⓓ Ⓔ
38 Ⓐ Ⓑ Ⓒ Ⓓ Ⓔ
39 Ⓐ Ⓑ Ⓒ Ⓓ Ⓔ
40 Ⓐ Ⓑ Ⓒ Ⓓ Ⓔ

Writing

1 Ⓐ Ⓑ Ⓒ Ⓓ Ⓔ
2 Ⓐ Ⓑ Ⓒ Ⓓ Ⓔ
3 Ⓐ Ⓑ Ⓒ Ⓓ Ⓔ
4 Ⓐ Ⓑ Ⓒ Ⓓ Ⓔ
5 Ⓐ Ⓑ Ⓒ Ⓓ Ⓔ
6 Ⓐ Ⓑ Ⓒ Ⓓ Ⓔ
7 Ⓐ Ⓑ Ⓒ Ⓓ Ⓔ
8 Ⓐ Ⓑ Ⓒ Ⓓ Ⓔ
9 Ⓐ Ⓑ Ⓒ Ⓓ Ⓔ
10 Ⓐ Ⓑ Ⓒ Ⓓ Ⓔ
11 Ⓐ Ⓑ Ⓒ Ⓓ Ⓔ
12 Ⓐ Ⓑ Ⓒ Ⓓ Ⓔ
13 Ⓐ Ⓑ Ⓒ Ⓓ Ⓔ
14 Ⓐ Ⓑ Ⓒ Ⓓ Ⓔ
15 Ⓐ Ⓑ Ⓒ Ⓓ Ⓔ
16 Ⓐ Ⓑ Ⓒ Ⓓ Ⓔ
17 Ⓐ Ⓑ Ⓒ Ⓓ Ⓔ
18 Ⓐ Ⓑ Ⓒ Ⓓ Ⓔ
19 Ⓐ Ⓑ Ⓒ Ⓓ Ⓔ
20 Ⓐ Ⓑ Ⓒ Ⓓ Ⓔ
21 Ⓐ Ⓑ Ⓒ Ⓓ Ⓔ
22 Ⓐ Ⓑ Ⓒ Ⓓ Ⓔ
23 Ⓐ Ⓑ Ⓒ Ⓓ Ⓔ
24 Ⓐ Ⓑ Ⓒ Ⓓ Ⓔ
25 Ⓐ Ⓑ Ⓒ Ⓓ Ⓔ
26 Ⓐ Ⓑ Ⓒ Ⓓ Ⓔ
27 Ⓐ Ⓑ Ⓒ Ⓓ Ⓔ
28 Ⓐ Ⓑ Ⓒ Ⓓ Ⓔ
29 Ⓐ Ⓑ Ⓒ Ⓓ Ⓔ
30 Ⓐ Ⓑ Ⓒ Ⓓ Ⓔ
31 Ⓐ Ⓑ Ⓒ Ⓓ Ⓔ
32 Ⓐ Ⓑ Ⓒ Ⓓ Ⓔ
33 Ⓐ Ⓑ Ⓒ Ⓓ Ⓔ
34 Ⓐ Ⓑ Ⓒ Ⓓ Ⓔ
35 Ⓐ Ⓑ Ⓒ Ⓓ Ⓔ
36 Ⓐ Ⓑ Ⓒ Ⓓ Ⓔ
37 Ⓐ Ⓑ Ⓒ Ⓓ Ⓔ
38 Ⓐ Ⓑ Ⓒ Ⓓ Ⓔ
39 Ⓐ Ⓑ Ⓒ Ⓓ Ⓔ
40 Ⓐ Ⓑ Ⓒ Ⓓ Ⓔ
41 Ⓐ Ⓑ Ⓒ Ⓓ Ⓔ
42 Ⓐ Ⓑ Ⓒ Ⓓ Ⓔ
43 Ⓐ Ⓑ Ⓒ Ⓓ Ⓔ
44 Ⓐ Ⓑ Ⓒ Ⓓ Ⓔ
45 Ⓐ Ⓑ Ⓒ Ⓓ Ⓔ

PPST PRACTICE TEST 2

READING

60 Minutes—40 Questions

Directions: Each passage in this test is followed by a question or questions based on its content. Read each passage and answer the accompanying questions by choosing the best answer from among the five choices given. Base your answers on what is *stated* or *implied* in the passage.

1. With the exception of Earth, all of the planets in our solar system are named for gods and goddesses in Greek or Roman legends. This is because the other planets were thought to be in heaven like the gods and our planet lay beneath, like the ground.

   The paragraph best supports the statement that all the planets except Earth

   (A) were part of Greek and Roman legends
   (B) were thought to be in heaven
   (C) are part of the same solar system
   (D) were thought to be gods
   (E) were worshipped as gods

2. The game of Monopoly is a frustrated capitalist's delight. One rushes around a board trying to amass property and drive one's competitors into bankruptcy. I think it is no wonder that the game was invented by an unemployed man during the Depression, and that the game immediately caught the fancy of poverty-stricken America.

   The author would probably agree that

   (A) poor people enjoy Monopoly more than do middle-class people
   (B) Monopoly's popularity declines in more prosperous times
   (C) unemployed people are more creative than employed people
   (D) when Monopoly was invented, it was played more often by unemployed than by employed people
   (E) Monopoly was more likely to have been a success introduced when it was than during prosperous times

Questions 3–4

I would like to speak tonight in defense of a much-maligned subject, elitism. The past decades have seen a steady withering away of our commitment to excellence and the growth of egalitarianism. This philosophy believes that it is somehow evil to distinguish between people on the basis of their performance by giving grades and the like. I do not refer to equal opportunity programs, in which disadvantaged people get compensatory advantages, but instead to colleges and graduate schools, which have been content simply to give a "pass" or a "fail" to a student, thus guaranteeing that most will work less hard. Pass-fail decreases competition, and I see that as bad. This country was founded on the principle that free people should compete on equal terms, . . .

3. With which of the following statements would the author be most likely to agree?

   (A) People who advocate egalitarianism are probably underachievers.
   (B) Elitism is coming back into popularity.
   (C) Pass-fail grading is un-American.
   (D) It is good to make students work hard.
   (E) Equal opportunity programs unfairly promote those with lesser achievements.

4. Which of the following provides the best continuation for the paragraph?

   (A) and I'm all for that
   (B) and it was expected that everyone would end equally, too
   (C) but competition is harmful in many ways
   (D) and elitism and competition are not contradictory
   (E) but it was always assumed that the results of the competition would vary between people

5. It's dangerous to change the weather and the climate. We do not know enough about how such changes will affect the earth. What may seem good for one area may be bad for another. If you change a grassland into a vegetable farm, where will the cattle in that area graze? Before we tinker with our natural environment, we should be very sure of what we are doing.

The writer believes that

(A) changes in climate and weather may be harmful
(B) changing climate and weather will improve the earth's surface
(C) man should never meddle with his natural environment
(D) it's easy to figure out what will happen when you change the weather
(E) steady, unchanging weather is better for cattle

Questions 6–10

Dr. Horace O. Parrack of the United States Air Force Medical Laboratory has been studying the effect on airmen of jet propulsion and other modern aircraft engines. The Army wants to know whether or not high-pitched sounds generated by the new power planes are hazardous. Jet-engine noise may temporarily deafen a man even after brief exposures, and repeated exposure may result in permanent deafness.

Dr. Parrack finds that rats and guinea pigs can be killed with high-frequency sound waves, but that man is safe against them because he has no fur. With the fur-bearing animals the sound energy is turned into heat. They die from high-frequency noise because they get so hot that the body proteins coagulate. When the hair is shaved off, there is no such coagulating effect. Man, with his much more efficient skin ventilating system, is safe at energy levels 120 times greater than rats are.

6. The ultimate purpose of Dr. Parrack's study is

(A) to suggest safer flying methods
(B) to reduce loss of life in animals
(C) to study causes of deafness
(D) to decrease danger to aviators who fly jet-propelled planes
(E) to increase speeds of planes

7. According to this study

(A) high-pitched sounds are not at all dangerous
(B) high-pitched sounds can be fatal to man
(C) high-pitched sounds often cause deafness

(D) high-pitched sounds decrease body heat
(E) high-pitched sounds must be eliminated from engines

8. Animals like rats and guinea pigs may be killed by high-frequency sounds because

(A) their fur gets hot
(B) their blood gets too hot
(C) their fur does not allow body heat to escape
(D) they are fed on proteins
(E) their blood coagulates

9. Coagulation means most nearly

(A) thin out
(B) clot
(C) boil
(D) burn
(E) speed up

10. The efficient ventilating system that man has includes

(A) intestines
(B) throat
(C) skin pores
(D) mouth
(E) clothing

11. Without innovation, society cannot progress. Yet without an intellectual tradition to follow, real innovation is not possible. A free-thinking society with no cultural heritage will flounder just as surely as will a tradition-bound society with no independent thought.

The author would be most likely to oppose a philosophy that

(A) advocates building a new society upon the ashes of the old one
(B) advocates remedying historical wrongs by overturning the existing social order
(C) holds imagination to be more valuable than tradition
(D) venerates ancestors
(E) does not venerate ancestors

12. Restlessness such as ours, success such as ours, do not make for beauty. Other things must come first: good cookery; cottages that are homes, not playthings; gardens; repose. These are first-rate things, and out of first-rate stuff art is made. It is possible that machinery has finished us as far as this is concerned. Nobody stays at home any more; nobody makes anything beautiful any more.

The author's argument is predicated on the assumption that

(A) an artist must be a gourmet
(B) beauty depends on utility
(C) there are no successful artists any more
(D) the true artist can never know peace
(E) industrialization is inimical to excellence

Questions 13–15

As of December, 1983, there were 391 species listed as endangered. Today over 650 have been listed including 282 mammals, 214 birds, 59 reptiles, 49 fishes, 26 mollusks, 16 amphibians, and 8 insects. We hope to provide protection to another 600 species by the end of 1988. Although only 4 species of plants have been designated as endangered, with the establishment of five botanist positions in 1985, it is expected that 200 will be listed by the end of 1987.

Success should not be measured by the number of species listed; the goal is to return the species to the point where they are no longer endangered. This Department would be just as negligent in the performance of its duties under the Act for not de-listing a species that has recovered as it would be for not listing a critical species. We have not had the manpower or funding to review all of the species listed at the time of the 1983 Act.

13. It can be inferred that very few plants had been listed by 1983 because

(A) very few are close to extinction
(B) the Department doesn't classify plants
(C) no botanists were on the staff at the time
(D) some endangered mammals eat plants
(E) the Department had a surplus of funds

14. Which of the following is not stated in the passage?

(A) Eight insects have been listed as endangered.
(B) By the end of 1987, many plants will be added to the list.
(C) The Department considers listing species more important than de-listing them.
(D) The Department lacked manpower to review all listed species.
(E) Four species have been "reclassified."

15. "Success should not be measured by the number . . . ." What is a reasonable inference concerning the purpose of this statement?

(A) to avoid mentioning that the computer that kept count malfunctioned

(B) because measurement is always statistically difficult
(C) because the concept of success has been abused in recent years
(D) to counteract criticism that the Department was not listing enough species
(E) to indicate that the Department should not be successful

16. Only about one tenth of an iceberg is visible above the water. Eight to nine times as much ice is hidden below the water line. In the Antarctic Ocean, near the South Pole, there are icebergs that rise as high as 300 feet above the water.

The paragraph best supports the statement that icebergs in the Antarctic Ocean

(A) are usually 300 feet high
(B) can be as much as 3000 feet in total height
(C) are difficult to spot
(D) are a hazard to navigation
(E) are near the South Pole

17. It is a common assumption that city directories are prepared and published by the cities concerned. However, the directory business is as much a private business as is the publishing of dictionaries and encyclopedias. The companies financing the publication make their profits through the sales of the directories themselves and through the advertising in them.

The paragraph best supports the statement that

(A) the publication of a city directory is a commercial enterprise
(B) the size of a city directory limits the space devoted to advertising
(C) many city directories are published by dictionary and encyclopedia concerns
(D) city directories are sold at cost to local residents and businessmen
(E) city directories are published by nonprofit organizations

Questions 18–22

French portrait painting in the years immediately following the French Revolution developed a character all its own. The bitter experience of the Revolution created a people who had lost their ability to idealize, and could only recognize a reality they could see. Naturalism became a jealous god that purged completely the elements of Romanticism—be they classical, Walterian, Bolati, or whatever—with which it had found a certain compatibility in the first half of the century. We can see naturalism as an end in itself in the late portraits of Francis Peters, where the earlier Walterian ideal was swept aside. It can also be seen in the work of James Ellis Green, whose portrait of General Lefete is no match for his marvelous equestrian "Welton." And it can be recognized in countless other painters of the period. It has gained for the sixties and seventies the reputation of an art that is crass and banal in its naturalism, devoid of any poetry. With some justification, the question has been asked whether a painter that was so captivated by objectivism and the pursuit of reality could attain the level of the highest form of art. The painted portrait in America experienced the same disastrous result. An excessive naturalism had been encouraged by the appearance of the camera, which produced an image of total objectivity and accuracy, and unfortunately both patron and artist accepted this as the true form of art. The photographic naturalism of the painted portrait was not to be outdone by the modeled portrait, and American portraiture had to await the arrival of such men as Jerome Singer, John Elkin, and Jerode Balter to restore Art with a capital A upon the throne usurped by Naturalism with a capital N. To rise above the dull mediocrity it had achieved, naturalism had to be revitalized with elegance and heroism.

18. According to the author, after the French Revolution French portrait painting

    (A) was returned to the common man
    (B) improved its idealism
    (C) decreased in quality
    (D) developed into a modern classicism
    (E) returned to Romanticism

19. Each of the following is mentioned as affecting art in the 1870s EXCEPT

    (A) photography
    (B) war
    (C) objectivism
    (D) naturalism
    (E) religion

20. It seems to be that the thing the author dislikes most about the art following the French Revolution is its

    (A) inability to make changes
    (B) use of naturalism
    (C) poor craftsmanship
    (D) lack of elegance
    (E) poor choice of subject matter

21. The author implies that he or she liked least the works of

    (A) Green
    (B) Singer

    (C) Peters
    (D) Bolati
    (E) Walter

22. The article's main purpose is to

    (A) discuss the reasons for the changes in some of the art of the mid-1800s
    (B) show how war can destroy art
    (C) urge that art take a turn from naturalism
    (D) show how classical art and modern art are alike
    (E) explain the unpopularity of the art of the mid-1880s

23. The existence of a vacuum is impossible. For there to be a vacuum, for example, in a container, nothing material must be present in it. But if nothing material is in the container, then there is nothing between any pair of opposite points on the inner surface of the container. Consequently, no distance separates these two points, so that the two points would be one. This, of course, is absurd.

The best summary of the above argument is:

    (A) Because a container must contain something, no vacuum can exist.
    (B) Since, on the assumption that a vacuum exists in a container, the nonexistence of the container logically follows, there can be no vacuum.
    (C) Since it has been shown logically that, if a vacuum exists, there can be no containers, a vacuum must exist outside a container.
    (D) If we carefully examine a container by observing its contents, we will see that it is never really empty.
    (E) Since nothing can be removed from a container if the parts of its inner surface are not separated from each other, no vacuum can be produced.

24. The great thing about watching a sporting event is its unpredictability. No one knows what is going to happen next; at any point something may happen that has never happened before.

Which of the following provides the most logical continuation of the paragraph?

    (A) When you read a good book, you do not know what is coming next.
    (B) Professional wrestling features "matches" that are really rehearsed acts.
    (C) Football is better suited to television than is baseball.

(D) This compares favorably with such activities as watching formulaic television comedies and listening to the tired clichés of political speeches.
(E) Sports watching has developed into a national epidemic, helping to produce a nation accustomed to letting other people get their exercise for them.

25. The coloration of textile fabrics composed of cotton and wool generally requires two processes, as the process used in dyeing wool is seldom capable of fixing the color upon cotton. The usual method is to immerse the fabric in the requisite baths to dye the wool and then to test the partially dyed material in the manner found suitable for cotton.

The paragraph best supports the statement that the dyeing of textile fabrics composed of cotton and wool

(A) is more successful when the material contains more cotton than wool
(B) is more successful when the material contains more wool than cotton
(C) is not satisfactory when solid colors are desired
(D) is restricted to two colors for any one fabric
(E) is based on the methods required for dyeing the different materials

Questions 26–29

Private enterprise is no stranger to the American prison. When the United States replaced corporal punishment with confinement as the primary punishment for criminals in the early 19th century, the private sector was the most frequent employer of convict labor. Prisoners were typically either leased to private companies who set up shop in the prison or used by prison officials to produce finished goods for a manufacturer who supplied the raw materials to the prison. The former arrangement was called the contract system, while the latter came to be known as the piece-price system. In both instances, a private company paid the prison a fee for the use of prison labor, which was used to partially offset the expense of operating the prison. Blatant exploitation of inmates sometimes developed as a consequence of these systems.

Opposition to the use of prison labor from rival manufacturers and from the growing organized labor movement began to emerge in the latter part of the 19th century as more and more prisoners were put to work for the private sector. Opposition reached a peak during the Great Depression when Congress passed a series of laws designed to prohibit the movement of prison-made goods in interstate commerce, thus insuring that these products would not compete with those made by outside labor. Many state legislatures followed suit, forbidding the open market sale or importation of prison-made goods within their borders and effectively barring the private sector from the prison. As a consequence, prison-based manufacturing operations became state-owned and -operated businesses, selling goods in a highly restricted market.

26. Prisons stopped producing readily available goods due to all of the following *except*

(A) laws passed by state legislatures
(B) laws passed by the Congress of the United States
(C) opposition from organized labor
(D) dissatisfaction of the prisoners
(E) opposition from rival manufacturers

27. In the arrangement known as the "contract system"

(A) companies set up shop inside a prison and used prisoners for labor
(B) manufacturers supplied raw materials to the prison
(C) all of the prisoners signed a contract to produce a certain amount of goods
(D) prisoners with suitable skills would contact the companies
(E) exploitation inevitably ensued

28. According to the passage, which of the following was instrumental in the development of the private sector in prison?

(A) seed money from the federal government
(B) the replacement of corporal punishment with confinement
(C) the crudeness of the original prison system
(D) the constant exploitation of the prisoners by manufacturers
(E) the piece-price and contract system

29. Which of the following statements can be inferred from the passage?

(A) There is no longer any private sector work done in prisons.
(B) Legislatures are ready to repeal the previously passed prison laws.
(C) Prison systems were once fully supported by the fees paid by the private sector.
(D) The Great Depression was caused by excessive prison labor.
(E) Piece-price was more profitable than the contract system.

30. Certain genetic conditions such as albinism can theoretically be eliminated by preventing those affected from reproducing and thereby passing on the deleterious gene. An important genetic consideration exists, however, which makes this scheme impractical.

Which of the following sentences would provide the most logical continuation of this paragraph?

(A) The recessive gene that causes conditions such as albinism is found much more often in people who appear normal than in people manifesting the condition.
(B) Most diseases are not genetic.
(C) Even genetic conditions may not be manifested if the person affected has some overriding condition.
(D) Such a scheme would violate the civil rights of those barred from reproducing.
(E) Albinos have normal intelligence.

31. In response to those who say that the introduction of nuclear weapons into the area would destabilize conditions and lead to greater danger for its inhabitants, I say that the best defense is the capability for a strong offense, and I remind you that no one ever won a football game without scoring any points.

The speaker apparently believes that

(A) football games should be played with atomic weapons
(B) nuclear weapons are good things
(C) the introduction of nuclear weapons would not destabilize conditions in the area under discussion
(D) relations between countries are analogous to a game
(E) all inhabitants of the area would be safer if nuclear weapons were introduced there.

Questions 32–33

People like to say that there is no more frontier, except Alaska, for America. I would like to remind people of space: that is, *outer* space. The potential of the industrial space age is enormous. People will settle in company or government towns in orbit or on the moon, and will produce far more than the expense required to put them there. One study shows that if NASA spent $1 billion per year more for the next twelve years, $144 billion would be returned to the economy over the same time span, so that taxes from this additional income would make the federal government's expenditure fiscally worthwhile.

32. It can be inferred that the author believes that

(A) Alaska is not a true frontier
(B) development of Alaska is not economically appealing
(C) the oceans do not represent or contain a true frontier
(D) it is militarily important for the United States to control outer space
(E) the aesthetic and spiritual pleasures of settling outer space are less important than the economic reasons

33. Which of the following is (are) the author likely to support?

I. Regulation of profits made by private companies in outer space
II. Increased exploration for mineral wealth in Alaska
III. Some federal actions that aid in private businesses with operations in space

(A) I
(B) III
(C) I and II
(D) II and III
(E) I, II, and III

Questions 34–35

It is commonly thought that we can single out each of our beliefs apart from the rest and discover if it is true or false. To have a belief, however, we must first have some idea of what it is we believe to be the case. But no single one of our ideas can exist in isolation from at least some of our other ideas. So, for example, if we believe that Fido is a spaniel, we must have some idea of what a spaniel is and this idea is obviously connected with other ideas: e.g., of an animal; of a canine animal; of a barking canine animal, etc. Therefore, for us to verify that Fido is a spaniel—our original belief—we must also verify the beliefs that Fido is an animal, a canine animal, etc.

34. The conclusion implied by the author's argument is:

(A) Each idea we have is connected with every one of our ideas.
(B) We cannot verify any single one of our beliefs unless we can verify every one of them.
(C) No one of our beliefs can be verified without verifying some of our other beliefs.
(D) We cannot be sure of anything because we would have to know everything.
(E) Whenever we have a belief about anything, we also have an infinite number of interconnected ideas about it.

35. The author's argument would be considerably weakened if which of the following statements were true?

(A) To every idea connected with a given idea, there corresponds a belief requiring verification.

(B) Ideas are connected with other ideas.

(C) By verifying one belief, we at the same time verify several other beliefs that are connected with it.

(D) To every belief there corresponds at least one idea, and to every idea there corresponds at least one belief.

(E) No one can believe anything unless he or she has an idea about what it is he or she believes.

Questions 36–40

There is evidence that the usual variety of high blood pressure is, in part, a familial disease. Since families have similar genes as well as similar environments, familial diseases could be due to shared genetic influences, to shared environmental factors, or to both. For some years, the role of one environmental factor commonly shared by families, namely dietary salt (i.e., sodium chloride), has been studied at Brookhaven National Laboratory. These studies suggest that chronic excess salt ingestion can lead to high blood pressure in man and animals. Some individuals, however, and some rats consume large amounts of salt without developing high blood pressure. No matter how strictly all environmental factors were controlled in these experiments, some salt-fed animals never developed hypertension whereas a few rapidly developed very severe hypertension followed by early death. These marked variations were interpreted to result from differences in genetic constitution.

By mating in successive generations only those animals that failed to develop hypertension from salt ingestion, a resistant strain (the ''R'' strain) has been evolved in which consumption of large quantities of salt fails to influence the blood pressure significantly. In contrast, by mating only animals that quickly develop hypertension from salt, a sensitive strain (''S'' strain) has also been developed.

The availability of these two strains permits investigations not heretofore possible. They provide a plausible laboratory model on which to investigate some clinical aspects of the human prototypes of hypertension. More important, there might be the possibility of developing methods by which genetic susceptibility of human beings to high blood pressure can be defined without waiting for its appearance. Radioactive Sodium 22 was an important ''tool'' in working out the characteristics of the sodium chloride metabolism.

36. The statement that best relates the main idea of this article is:

(A) When salt is added to their diets, rats and humans react in much the same way.

(B) The near future will see a cure for high blood pressure.

(C) The medical field is desperately in need of research.

(D) Modern research has shown that high blood pressure is a result of salt in the diet.

(E) A tendency toward high blood pressure may be a hereditary factor.

37. The study of the effects of salt on high blood pressure was carried out

(A) because members of the same family tend to use similar amounts of salt

(B) to explore the long-term use of a sodium-based substance

(C) because it was proven that salt caused high blood pressure

(D) because of the availability of chemically pure salt and its derivatives

(E) because studies show an increase in the human consumption of salt

38. It can be implied that the main difference between ''S'' and ''R'' rats is their

(A) need for Sodium 22

(B) rate of mating

(C) reaction to salt

(D) type of blood

(E) general health condition

39. The reader can infer from the article that Sodium 22 can be used to

(A) cure high blood pressure caused by salt

(B) tell the ''S'' rats from the ''R'' rats

(C) determine what a sodium chloride metabolism is like

(D) control high blood pressure

(E) determine the amount of salt needed to improve our metabolism

40. Among the results of the research discussed in this article, the most beneficial might be

(A) the early identification of potential high blood pressure victims

(B) development of diets free of salt

(C) an early cure for high blood pressure

(D) control of genetic agents that cause high blood pressure

(E) improved laboratory breeding methods

MATHEMATICS

60 Minutes—40 Questions

Directions: Each of the questions or statements below is followed by five suggested answers. Choose the one that is best in each case.

1. George has a five-dollar bill and a ten-dollar bill. If he buys one item costing $7.32 and another item costing $1.68, how much money will he have left?

   (A) $1.10   (D) $9.00
   (B) $5.64   (E) $9.90
   (C) $6.00

2. If 20% of a number is 8, what is 25% of the number?

   (A) 2   (D) 11
   (B) 10   (E) 15
   (C) 12

3. Between 9 A.M. and noon, how many degrees does the hour hand of a clock move?

   (A) 30
   (B) 60
   (C) 90
   (D) 180
   (E) 360

4. The perimeter of figure *ABCDE* is

   (A) 18
   (B) 25
   (C) 38
   (D) 44
   (E) 45

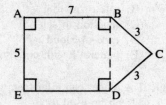

5. The total number of eighths in two wholes and three fourths is

   (A) 11
   (B) 14
   (C) 19
   (D) 22
   (E) 24

6. If $a = 2b$ and $4b = 6c$, then $a =$

   (A) 3c   (D) 4c
   (B) 6c   (E) 12c
   (C) 2.5c

7. A drawer contains 4 red socks and 4 blue socks. Find the least number of socks that must be drawn from the drawer to be assured of having a pair of red socks.

   (A) 2   (D) 5
   (B) 3   (E) 6
   (C) 4

8. A rectangular swimming pool is to be filled with water to a depth of 10 feet. If the pool is 30 feet long by 20 feet wide, how many cubic feet of water will be needed to fill the pool?

   (A) 500   (D) 5000
   (B) 600   (E) 6000
   (C) 2000

9. A college graduate goes to work for $x per week. After several months the company gives all the employees a 10% pay cut. A few months later the company gives all the employees a 10% raise. What is the college graduate's new salary?

   (A) .90 $x   (D) 1.01 $x
   (B) .99 $x   (E) 1.11 $x
   (C) $x

10. 10 to the fifth power may correctly be expressed as

   (A) $10^{10} \div 10^2$
   (B) 5^{10}
   (C) $10 \times 10 \times 10 \times 10 \times 10$
   (D) 10×5
   (E) $5\sqrt{10}$

11. Working alone, Jane put the first coat of paint on her living room walls in 5 hours 13 minutes. Four friends came to help with the second coat, and together they finished in 3 hours 49 minutes. How much time was saved by using her friends to help paint the room?

   (A) 1 hour 5 minutes
   (B) 1 hour 10 minutes
   (C) 1 hour 18 minutes
   (D) 1 hour 24 minutes
   (E) 1 hour 30 minutes

Items 12–15 refer to the following information.

Equipment, supplies, and salaries were the only three categories for which the bureau spent money.

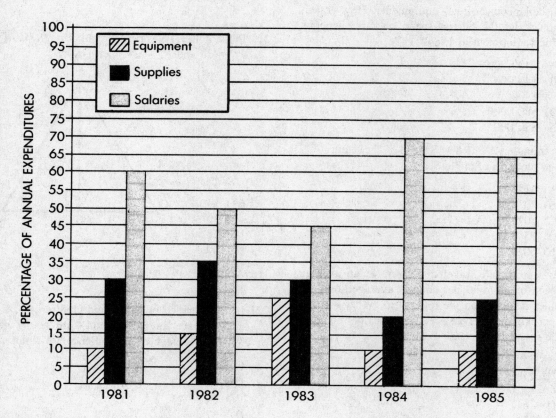

The bureau's annual expenditures for the years 1981–1985 are shown in the following table.

YEAR	EXPENDITURES
1981	$ 800,000
1982	1,200,000
1983	1,500,000
1984	1,000,000
1985	1,200,000

12. If the percentage of expenditures for salaries in one year is added to the percentage of expenditures for equipment in that year, a total of the two percentages for that year is obtained. The two years for which this total is the same are

(A) 1981 and 1983
(B) 1981 and 1984
(C) 1982 and 1984
(D) 1982 and 1985
(E) 1983 and 1985

13. Of the following, the year in which the bureau spent the greatest amount of money on supplies was

(A) 1985
(B) 1984
(C) 1983
(D) 1982
(E) 1981

14. Of the following years, the one in which there was the greatest increase over the preceding year in the amount of money spent on salaries is

(A) 1981
(B) 1984
(C) 1985
(D) 1982
(E) 1983

15. Of the bureau's expenditures for equipment in 1985, one third was used for the purchase of mailroom equipment and the remainder was spent on miscellaneous office equipment. How much money did the bureau spend on miscellaneous office equipment in 1985?

(A) $400,000
(B) $40,000
(C) $4000
(D) $800,000
(E) $80,000

16. In triangle RST, $\overline{RS} = \overline{ST}$ and $\angle T$ contains 70°. The measure of angle S is

(A) 70°
(B) 40°
(C) 50°
(D) 55°
(E) 60°

17. An automobile traveled 6 hours at an average speed of 40 miles per hour. It averaged only 30 miles per hour on the return trip. What was the approximate average speed in miles per hour for the round trip?

(A) 33
(B) 34
(C) 35
(D) 36
(E) 37

18. In the fraction $\frac{1}{\triangle}$, $\triangle$ could be replaced by all of the following except

(A) 1
(B) 0
(C) 10
(D) 4.2
(E) 9

19. A micromillimeter is defined as one millionth of a millimeter. A length of 17 micromillimeters may be represented by

(A) .00017 millimeters
(B) .0000017 millimeters
(C) .000017 millimeters
(D) .00000017 millimeters
(E) .017 millimeters

20. If 7 feet 9 inches is cut from a piece of wood that is 9 feet 6 inches, how long is the remaining piece?

(A) 1 foot 9 inches
(B) 1 foot 10 inches

(C) 2 feet 2 inches
(D) 2 feet 5 inches
(E) 3 feet

21. In the figure, $\overline{PS}$ is perpendicular to $\overline{QR}$. If $\overline{PQ} = \overline{PR} = 26$ and $\overline{PS} = 24$, then $\overline{QR} =$

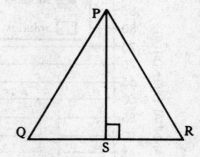

(A) 14
(B) 16
(C) 18
(D) 20
(E) 22

22. In an audience of adults and children, $\frac{1}{6}$ of the audience are young boys and $\frac{1}{3}$ are young girls. What percentage of the audience are children?

(A) $66\frac{2}{3}$
(B) 50
(C) 40
(D) $37\frac{1}{2}$
(E) $33\frac{1}{3}$

23. Of the following, the one that may be used correctly to compute $26 \times 3\frac{1}{2}$ is

(A) $(26 \times 30) + (26 \times \frac{1}{2})$
(B) $(20 \times 3) + (6 \times 3\frac{1}{2})$
(C) $(20 \times 3\frac{1}{2}) + (6 \times 3)$
(D) $(20 \times 3) + (26 \times \frac{1}{2}) + (6 \times 3\frac{1}{2})$
(E) $(26 \times \frac{1}{2}) + (20 \times 3) + (6 \times 3)$

24. The cost of 30 onions is d dollars. At this rate, how many onions can you buy for 80 cents?

(A) $\frac{24}{d}$
(B) $\frac{240}{d}$
(C) $24d$
(D) $\frac{3d}{8}$
(E) $\frac{8d}{3}$

25. On a map having a scale of $\frac{1}{4}$ inch = 20 miles, how many inches should there be between towns 325 miles apart?

(A) $4\frac{1}{16}$

(B) $16\frac{1}{4}$

(C) $81\frac{1}{4}$

(D) $32\frac{1}{2}$

(E) $6\frac{1}{4}$

26. Of the following, the unit that would most likely be used to measure the distance from New York to Albany is the

(A) liter
(B) kilometer
(C) centigram
(D) millimeter
(E) degree Celsius

27. During a ten-day museum exhibit the number of visitors doubled each day. If the exhibit opened on Tuesday and the attendance on Friday of the same week was 1000, what was the attendance on opening day?

(A) 1000
(B) 500
(C) 250
(D) 125
(E) 100

28. What is the next number in the series 27, 9, 36, 12, 48, –?

(A) 8
(B) 16
(C) 24
(D) 32
(E) 36

29. A dealer buys a TV set for $550 and wishes to sell it at a 20% profit. What should his selling price be?

(A) $570
(B) $600
(C) $620
(D) $640
(E) $660

30. If $\frac{a}{b} = \frac{3}{4}$ then $12a =$

(A) $3b$
(B) b
(C) $9b$

(D) $12b$
(E) $16b$

31. In the graph, the axes and the origin are not shown. If point P has coordinates (3,7), what are the coordinates of point Q?

(A) (5,6)
(B) (1,10)
(C) (6,9)
(D) (6,5)
(E) (5,10)

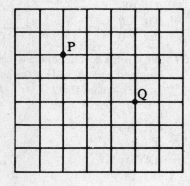

32. Which fraction is equal to .25%?

(A) $\frac{1}{400}$

(B) $\frac{1}{40}$

(C) $\frac{1}{4}$

(D) $\frac{5}{2}$

(E) $\frac{50}{2}$

33. If we double the value of a and c in the fraction $\frac{ab}{c}$, the value of the fraction is

(A) doubled
(B) tripled
(C) multiplied by 4
(D) halved
(E) unchanged

34. If a steel bar is 0.39 feet long, its length in inches is

(A) less than 4
(B) between 4 and $4\frac{1}{2}$
(C) between $4\frac{1}{2}$ and 5
(D) between 5 and 6
(E) more than 6

35. Michael earns $50 for 8 hours of work. At the same rate of pay, how much will he earn for 28 hours of work?

(A) $150
(B) $175
(C) $186
(D) $232
(E) $250

36. Two cars leave the same location at 2:00 P.M. If one car travels north at the rate of 30 mph and the other travels east at the rate of 40 mph, how many miles apart are the two cars at 4:00 P.M.?

(A) 50
(B) 500
(C) 100
(D) 120
(E) 150

Car 1
Car 2

37. What is the cost in dollars to carpet a room x yards long and y yards wide if the carpet costs two dollars per square foot?

(A) xy
(B) $2xy$
(C) $3xy$
(D) $6xy$
(E) $18xy$

38. Which of the following is equal to 3.14×10^6?

(A) 314
(B) 3140
(C) 31,400
(D) 314,000
(E) 3,140,000

39. If $3x + 3x - 3x = 12$, find $3x + 1$.

(A) 4
(B) 5
(C) 10
(D) 13
(E) 37

40. In May, Carter's Appliances sold 40 washing machines. In June, because of a special promotion, the store sold 80 washing machines. The percent of increase in the number of washing machines sold is

(A) 100
(B) 50
(C) 200
(D) 40
(E) 80

WRITING: SECTION 1

30 Minutes—45 Questions

Part A

25 Questions: Suggested time—10 Minutes

Directions: The sentences below may contain errors in punctuation, capitalization, grammar, usage, word choice, and idiom. Parts of each sentence are underlined and lettered. Decide which underlined part contains the error, and choose the corresponding letter as your answer choice. If the sentence is correct as it stands, choose E. No sentence contains more than one error.

1. In 1901 McKinley was fatally shot dead and, at
A
age forty-three, Teddy Roosevelt became Presi-
B   C   D
dent. No error
E

2. Of the four women in the quartet, Cindy has the
A   B
lower vocal range. No error
C   D   E

3. Unlike lightweight flying firds, penguins have
A
solid bones that help them in diving. No error
B   C   D   E

4. My friend considers cooking a great joy and to
A   B   to
wash dishes a great hardship. No error
C   D   E

5. By the time the storm subsided the majority of
A   B   C
the passengers been seasick. No error
D   E

6. The Atlantic salmon, once common in New En-
A   B
gland, is spawned in rivers but lives most of
C
it's life in the sea. No error
D   E

7. Miguel's looks are very similar to his brother; the
A   B
family resemblance is truly striking. No error
C   D   E

8. It is all together too early to forecast accurately
A   B
what the rate of inflation will be by year's end.
C   B
No error
E

9. Traditionally, the street number of a house in a
A
Japanese town reflected the relative antiquity of

the building rather than its location; the oldest
B   C
house was number one, the next oldest number
two, and so forth. No error
D   E

10. The influence of Beethoven's musical innova-
A
tions on later composers were pervasive. No
B   C   D
error
E

11. Opera singers admit that they tone down their
A   B
performances for the television camera, what is
C
effective on the stage often looks exaggerated
D
and ludicrous on the small screen. No error
E

12. Most animals cannot recognize their reflection
A
in a mirror as themselves; they usually react like
B
if confronted by another member of their
C
species. No error
D   E

13. People who are too credulous are liable to be
A   B   C
deceived by unscrupulous individuals. No error
D   E

14. I read where smoking tobacco can affect the
A   B   C
body's ability to utilize certain drugs. No error
D   E

15. To be the best at anything it demands a lot
A   B   C
more than talent. No error
D   E

16. Because the safety gear had been proved
                                A   B
to reduce the amount of accidents, it was made
                C
mandatory. No error
     D   E

17. The word "atom" comes from the Greek word
                                         A
meaning "not divisible," reflecting the belief
  B
that the atom was the most smallest unit of mat-
  C   D
ter. No error
     E

18. A *roman à clef* is a novel in which the fictional
                   A   B
characters and plot based closely on actual per-
                C   D
sons and events. No error
          E

19. Although I attended College until recently,
                A   B
I left without getting my degree. No error
  C   D   E

20. Airline executives hope that a more efficient
                             A
use of fuel will actually decrease the cost of air
  B   C
travel in the next decade. No error
  D   E

21. One of the cornerstones of modern physics, the
        A

principle of the conservation of energy
  B   C
was formulated by Leibnitz in the seventeenth
  D
century. No error
     E

22. The number of laboratories testing for Lyme
disease have grown throughout the country, but
A   B   C
some fail to follow the procedures necessary
to ensure accurate results. No error
  D   E

23. The storm was not severe enough to be
classified as a hurricane, yet it did considerable
  A   B   C
damage for the coastal settlements. No error
  D   E

24. The noise of him typing so disturbed the other
            A   B
tenants that he was asked to leave. No error
  C   D   E

25. Some researchers advocate the use in America of
                A
specially trained dogs to herd sheep and
  B
for protecting them from predators such as
  C   D
coyotes and bears. No error
            E

Part B

20 Questions: Suggested time—20 Minutes

Directions: The sentences below may contain errors in grammar, sentence construction, word choice, and punctuation. Part or all of each sentence is underlined. Select the lettered answer that contains the best version of the underlined section. Answer A always repeats the original underlined section exactly. If the sentence is correct as it stands, select A.

26. The Freedom of Information Act gives private citizens access of government files.

  (A) citizens access of
  (B) citizens access to
  (C) citizens' access to
  (D) citizens' access of
  (E) citizen's access of

27. By analyzing the remains of Stone Age cultures show that some preagricultural people probably chewed, but did not smoke, tobacco.

  (A) By analyzing the remains of Stone Age cultures show
  (B) By analyzing the remains of Stone Age cultures shows
  (C) Analyzing the remains of Stone Age cultures shows
  (D) Analyzing the remains of Stone Age cultures to show
  (E) Analysis of the remains of Stone Age cultures which show

28. Many critics consider James Joyce's *Ulysses,* a novel once banned as obscene, to be the greatest novel of the twentieth century.

  (A) *Ulysses*, a novel once banned as obscene, to be
  (B) *Ulysses*, a novel once banned as obscene, to be
  (C) *Ulysses*, once a novel banned as obscene, that it is
  (D) *Ulysses*, a once banned as obscene novel, to be
  (E) *Ulysses,* a novel once banned as obscene, as being

29. Athletes are less likely to develop sore muscles after vigorous exercise as others, partly because their muscles repair theirselves quickly after being strained or damaged.

  (A) as others, partly because their muscles repair theirselves quickly
  (B) as are others; partly because their muscles repair themselves quick
  (C) than others; partly because their muscles quickly repair theirselves
  (D) than do others, partly because their muscles repair theirselves quick
  (E) than are others, partly because their muscles quickly repair themselves

30. Having raked the beach for hours, the search for the lost ring was abandoned.

  (A) Having raked the beach
  (B) Having the beach raked
  (C) After we had raked the beach
  (D) Having raked, the beach
  (E) Raking the beach

31. Both being overweight and to smoke cigarettes increase one's chances of suffering some form of heart disease.

  (A) being overweight and to smoke cigarettes increase one's chances
  (B) being overweight and to smoke cigarettes increases one's chances
  (C) to be overweight and the smoking of cigarettes increase one's chances
  (D) being overweight and smoking cigarettes increase one's chances
  (E) being overweight and to smoke cigarettes increase ones chances

32. Because the animal was almost extinct so they were placed on the endangered species list.

  (A) extinct so they were
  (B) extinct; they were
  (C) nearly extinct so they were
  (D) extinct, it was
  (E) extinct, they were

33. Female attorneys at some of the nation's largest law firms say that, although their pay, they believe, is equal to their male counterparts, they are not promoted or offered partnerships at the same rate.

  (A) although their pay, they believe, is equal to
  (B) although they believe their pay equals that of
  (C) although their belief is that of equivalent pay to
  (D) despite their belief of pay equaling
  (E) despite pay they believe is equal as that of

34. Completed in 1957, the bridge was not only the longest suspension bridge in the world and also one of the most expensive, it cost over 99 million dollars to build.

  (A) and also one of the most expensive, it cost
  (B) and it was also one of the most expensive, costing
  (C) but was one of the most expensive, the cost of it
  (D) but one of the most expensive also, its cost being
  (E) but also one of the most expensive, costing

35. Whoever leaves last ought to turn out the lights.

  (A) Whoever
  (B) Who ever
  (C) Whomever
  (D) Whatever person
  (E) Who

36. Scientists who study sleep patterns and behavior have found that a majority of people are sleeping at least an hour to 90 minutes too little each night as what they should.

  (A) too little each night as what they should
  (B) too little each night than they should be
  (C) less each night as they should
  (D) less each night than they should
  (E) less each night than what they should be

37. Using <u>them as intended</u>, the tools will last a life-time.

    (A) Using them as intended
    (B) Because of intended use
    (C) Used as intended
    (D) Using them as they were intended to be used
    (E) Using them intentionally

38. <u>Contrary to</u> widespread belief, doctors are not required to take the Hippocratic oath in order to practice medicine.

    (A) Contrary to
    (B) Contrarily to
    (C) As opposed to
    (D) In opposition of
    (E) Against

39. The geometrical design of the quilt was tradition-al, but <u>using strikingly modern fabrics</u>.

    (A) using strikingly modern fabrics
    (B) strikingly modern fabrics were used
    (C) using striking modern fabrics
    (D) making use of strikingly modern fabrics
    (E) the fabrics used were strikingly modern

40. There should be no objection <u>to him winning</u> the most valuable player award, since all the coaches in the league voted for him.

    (A) to him winning
    (B) to his winning
    (C) to his having had won
    (D) of him winning
    (E) at him winning

41. The computer <u>has the capability for processing</u> all the relevant data within a half hour.

    (A) has the capability for processing
    (B) has the capacity for processing
    (C) has the capability in processing
    (D) can process
    (E) processes

42. <u>If I would have realized how much</u> the music dis-turbed her, I would have turned the volume down.

    (A) If I would have realized how much
    (B) If I realize how much
    (C) Had I realized how much
    (D) When I realized how much
    (E) If I would have realized to what extent

43. Passengers are requested <u>that they don't smoke excepting</u> in the designated area.

    (A) that they don't smoke excepting
    (B) do not smoke except if
    (C) not to smoke except
    (D) not to be smoking except that
    (E) that they are not smoking except

44. Animals exposed to high levels of some chlori-nated pesticides such as DDT display symptoms ranging from <u>suppression of the immune system to disruption of cell growth.</u>

    (A) suppression of the immune system to disrup-tion of cell growth
    (B) suppression of the immune system to cell growth being disrupted
    (C) suppressed immune systems up to disrupted cell growth
    (D) their immune systems being suppressed to disruption of cell growth
    (E) immune system suppression up to cell-growth disruption

45. It is essential <u>that tenants be understanding</u> how best to handle these complex rent increase notifi-cations.

    (A) that tenants be understanding
    (B) for tenants to understand
    (C) that the tenants have an ability to under-stand
    (D) for understanding tenants
    (E) , for those who have an understanding of ten-ants,

WRITING: SECTION 2

Essay

Time—30 Minutes

Directions: You will have thirty minutes to plan and write an essay on the topic given below. Read the topic carefully, and organize your ideas before you start writing. Remember to use specific examples and details where appropriate.

Many people have criticized television for presenting little of value. They claim television is a "vast wasteland" and we, as viewers, are little more than a "plugged-in" generation, unable to think for ourselves. Do you agree that television has little to offer? State your opinion and support it with specific reasons and examples.

The space below is for any notes you may wish to make. Begin your essay on a separate sheet of paper.

ANSWER KEY FOR PRACTICE TEST 2

Reading

1. B	21. C
2. E	22. A
3. D	23. B
4. E	24. D
5. A	25. E
6. D	26. D
7. C	27. A
8. C	28. B
9. B	29. A
10. C	30. A
11. A	31. D
12. E	32. E
13. C	33. B
14. C	34. C
15. D	35. C
16. B	36. E
17. A	37. A
18. C	38. C
19. E	39. C
20. D	40. A

Mathematics

1. C	21. D
2. B	22. B
3. C	23. E
4. B	24. A
5. D	25. A
6. A	26. B
7. E	27. D
8. E	28. B
9. B	29. E
10. C	30. C
11. D	31. D
12. A	32. A
13. C	33. E
14. D	34. C
15. E	35. B
16. B	36. C
17. B	37. E
18. B	38. E
19. C	39. D
20. A	40. A

Writing

1. A	24. A
2. C	25. C
3. E	26. B
4. C	27. C
5. D	28. A
6. D	29. E
7. B	30. C
8. A	31. D
9. E	32. D
10. D	33. B
11. C	34. E
12. C	35. A
13. E	36. D
14. A	37. C
15. B	38. A
16. C	39. E
17. D	40. B
18. C	41. D
19. A	42. C
20. E	43. C
21. E	44. A
22. B	45. B
23. D	

EXPLANATORY ANSWERS FOR PRACTICE TEST 2

Reading

1. (B) This paragraph takes careful reading, but it clearly states that the planets were thought to be in heaven like the gods, not that they were thought to be gods or that they were worshipped like gods.

2. (E) The final sentence expresses the idea that Monopoly was especially likely to be invented and to be a success in a country suffering from economic woes; (E) also expresses this idea. (B) is somewhat similar, but refers to the popularity of Monopoly after it became a success, a subject not addressed in the passage. (A), (C), and (D) are far from the author's topic.

3. (D) The tenor of the passage supports the idea that students should work hard. (A) is incorrect because the author does not impugn the motives or achievements of those who advocate egalitarianism. (B) is not suggested. (C) is incorrect because it is too extreme; while the author points to an old American principle in arguing against pass-fail, he or she does not go so far as to suggest that pass-fail is un-American. (E) is incorrect because the author does not state or imply that equal opportunity programs are unfair.

4. (E) (A) presents a vapid, repetitious continuation. (B) is contrary to the author's drift. (C) is not good because the author is arguing for competition, not against it. (D) is consistent with the author's beliefs, but does not belong in a sentence still attempting to justify competition. Simply claiming competition to be consistent with the main topic helps justify neither. (E) presents the logical continuation of the paragraph, one which argues for competition while continuing the reference to the country's founding principles and the philosophy behind them.

5. (A) The statement warns of the dangers that may result from changes in weather and climate. It does not say that we should *never* meddle with the environment.

6. (D) This is a good summary of the first two sentences.

7. (C) The only one of these conclusions supported by this study is (C).

8. (C) The clue to this as the correct answer comes in the statement that man has a "much more efficient skin-ventilating system." (D) would be ridiculous because man is also "fed on proteins." (E) is wrong because it's the proteins that coagulate. (A) and (B) may be true, but they are not cited as the ultimate cause of death.

9. (B) To coagulate is to change from a liquid to a more solid state. (E) is irrelevant; (A), the exact opposite of the truth; (C) and (D) involve processes counter to coagulation.

10. (C) This inference is drawn from two facts: 1) it's a *skin*-ventilating system, and 2) skin is the body part closest, in other animals, to their fur.

11. (A) The author stresses the importance of tradition, and thus would probably oppose destroying society. The author's opinions on revolution and the relative values of imagination and tradition are not stated or implied. His or her opinions on veneration (worship) of ancestors are likewise not mentioned; he need not oppose a lack of ancestor-worship simply because he stresses the importance of tradition.

12. (E) The author's conclusion follows from his or her premises only if the mechanization of modern society precludes "first-rate things." (A), (C), and (D) are incorrect because the passage discusses the social climate for appreciating beauty, not the characteristics of artists. (B) is incorrect because the passage describes the prerequisites for the creation of beauty, not a definition of it.

13. (C) We are told that five positions for botanists have been created. The indication is that they were new positions.

14. (C) The Department says that listing and de-listing species are equally important.

15. (D) Out of these five answer choices, this would seem the most likely. The speaker is anticipating a criticism and answering it in advance.

16. (B) If an iceberg towers 300 feet above the water line and only one tenth of its height is visible, its total height may well be 3000 feet. Choices (A) and (C) are clearly incorrect. (D) may well be a correct statement, but it is not supported by the paragraph. Choice (E) is too limiting. Icebergs range throughout the Antarctic Ocean, not just near the South Pole.

17. (A) The business of publishing city directories is a private business operated for profit. As such, it is a commercial enterprise.

18. (C) The author does not like the art of the period following the French Revolution, so answers (B), (D), and (E), suggestive of development, improvement, or appeal, are wrong responses. As there is no evidence to support choice (A), and answer (C) is appropriately negative, answer (C) is the correct response.

19. (E) Only answer (E)—religion—was not specifically mentioned as affecting art in the 1870s. This, then, is the correct response. The author felt that photography (A) produced total accuracy, that the war (B) brought about a loss of ability to idealize, and that objectivism (C) no longer existed. His or her harshest comments were directed toward the trend of naturalism (D) in art.

20. (D) Although answer (B) seems to be the appropriate response, it is not correct. The naturalism that the author so vehemently attacks is repulsive to him or her because it is "devoid of poetry" and needs to be revitalized with elegance. It is not so much the naturalism he or she dislikes as it is the apparent lack of elegance. Choice (D) is therefore the best answer here.

21. (C) The author likes least the portraits of Francis Peters, wherein he or she sees naturalism as an end in itself. (C) is the correct answer. The author is not pleased with Green (A) but writes less harshly of him. He or she writes positively of Singer (B), Bolati (D), and Walter (E); however, these are poor responses to the question.

22. (A) The author writes of the war, naturalism, and photography as having disastrous effects on the art of the mid-1800s. The main purpose, then, is to discuss the reasons for these phenomena, and answer (A) is the appropriate choice. Answers (B) and (C), although discussed quite fully, do not express the thrust of the entire passage. (D) and (E) cannot be supported from the information given.

23. (B) The argument is a reduction to absurdity. An obviously false conclusion is deduced from the assumption the author wants to disprove, thus implying that it is false. (A) oversimplifies the argument. (C) states a different argument with a somewhat preposterous conclusion. (D) is wrong, since the argument above makes no appeal to observation. (E) is at best a parody of the argument.

24. (D) The author is praising sports for the spontaneity, so that criticizing certain aspects of sports, as (B) and (E) do, is contradictory to the tone of the original statement. (A) is true, but it is not well connected to the previous thoughts; there is no special reason to mention books unless they are related to sports. (C)

brings in an irrelevant comparison. (D) continues the train of thought, pointing out that the excitement to be found in a sporting event is lacking in such other activities as watching situation comedies or listening to political speeches.

25. (E) The paragraph tells us that the dyeing of wool requires a process quite different from that for dyeing cotton. Fabric that contains both wool and cotton fibers must go through both processes, one after the other.

26. (D) There is no mention of prisoner satisfaction or dissatisfaction.

27. (A) The "contract system" and the "piece-price system" are discussed in the first paragraph.

28. (B) This is stated in the second sentence.

29. (A) The last sentence states that the operations became state owned.

30. (A) Choice (A) mentions an important *genetic* consideration that makes the idea impractical. (D) does not refer to a genetic consideration. (B) and (E) are irrelevant. (C) is at best peripherally relevant; it does not address the question of what consideration makes the scheme impractical.

31. (D) The war-peace topic of the sentence is compared to a football game. (A) is clearly incorrect. (B) is incorrect because the author does not clearly approve of nuclear weapons *per se;* he or she approves of their introduction into the area, a view based on the assumption that the weapons exist. (C) is incorrect because the author does not deny that nuclear weapons would destabilize the area. Similarly, (E) is wrong because the question of safety is not addressed; it may be assumed that the author believes that at least *some* inhabitants of the area would be made safer if nuclear weapons were introduced, but it is possible that the author believes that the inhabitants of countries lacking such weapons would be made less safe.

32. (E) The author calls Alaska a frontier, so (A) is incorrect. He or she does not speak of the economic development of Alaska, so (B) is incorrect. Since he or she does not say that Alaska and outer space are the only frontiers left, (C) is incorrect. (D) is incorrect because the passage makes no mention of the military importance of outer space. Because the author's argument for settling outer space is solely economic, it is reasonable to assume that the author considers economic reasons more important than aesthetic or spiritual reasons for developing outer space (E).

33. (B) Since the author mentions that the increased tax revenues from business stimulated by an increase in NASA's budget will make the investment profitable for the government, it is probable that he or she does not favor regulating profits made by private companies in outer space. It certainly cannot be said that the author does favor regulation of profits, so Statement I is wrong. Since the author ignores Alaska, there is no evidence except the act of ignoring it that bears upon Statement II and, therefore, it too should be considered incorrect. Statement III is clearly correct, for the author advocates that federal research into space development be followed by the establishment of "company or government towns in orbit or on the moon" that are both productive and profitable.

34. (C) (A) is wrong, since the author has not committed to so extreme a position; likewise (B). (D) is wrong, since it presupposes (B). (E) is a more extreme version of (A).

35. (C) The author is arguing that separate verification is required for every belief connected with a given belief and thus tacitly assumes that one cannot verify these beliefs by verifying the given belief. (A) is what the author is tacitly assuming. (B) is a stated assumption in the argument; likewise (D) and (E).

36. (E) Choices (A) and (D) are true statements but are only details, not the main idea, of the passage. There is no evidence to support answers (B) or (C).

Choice (E) is the best expression of the main idea of the article and is also the hypothesis of the study.

37. (A) The basis of the Brookhaven study was to determine the extent of familial diseases and, in particular, high blood pressure. Choice (A), then, is the best answer. Although answers (B), (C), (D), and (E) also seem correct, familial ties are not included in any of them, so they cannot be considered correct.

38. (C) Both the "R" and "S" strains of rats were injected with salt. It was each group's varying reaction to the salt that provided the main difference between the two groups. (C) is the correct answer.

39. (C) Sodium 22 does not cure or control high blood pressure; therefore, choices (A) and (D) are wrong. The "S" rats and the "R" rats were a known factor in the study, so answer (B) is also incorrect. Choice (E) is a ridiculous statement: Salt does not improve metabolism. The best answer is (C), and it is directly stated in the last sentence of the passage.

40. (A) Because the study was concerned with high blood pressure strains within families, this can lead to an early identification of the problem in family members, and preventive measures can be taken. This is most beneficial and best explained in answer (A), which is the correct answer. Answers (B) and (D) can be a result (thus secondary) of the early identification. Answer (C) is wrong, as the study did not lead to a cure. Answer (E) is irrelevant.

Mathematics

1. (C) George has $15.00. His total purchase is:

$$\begin{array}{r} \$7.32 \\ +\ 1.68 \\ \hline \$9.00 \end{array}$$

He will have $15.00 - $9.00 = $6.00 left.

2. (B) $\frac{1}{5}x = 8$
  $x = 40$
  $\frac{1}{4}(40) = 10$

3. (C) The hour hand makes a complete revolution (360°) in 12 hours. Therefore, it rotates $\frac{1}{12} \times 360°$ or 30° per hour. In 3 hours, the hour hand will rotate $30° \times 3 = 90°$.

4. (B) The perimeter is the sum of all the sides of the figure. ABDE is a rectangle, so side DE = 7.

  Perimeter = 7 + 5 + 7 + 3 + 3 = 25

5. (D) $2\frac{3}{4} \div \frac{1}{8} = \frac{11}{4} \div \frac{1}{8} = \frac{11}{4} \times 8 = 22$.

6. (A) If $4b = 6c$, then $2b = 3c$
If $a = 2b = 3c$, then $a = 3c$

7. (E) It is possible for the first four to be blue, then the next two *must* be red. Of course it is possible that two red socks could be drawn earlier, but with six we are *assured* of a pair of red socks.

8. (E) Use the formula page for volume of a rectangular container, $V = L \times W \times H$. Substituting, $V = 30 \times 20 \times 10 = 6000$.

9. (B) The graduate starts at $x per week. After the pay cut the graduate receives 90% of the original salary. The 10% raise adds 9% to the salary (10% of 90%), so the new salary is .99 $x.

10. (C) 10^5 is defined as $10 \times 10 \times 10 \times 10 \times 10$, or 100,000. $10 \times 5 = 50$. $5^{10} = 25^5$, $5\sqrt{10}$ is between 1 and 2, and $10^{10} \div 10^2 = 10^6$.

11. (D)
$$\begin{array}{r} 5 \text{ hours } 13 \text{ minutes } = \quad 4 \text{ hours } 73 \text{ minutes} \\ -3 \text{ hours } 49 \text{ minutes } = -3 \text{ hours } 49 \text{ minutes} \\ \hline 1 \text{ hour } 24 \text{ minutes} \end{array}$$

12. (A) Add the percentages for salaries and equipment. The totals are the same for 1981 and 1983.

1981 Salaries = 10%	1983 Salaries = 25%
Equipment = 60%	Equipment = 45%
Total 70%	Total 70%

13. (C) You must look at both charts to answer this question. Money spent on supplies:

1985—25% of $1,200,000 = $300,000
1984—20% of $1,000,000 = $200,000
1983—30% of $1,500,000 = $450,000
1982—35% of $1,200,000 = $420,000
1981—30% of $ 800,000 = $240,000

The greatest amount of money was spent on supplies in 1983.

14. (D) Money spent on salaries

1981—60% of $ 800,000 = $480,000
1982—50% of $1,200,000 = $600,000
             Difference + $120,000
1983—45% of $1,500,000 = $675,000
             Difference + $75,000
1984—70% of $1,000,000 = $700,000
             Difference + $25,000
1985—65% of $1,200,000 = $780,000
             Difference + $80,000

In 1982 there was an increase of $120,000 from the amount spent the preceding year on salaries. This amount represented the greatest increase of the years given.

15. (E) The total expenditure for equipment in 1985 was 10% of the annual budget. The budget was $1,200,000 (see lower chart). 10% represents .10 × 1,200,000 = $120,000. $\frac{1}{3}$ was spent on mailroom equipment and the remaining $\frac{2}{3}$ was spent on miscellaneous, or $\frac{2}{3} \times 120,000 = 80,000$.

16. (B)

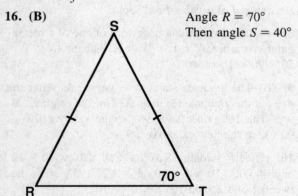

Angle $R = 70°$
Then angle $S = 40°$

17. (B) The distance, one way, is 40 mph × 6 h = 240 miles. The time to return was 240 mi ÷ 30 mph = 8 hours. The total distance is 480 miles, and the total

time is 14 hours; therefore, the average speed was 480 mi. ÷ 14 hours = 34 mph.

18. (B) The denominator of a fraction can never be equivalent to zero. Division by zero has no meaning in mathematics.

19. (C)   1 micromillimeter = .000001 mm
17 micromillimeters = 17 × .000001 mm
                     = .000017 mm

20. (A)   9 ft 6 in =   8 ft 18 in
     −7 ft 9 in = −7 ft 9 in
                     1 ft   9 in

21. (D)

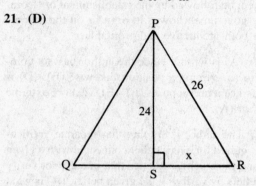

In the figure, $\overline{PS} \perp \overline{QR}$. Then, in right triangle PSR,
$$x^2 + 24^2 = 26^2$$
$$x^2 = 26^2 - 24^2$$
$$= (26 + 24)(26 - 24)$$
$$x^2 = 50 \cdot 2 = 100$$
$$x = 10$$
Thus, $\overline{QR} = 20$

22. (B) Let x = number of people in the audience.
     $\frac{1}{6}x$ = number of boys
     $\frac{1}{3}x$ = number of girls
$\frac{1}{6}x + \frac{1}{3}x = \frac{1}{6}x + \frac{2}{6}x = \frac{3}{6}x =$
$\frac{1}{2}x$ = number of children
$\frac{1}{2}$ = 50%

23. (E) $26 \times 3\frac{1}{2} = (26 \times 3) + (26 \times \frac{1}{2})$ by the distributive law. $26 \times 3 = (20 \times 3) + (6 \times 3)$ by the distributive law. Therefore, $26 \times 3\frac{1}{2} = (26 \times \frac{1}{2}) + (20 \times 3) + (6 \times 3)$.

24. (A) Let x = the number of onions you can buy for 80 cents.

$$\frac{30}{100d} = \frac{x}{80}$$
$$100dx = 2400$$
$$x = \frac{24}{d}$$

25. (A) Use a proportion comparing inches to miles.

$$\frac{\frac{1}{4}}{20} = \frac{x}{325}$$
$$20x = \frac{325}{4}$$
$$x = \frac{325}{4} \cdot \frac{1}{20} = \frac{325}{80} = 4\frac{5}{80} = 4\frac{1}{16}$$

26. (B) Kilometers are used to measure long distances.

27. (D) Counting backward and halving each new attendance, we get

Friday	1000
Thurs.	500
Wed.	250
Tues.	125

28. (B) The pattern is to divide by 3 and then multiply by 4. Thus the next number is $48 \div 3 = 16$.

29. (E) His selling price will be $(100\% + 20\%)$ of his cost price.
$$120\% \text{ of } \$550 = 1.20(\$550)$$
$$= \$660$$

30. (C) Cross multiply.
$4a = 3b$
Multiply by 3.
$12a = 9b$

31. (D) The abscissa of Q is 3 more than that of P. The ordinate of Q is 2 less than that of P. Hence, coordinates of Q are $(3 + 3, 7 - 2) = (6,5)$

32. (A) $.25\% = .0025$
$$= \frac{25}{10000}$$
$$= \frac{1}{400}$$

33. (E) By doubling the size of one of the factors of the numerator and the size of the denominator, we do not change the value of the fraction. We are actually writing an equivalent fraction. Try this with fractions having numerical values for the numerator and denominator.

34. (C) $12 \times .39 = 4.68$ inches; that is, between $4\frac{1}{2}$ and 5.

35. (B) The amount earned is proportional to the number of hours worked.
Let m = unknown pay

$8m = 28 \times 50$ — The product of the means is equal to the product of the extremes.
$$\frac{8m}{8} = \frac{1400}{8}$$
$$m = 175$$

36. (C)

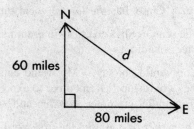

The car traveling north travels 30 mph $\times$ 2 hrs. = 60 mi. The car traveling east travels 40 mph $\times$ 2 hrs. = 80 mi. Using the Pythagorean Theorem,
$$60^2 + 80^2 = d^2$$
$$3600 + 6400 = d^2$$
$$10000 = d^2$$
$$\sqrt{10000} = d$$
$$100 = d$$

37. (E)

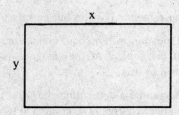

$$\text{Area} = xy \text{ sq. yd.}$$
$$= 9xy \text{ sq. ft.}$$
$$9xy \cdot 2 = 18\ xy$$

38. (E) $3.14 \times 10^6 = 3.14 \times 1,000,000$
$$= 3,140,000$$

39. (D) $3x = 12$
$x = 4$
$3x + 1 = 13$

40. (A) Increase of 40

$$\text{Percent of Increase} = \frac{\text{Amount of increase}}{\text{Original}} \cdot 100\%$$

$$\frac{40}{40} \cdot 100\% = 100\%$$

Writing

1. (A) The phrase *fatally shot dead* is redundant, since *fatally shot* and *shot dead* mean the same thing. Either *fatally* or *dead* should be deleted.

2. (C) The adjective *lower* is in the comparative form, used to compare two things or persons. If there are three or more, as in a quartet, you need the superlative form: "Cindy has *the lowest* vocal range."

3. (E) The sentence has no errors in grammar, usage, word choice, or idiom.

4. (C) You would not say, "My friend considers to wash dishes a hardship." Remember to express parallel ideas in parallel grammar: *cooking* and *washing*.

5. (D) The writer has omitted the first word from the past perfect *had been*.

6. (D) The apostrophe in *it's* signifies that the word is a contraction of *it is*. The possessive form *its,* clearly the sense intended here, does not take an apostrophe.

7. (B) The writer carelessly compares *looks* with a *person,* a part with the whole. "Miguel's looks are very similar to his *brother's*."

8. (A) The writer has confused *all together* with *altogether*. *All together* is used to describe persons or things that stand in close physical or psychological proximity. *Altogether* means entirely, completely.

9. (E) The sentence is plain but correct.

10. (D) True, *innovations* and *composers* are plural nouns, but the subject of the sentence is *influence*. Change *were* to *was*.

11. (C) A comma alone cannot be used to separate two independent clauses. The comma at (C) should be replaced by a semicolon.

12. (C) When *like* means *similar to*, it is a preposition and should be followed by a noun or a noun phrase. The correct usage in this sentence is *as if; as* is a subordinating conjunction that can properly introduce the subordinate clause.

13. (E) This sentence is correct.

14. (A) The writer doesn't mean *where;* he or she means *that*.

15. (B) The *it* is superfluous.

16. (C) You should say, "the *number* of accidents." Idiomatic usage requires that you use *number* with things or creatures that are separate units and can be counted. Use *amount* with things that come in masses: "the *amount* of butter" or "the *amount* of gasoline."

17. (D) The *most* in this sentence is redundant. The superlative form of the adjective *small* is already indicated by the *-est* ending. The word *most* is required for the superlative of some two-syllable and most longer adjectives, but then the *-est* ending is not used.

18. (C) The verb form is incomplete: it should be *are based*. Without the auxiliary *are* the statement is a sentence fragment.

19. (A) Since no specific educational institution is named, the word *college* should not be capitalized. The word *college* in this sentence functions as a common, not a proper, noun.

20. (E) This sentence is correct.

21. (E) This sentence is correct.

22. (B) In order to agree with the singular subject *number,* the conjugated verb of the sentence should also be in the singular. Therefore, the plural form *have grown* is incorrect; the correct form is *has grown*.

23. (D) Idiomatic usage is *damage to*.

24. (A) The writer is referring not to *him* but to *his* typing.

25. (C) The infinitive *to protect* is needed for parallel structure.

26. (B) The idiom is *access to*. In addition to using *of,* the wrong preposition, (D) and (E) incorrectly use the possessive, giving the impression that the act gives citizens access to—somebody else? (C) also incorrectly uses the possessive.

27. (C) Only (C) contains a subject (*Analyzing the remains . . .*) matched with a correctly conjugated verb (*shows*). Therefore, only (C) presents a grammatically complete sentence. The other choices are all long and elaborate sentence fragments.

28. (A) The original sentence is correct.

29. (E) Sentence (E) is best. Both (A) and (B) incorrectly use *as* instead of *than* as the idiom of comparison required by the sentence. (B) and (C) incorrectly use a semicolon instead of a comma to join an independent and a dependent clause, and (B) and (D) incorrectly use the adjective *quick* instead of the adverb *quickly* to modify the verb *repair*. In (A), (C), and (D) the form of the reflexive pronoun should be *themselves; theirselves* is not a word. Additionally in (D), *than do others* creates an illogical comparison, because the conjugated verb in the first part of the sentence is *are*. Only (E) is grammatically correct.

30. (C) The original dangling phrase may be corrected by substituting a dependent clause with its own subject (*we*).

31. (D) The parts of a compound subject ought to be parallel. *Smoking* is in the same grammatical form as *being*.

32. (D) *Animal* is singular, so *it* should be the subject.

33. (B) Sentences (A), (C), and (D) all present illogical comparisons, because they compare the female attorneys' pay to *male counterparts,* not to the *pay* of the male counterparts. (E) is awkward and unidiomatic.

34. (E) Sentence (E) is correct; *but also* is the idiomatic correlative for *not only,* and the present participle of the verb (*costing*) is correctly used to introduce the last phrase of the sentence, which serves to modify the bridge. Choices (A), (B), and (D) are unidiomatic and awkward; (A) and (C) are also examples of comma splices.

35. (A) If you do not know exactly *who* will be the last to leave, you use the generalized *whoever*. You do not use *whomever* (C) because what is needed is a subject (nominative case), not an object (objective case). (B) would change the meaning of the expression from "who, generally speaking," to "who, at any time." (D) would have to be *whichever person* but, compared with (A), it's wordy and stuffy.

36. (D) This sentence compares the amount of sleep most people get to the amount of sleep they should get. The comparative form of *little* is *less,* and the correct idiom for the comparison is "less x than y." The *what* in (A) and (E) and *be* in (B) and (E) are unnecessary and intrusive. Only (D) is correct.

37. (C) *Who* or *what* is using *them?* The tools? That's the subject of the original (A), and it's the noun nearest the introductory participle, so the writer has said, willy-nilly, that it's the tools that use the tools.

(A), (D), and (E) all err in the same way: *Using . . .* cannot modify *tools;* but *Used . . .* can. (B) is especially nonsensical.

38. (A) The original sentence is correct; the other choices are unidiomatic.

39. (E) The design and the fabrics are being compared. The first is traditional, the second, modern. The inevitable form is parallel structure, as in (E). (B) only appears to be parallel: it would put the second clause in the passive voice instead of in a simple linking-verb construction like the first clause.

40. (B) A gerund (*winning*) is modified by a possessive pronoun (*his*).

41. (D) The original uses four words where one will do: eleven syllables where three suffice.

42. (C) The sentence deals with a condition that is not a fact but a possibility. The verb used to express the condition contrary to fact should be in the subjunctive mood; the verb used to explain the possible conclusion should be in the conditional mood. But the writer of this sentence put both verbs in the conditional. The first clause should read: *Had I realized* or *If I had realized*. Remember, the past subjunctive corresponds to the past-perfect indicative.

43. (C) In the active voice, the verb *request* is used with *that:* "He *requested that* they not smoke." In the passive voice, it's used with the infinitive form of the verb: "They were requested not to smoke." Thus, (C) is the only correct choice. (A), (B), (D), and (E) are all structurally flawed, and, in addition, *excepting* in (A) is too colloquial.

44. (A) The original sentence is correct. The *up to* in (C) and (E) is unidiomatic; the correct expression is merely "from x to y." (B) and (D) violate parallelism, since the terms exemplifying the range of symptoms should be presented in parallel form.

45. (B) Substituting in the choices makes it easy to eliminate the wrong answers. All but (B) are unidiomatic and awkward.

ANSWER SHEET FOR PRACTICE TEST 3

	Reading		Mathematics		Writing
1	Ⓐ Ⓑ Ⓒ Ⓓ Ⓔ	1	Ⓐ Ⓑ Ⓒ Ⓓ Ⓔ	1	Ⓐ Ⓑ Ⓒ Ⓓ Ⓔ
2	Ⓐ Ⓑ Ⓒ Ⓓ Ⓔ	2	Ⓐ Ⓑ Ⓒ Ⓓ Ⓔ	2	Ⓐ Ⓑ Ⓒ Ⓓ Ⓔ
3	Ⓐ Ⓑ Ⓒ Ⓓ Ⓔ	3	Ⓐ Ⓑ Ⓒ Ⓓ Ⓔ	3	Ⓐ Ⓑ Ⓒ Ⓓ Ⓔ
4	Ⓐ Ⓑ Ⓒ Ⓓ Ⓔ	4	Ⓐ Ⓑ Ⓒ Ⓓ Ⓔ	4	Ⓐ Ⓑ Ⓒ Ⓓ Ⓔ
5	Ⓐ Ⓑ Ⓒ Ⓓ Ⓔ	5	Ⓐ Ⓑ Ⓒ Ⓓ Ⓔ	5	Ⓐ Ⓑ Ⓒ Ⓓ Ⓔ
6	Ⓐ Ⓑ Ⓒ Ⓓ Ⓔ	6	Ⓐ Ⓑ Ⓒ Ⓓ Ⓔ	6	Ⓐ Ⓑ Ⓒ Ⓓ Ⓔ
7	Ⓐ Ⓑ Ⓒ Ⓓ Ⓔ	7	Ⓐ Ⓑ Ⓒ Ⓓ Ⓔ	7	Ⓐ Ⓑ Ⓒ Ⓓ Ⓔ
8	Ⓐ Ⓑ Ⓒ Ⓓ Ⓔ	8	Ⓐ Ⓑ Ⓒ Ⓓ Ⓔ	8	Ⓐ Ⓑ Ⓒ Ⓓ Ⓔ
9	Ⓐ Ⓑ Ⓒ Ⓓ Ⓔ	9	Ⓐ Ⓑ Ⓒ Ⓓ Ⓔ	9	Ⓐ Ⓑ Ⓒ Ⓓ Ⓔ
10	Ⓐ Ⓑ Ⓒ Ⓓ Ⓔ	10	Ⓐ Ⓑ Ⓒ Ⓓ Ⓔ	10	Ⓐ Ⓑ Ⓒ Ⓓ Ⓔ
11	Ⓐ Ⓑ Ⓒ Ⓓ Ⓔ	11	Ⓐ Ⓑ Ⓒ Ⓓ Ⓔ	11	Ⓐ Ⓑ Ⓒ Ⓓ Ⓔ
12	Ⓐ Ⓑ Ⓒ Ⓓ Ⓔ	12	Ⓐ Ⓑ Ⓒ Ⓓ Ⓔ	12	Ⓐ Ⓑ Ⓒ Ⓓ Ⓔ
13	Ⓐ Ⓑ Ⓒ Ⓓ Ⓔ	13	Ⓐ Ⓑ Ⓒ Ⓓ Ⓔ	13	Ⓐ Ⓑ Ⓒ Ⓓ Ⓔ
14	Ⓐ Ⓑ Ⓒ Ⓓ Ⓔ	14	Ⓐ Ⓑ Ⓒ Ⓓ Ⓔ	14	Ⓐ Ⓑ Ⓒ Ⓓ Ⓔ
15	Ⓐ Ⓑ Ⓒ Ⓓ Ⓔ	15	Ⓐ Ⓑ Ⓒ Ⓓ Ⓔ	15	Ⓐ Ⓑ Ⓒ Ⓓ Ⓔ
16	Ⓐ Ⓑ Ⓒ Ⓓ Ⓔ	16	Ⓐ Ⓑ Ⓒ Ⓓ Ⓔ	16	Ⓐ Ⓑ Ⓒ Ⓓ Ⓔ
17	Ⓐ Ⓑ Ⓒ Ⓓ Ⓔ	17	Ⓐ Ⓑ Ⓒ Ⓓ Ⓔ	17	Ⓐ Ⓑ Ⓒ Ⓓ Ⓔ
18	Ⓐ Ⓑ Ⓒ Ⓓ Ⓔ	18	Ⓐ Ⓑ Ⓒ Ⓓ Ⓔ	18	Ⓐ Ⓑ Ⓒ Ⓓ Ⓔ
19	Ⓐ Ⓑ Ⓒ Ⓓ Ⓔ	19	Ⓐ Ⓑ Ⓒ Ⓓ Ⓔ	19	Ⓐ Ⓑ Ⓒ Ⓓ Ⓔ
20	Ⓐ Ⓑ Ⓒ Ⓓ Ⓔ	20	Ⓐ Ⓑ Ⓒ Ⓓ Ⓔ	20	Ⓐ Ⓑ Ⓒ Ⓓ Ⓔ
21	Ⓐ Ⓑ Ⓒ Ⓓ Ⓔ	21	Ⓐ Ⓑ Ⓒ Ⓓ Ⓔ	21	Ⓐ Ⓑ Ⓒ Ⓓ Ⓔ
22	Ⓐ Ⓑ Ⓒ Ⓓ Ⓔ	22	Ⓐ Ⓑ Ⓒ Ⓓ Ⓔ	22	Ⓐ Ⓑ Ⓒ Ⓓ Ⓔ
23	Ⓐ Ⓑ Ⓒ Ⓓ Ⓔ	23	Ⓐ Ⓑ Ⓒ Ⓓ Ⓔ	23	Ⓐ Ⓑ Ⓒ Ⓓ Ⓔ
24	Ⓐ Ⓑ Ⓒ Ⓓ Ⓔ	24	Ⓐ Ⓑ Ⓒ Ⓓ Ⓔ	24	Ⓐ Ⓑ Ⓒ Ⓓ Ⓔ
25	Ⓐ Ⓑ Ⓒ Ⓓ Ⓔ	25	Ⓐ Ⓑ Ⓒ Ⓓ Ⓔ	25	Ⓐ Ⓑ Ⓒ Ⓓ Ⓔ
26	Ⓐ Ⓑ Ⓒ Ⓓ Ⓔ	26	Ⓐ Ⓑ Ⓒ Ⓓ Ⓔ	26	Ⓐ Ⓑ Ⓒ Ⓓ Ⓔ
27	Ⓐ Ⓑ Ⓒ Ⓓ Ⓔ	27	Ⓐ Ⓑ Ⓒ Ⓓ Ⓔ	27	Ⓐ Ⓑ Ⓒ Ⓓ Ⓔ
28	Ⓐ Ⓑ Ⓒ Ⓓ Ⓔ	28	Ⓐ Ⓑ Ⓒ Ⓓ Ⓔ	28	Ⓐ Ⓑ Ⓒ Ⓓ Ⓔ
29	Ⓐ Ⓑ Ⓒ Ⓓ Ⓔ	29	Ⓐ Ⓑ Ⓒ Ⓓ Ⓔ	29	Ⓐ Ⓑ Ⓒ Ⓓ Ⓔ
30	Ⓐ Ⓑ Ⓒ Ⓓ Ⓔ	30	Ⓐ Ⓑ Ⓒ Ⓓ Ⓔ	30	Ⓐ Ⓑ Ⓒ Ⓓ Ⓔ
31	Ⓐ Ⓑ Ⓒ Ⓓ Ⓔ	31	Ⓐ Ⓑ Ⓒ Ⓓ Ⓔ	31	Ⓐ Ⓑ Ⓒ Ⓓ Ⓔ
32	Ⓐ Ⓑ Ⓒ Ⓓ Ⓔ	32	Ⓐ Ⓑ Ⓒ Ⓓ Ⓔ	32	Ⓐ Ⓑ Ⓒ Ⓓ Ⓔ
33	Ⓐ Ⓑ Ⓒ Ⓓ Ⓔ	33	Ⓐ Ⓑ Ⓒ Ⓓ Ⓔ	33	Ⓐ Ⓑ Ⓒ Ⓓ Ⓔ
34	Ⓐ Ⓑ Ⓒ Ⓓ Ⓔ	34	Ⓐ Ⓑ Ⓒ Ⓓ Ⓔ	34	Ⓐ Ⓑ Ⓒ Ⓓ Ⓔ
35	Ⓐ Ⓑ Ⓒ Ⓓ Ⓔ	35	Ⓐ Ⓑ Ⓒ Ⓓ Ⓔ	35	Ⓐ Ⓑ Ⓒ Ⓓ Ⓔ
36	Ⓐ Ⓑ Ⓒ Ⓓ Ⓔ	36	Ⓐ Ⓑ Ⓒ Ⓓ Ⓔ	36	Ⓐ Ⓑ Ⓒ Ⓓ Ⓔ
37	Ⓐ Ⓑ Ⓒ Ⓓ Ⓔ	37	Ⓐ Ⓑ Ⓒ Ⓓ Ⓔ	37	Ⓐ Ⓑ Ⓒ Ⓓ Ⓔ
38	Ⓐ Ⓑ Ⓒ Ⓓ Ⓔ	38	Ⓐ Ⓑ Ⓒ Ⓓ Ⓔ	38	Ⓐ Ⓑ Ⓒ Ⓓ Ⓔ
39	Ⓐ Ⓑ Ⓒ Ⓓ Ⓔ	39	Ⓐ Ⓑ Ⓒ Ⓓ Ⓔ	39	Ⓐ Ⓑ Ⓒ Ⓓ Ⓔ
40	Ⓐ Ⓑ Ⓒ Ⓓ Ⓔ	40	Ⓐ Ⓑ Ⓒ Ⓓ Ⓔ	40	Ⓐ Ⓑ Ⓒ Ⓓ Ⓔ
				41	Ⓐ Ⓑ Ⓒ Ⓓ Ⓔ
				42	Ⓐ Ⓑ Ⓒ Ⓓ Ⓔ
				43	Ⓐ Ⓑ Ⓒ Ⓓ Ⓔ
				44	Ⓐ Ⓑ Ⓒ Ⓓ Ⓔ
				45	Ⓐ Ⓑ Ⓒ Ⓓ Ⓔ

PPST Practice Test 3

READING

60 minutes—40 Questions

Directions: Each passage in this test is followed by a question or questions based on its content. Read each passage and answer the accompanying questions by choosing the best answer from among the five choices given. Base your answers on what is *stated* or *implied* in the passage.

Questions 1–2

Adam Smith felt that the workings of the free marketplace inevitably produced results beneficial to society. He felt that free competition would reduce prices to the lowest possible levels, and that the law of supply and demand would cause production to be neither too little nor too great. The *laissez-faire* policies of the 19th century, in which government did not intervene in economic workings, resulted from Smith's theories. Finally, the excesses of the monopolists proved that the marketplace was not free, and government began regulating the marketplace. Today government is so large as to resemble an octopus, and it is debatable whether it or our monopolies would distress Smith more.

1. It may be inferred that the author believes that

   (A) octopuses are expecially large animals
   (B) *laissez faire* is a good economic policy
   (C) monopolies were destroyed by government regulation
   (D) the marketplace was freer a hundred years ago than it is today
   (E) government's economic influence is now extremely widespread

2. According to the author's description of Smith's views, which would Smith have been most likely to deplore?

   (A) Decreased production of wool due to a sheep epidemic
   (B) Merger of two economically unsound companies
   (C) Rules limiting the entry of producers into a market
   (D) Large purchases of goods by government
   (E) Labor unions with the power to call strikes

3. A year—the time it takes the Earth to go exactly once around the Sun—is not 365 days. It is actually 365 days 6 hours 9 minutes $9\frac{1}{2}$ seconds, or $365\frac{1}{4}$ days. Leap years make up for this discrepancy by adding an extra day once every four years.

The paragraph best supports the statement that the purpose of leap year is to

   (A) adjust for the fact that it takes $365\frac{1}{4}$ days for the Earth to circle the sun
   (B) make up for time lost in the work year
   (C) occur every four years
   (D) allow for differences in the length of a year in each time zone
   (E) allow the Earth to go exactly once around the Sun

Questions 4–6

A glance at five leading causes of death in 1900, 1910, and 1945, years representing in some measure the early and late practice of physicians of that time, shows a significant trend. In 1900 these causes were (1) tuberculosis, (2) pneumonia, (3) enteritis, typhoid fever, and other acute intestinal diseases, (4) heart diseases, and (5) cerebral hemorrhage and thrombosis. Ten years later the only change was that heart disease had moved from fourth to first place, tuberculosis now being second, and pneumonia third.

In 1945, however, the list had changed profoundly. Heart diseases were far out in front; cancer, which had come up from eighth place, was second; and cerebral hemorrhage and thrombosis, third. Fatal accidents, which had been well down the list, were now fourth, and nephritis was fifth. All of these are, of course, composites rather than single diseases, and it is significant that, except for accidents, they are characteristic of the advanced rather than the early or middle years of life.

4. Which of the following statements is best supported by the passage?

    (A) A cure for cancer will be found within this decade.

    (B) Many of the most prevalent medical problems of today are those experienced by the elderly.

    (C) Older persons are more accident-prone than are younger persons.

    (D) Tuberculosis has been all but eliminated.

    (E) Heart disease will be conquered within this decade.

5. It can be inferred from reading this passage that

    (A) longevity increased between 1900 and 1910

    (B) longevity increased between 1910 and 1945

    (C) longevity increased between 1900 and 1945

    (D) longevity was not a factor in these findings

    (E) the causes of death listed did not effect any increase in longevity

6. According to this passage, the incidence of cancer as a cause of death between 1900 and 1910

    (A) remained unchanged in rank

    (B) increased because smoking gained in popularity

    (C) decreased because of the relative increase in thrombosis

    (D) was not indicated

    (E) was unknown

Questions 7–11

"Blind judging" is a system of application by Arts Endowment panels in which panelists consider a sample of work without being given the artist's name and recommend grants solely on the basis of the work submitted. In the last two years, the move to blind judging has become something of a trend among endowment programs.

Recounting the Music Program's favorable experiences with the new system, Assistant Program Director, Paul Fran, said panelists felt that they could concentrate on the music and not spend time discussing past careers, that there was less favoritism, and that younger artists received a "fairer shake." The Jazz Panel, in particular, believed that famous artists had taken advantage of the previous system by submitting old works or sketchy tapes. Fran also pointed out that there is a tradition of blind auditions for orchestral positions.

Council member Buddy Jacobs argued that "there is a perceptual problem—panelists taking care of their friends—and blind judging is a way to overcome this false assumption." "We also need to encourage lesser known artists," Jacobs added. "The Endowment should strive toward the ideal of Olympic competition, where medals are awarded on the basis of present performance."

"I want panels to have as much information as possible," countered Toni Morrison. "Writers may send in their weakest work because that's what they're interested in at the time. Disregarding biographical information also means that the panel cannot consider the impact of the fellowship on the stage of the artist's career. The Olympic metaphor should not dominate. One high leap is not the only thing that matters."

"Do you really believe that judging is blind?" asked Robert Joffrey, calling attention to the polite fiction that these procedures turn into. "Panelists familiar enough with an art form to be good judges will inevitably recognize the anonymous creators."

7. The "Olympic metaphor" suggests that

    (A) the best artist at the present time should receive the award

    (B) objectivity is impossible

    (C) all artists should strive to do their best

    (D) Olympics are the highest achievement for an athlete

    (E) subjectivity is inevitable in any competition

8. It can be inferred that Morrison would agree with all of the following *except* that

    (A) the Olympic comparison is not valid in the arts

    (B) an artist should be judged on a lifetime of work

    (C) an artist should be free to work on an area that interests him or her

    (D) biographical information should not be given to Arts Endowment panels

    (E) an artist can improve slowly rather than in a spurt

9. Which of the following is an argument for the blind judging system?

    (A) It makes it difficult to concentrate on the work.

    (B) It prevents judges from helping their friends.

    (C) It is not used in orchestral auditions.

    (D) It stifles the development of lesser-known artists.

    (E) It places too much importance on biographical information.

10. One reason that blind judging for music was successful for the Endowment panels was that

(A) music is performed from memory
(B) music is essentially aural, not visual
(C) great composers were always judged that way
(D) the judges felt obligated to make it work
(E) orchestral auditions had long been run that way

11. Joffrey maintained that blind judging is not realistic because

(A) politeness would make it unworkable
(B) fiction does not allow for impartiality
(C) artists will attempt to call attention to themselves
(D) judges can often figure out the identity of the artist
(E) judges are people who failed as artists

12. Psychology has a lot to say but sometimes it says too much. In one experiment with dogs, a mild shock applied to the left leg caused a response in the right leg. The observers then claimed that a stimulation of one side of the body would cause a response on the opposite side, and these results were generalized to people. But when a researcher later applied the same mild shock to the right legs of the dogs, their left legs did not respond!

Which of the following best sums up the author's attitude?

(A) All psychologist draw unjustified conclusions from their data.
(B) Dogs are poor experimental animals for psychological tests.
(C) Scientists must be careful not to draw unsupported inferences.
(D) Dogs' right legs are less sensitive to shocks than are their left legs.
(E) Animal studies should not be applied to people; only studies on people are relevant to people.

Questions 13–14

Ecologists remind us of the limits of things and many of them ardently urge less growth. Oil is a commodity we are running out of, they say. So is arable land. So are iron, copper, tin, lead. Not to mention fresh water and good fishing grounds. Conserve, they say. Insulate your houses better and use solar energy. Drive smaller cars, drive more slowly. Have fewer children. Eat less. When will someone tell me that production

begets production, that poor people do not find small to be beautiful, that there is enough energy in the oceans to last millions of years, and that the consumption I forego is likely to be taken by some less principled resident of Spaceship Earth?

13. The author probably believes that

(A) arable land is not in short supply
(B) people should drive big cars
(C) research on how to extract energy from the oceans is important
(D) solar energy is uneconomical
(E) most ecologists are correct on the issue of growth

14. Which of the following apply (applies) to the passage's final sentence?

I. It is a rhetorical question, not meant to be answered literally.
II. It does not relate to the previous part of the passage.
III. It is inconsistent in tone with the previous part of the passage.

(A) I
(B) III
(C) I and II
(D) II and III
(E) I, II, and III

Questions 15–19

From historical records, we can document that earthquakes of a particular size and character have occurred at certain locations in the past. Under the assumption that history will repeat itself, the historic record allows an estimate of the size of earthquakes that may occur in the future. For example, on the basis of the 1906 San Francisco earthquake, the northern San Andreas fault in California may generate shocks as large as magnitude 8.3 out of a possible 10.0.

But historical records as such rarely consitute an adequate or, more important, reliable basis for estimating earthquake potential. In most regions of the world, recorded history is short relative to the time between the largest earthquakes. Thus, the fact that there have been no historic earthquakes larger than a given size does not make us confident that they will also be absent in the future. It may alternatively be due to the short length of available historical records relative to the long repeat time for large earthquakes. Clearly, the historic record is most valuable and reliable in regions of the world that have long written histories and high rates of seismicity. Two of the outstanding records have been described by Nicholas Ambraseys for the eastern Mediterranean region and by Clarence Allen for China. Conversely, the historic record is least reliable in regions like the eastern United States where the seismicity is relatively low and the written history dates back only two or three centuries.

15. The author would agree with all of the following statements *except*

    (A) Historical records can provide evidence of where earthquakes have occurred in the past.
    (B) Past records in the eastern United States are of little value for predicting future earthquakes.
    (C) If there is no record of a major earthquake in a region, then the region is certain to be free of earthquakes.
    (D) Large earthquakes generally occur infrequently in a given region.
    (E) History often repeats itself.

16. All of the following are implied *except*

    (A) China has a long history of written records
    (B) San Francisco is located near the San Andreas fault
    (C) earthquakes seldom occur in the eastern United States
    (D) it is certain that history will repeat itself
    (E) two centuries is not a long time when discussing earthquakes

17. It can be inferred that "seismicity" is

    (A) the size of an area on the fault
    (B) earthquake activity
    (C) the oral records of earthquake activity
    (D) the shock that people feel upon seeing an earthquake
    (E) the area of the world studied by Ambraseys and Allen

18. Which of the following statements is supported by the passage?

    (A) The Chinese culture was nearly destroyed by an earthquake.
    (B) It is possible to confidently predict earthquakes.
    (C) An earthquake with a magnitude of 8.3 is large.
    (D) Millions of years of written records help to predict earthquakes.
    (E) It is possible to estimate the size of future earthquakes.

19. According to the passage, historic records are most valuable in an area that

    I. stores records deep in caves
    II. has written records
    III. has a high earthquake activity

    (A) I only
    (B) II only
    (C) III only
    (D) I and II only
    (E) II and III only

20. The Supreme Court was established by Article 3 of the Constitution. Since 1869 it has been made up of nine members—the chief justice and eight associate justices—who are appointed for life. Supreme Court justices are named by the president and must be confirmed by the senate.

    The paragraph best supports the statement that the Supreme Court

    (A) consists of nine justices
    (B) was established in 1869
    (C) consists of justices appointed by the Senate
    (D) changes with each presidential election
    (E) consisted of fewer than nine justices before 1869

Questions 21–23

We often act as if past civilizations had no insights into the great scientific questions of our day. I was amazed when I discovered this passage written by a 13th century Chinese philosopher:

Heaven and earth are large, yet in the whole of space they are but as a small grain of rice. It is as if the whole of empty space were a tree, and heaven and earth were one of its fruits. Empty space is like a kingdom, and heaven and earth no more than a single individual person in that kingdom. Upon one tree there are many fruits, and in one kingdom many people. How unreasonable it would be to suppose that besides the heaven and earth which we can see there are no other heavens and no other earths.

21. Which of the following does the author use to describe the expansiveness of space?

    I. a tree with fruit
    II. a kingdom with people
    III. a grain of rice

    (A) I only
    (B) II only
    (C) III only

(D) I and III only
(E) I, II, and III

22. It can be inferred that the philosopher would agree with which of the following statements?

(A) We can easily measure the volume of space.
(B) It is unreasonable to think that there are other heavens and earths.
(C) Empty space is just that, empty.
(D) Space most likely contains many earths.
(E) Heaven and earth are like a kingdom.

23. Which of the following best paraphrases the first sentence of the philosopher's discourse?

(A) The author understood the significance of the Big Bang Theory.
(B) From our perspective, heaven and earth are overwhelming, but in reality they are miniscule.
(C) The whole of space is a predecessor to a black hole.
(D) Heaven and earth make the universe seem like a grain of rice.
(E) As a grain of rice grows, so does the universe.

24. Not only do nice guys finish last in sports, but they don't do so well in real life. It's the bad guys I know who get the girls, the good jobs, and the respect of society. The nice, good guys are praised but not respected, are liked by women and employers but are passed up by both in favor of the more aggressive, ambitious guy who doesn't care what people think of him just so long as he gets what he wants. Nice guys finish last and are dopes.

The author's description of nice guys and bad guys suggests that he believes

(A) that many people are neither nice nor bad
(B) it is good to be a bad guy
(C) that success in sports is a good predictor of success in other aspects of life
(D) aggressiveness and ambition are associated more with bad than with nice guys
(E) nice guys are bachelors

25. If the U.S. keeps on crusading for human rights around the world, it will wind up with a lot of sympathizers, none of whom will be in power.

Which of the following represents an assumption of the author?

(A) The U.S. should stop crusading for human rights.
(B) No political leader is at present sympathetic to the U.S. human rights crusade.
(C) The U.S. stand on human rights is approved of by many people.
(D) Any political leader now sympathetic to the U.S. human rights stand is certain to fall from power.
(E) Countries should act in their own self-interest.

Questions 26–30

Contemporary astronomy is ordinarily at least as much of an observational as a theoretical science. Sooner or later on the basis of observation and analysis, what astronomers detect finds its way into theory, or the theory is modified to accept it.

Neutrino astronomy doesn't fit this pattern. Its highly developed body of theory grew for thirty years without any possibility of verification. And despite the construction, finally, of a string of elaborate observatories, some buried in the earth from southern India to Utah to South Africa, the last five years as well have produced not a single, validated observation of an extraterrestrial neutrino.

It is a testament to the persistence of the neutrino astronomers and to the strength of their theoretical base that their intensive search for these ghost particles still goes on.

The neutrino is a particle with a vanishingly small mass and no charge. Having no charge, it does not interact with the fields around which most particle detection experiments are built; it can be detected only inferentially, by identification of the debris left following its rare interaction with matter.

Even such indirect observations need elaborate and highly sensitive equipment, which didn't begin to go into place until about five years ago. But the goal is worth the effort: once detected, extraterrestrial neutrinos will provide solid, firsthand information on the sources and conditions that spawned them.

Scientists are sure of this because of the sophistication of experiments on neutrino reactions in particle accelerators and other earth-bound apparatus. These experiments have been refined rigorously over the years, and neutrino theory based on them is an integral part of modern physics.

The existence of neutrinos was first postulated in the early 1930s, in order to explain a form of radioactive decay in which a beta particle—an electron—is emitted. Certain quantities that physicists insist should be the same after an interaction as before—momentum, energy, and angular momentum—could only be conserved if another particle of zero charge and negligible mass were emitted.

26. This article was written for the purpose of

    (A) detailing the work of astronomers
    (B) reviewing the search for neutrinos
    (C) discussing the theory of astronomy
    (D) describing the dangers of neutrinos
    (E) explaining the uses of neutrinos

27. The neutrino was first discovered by scientists through

    (A) actual observation
    (B) the use of telescopes
    (C) the use of a microscope
    (D) guessing
    (E) the use of a computer

28. In size the neutrino is

    (A) too small to be observed
    (B) slightly larger than a neutron
    (C) slightly larger than a proton
    (D) the smallest thing ever observed
    (E) the same size as the smallest atom

29. The author feels that neutrino theory

    (A) was developed to aid astronomers in space observation with their telescopes
    (B) will never be proven
    (C) has become a proven fact
    (D) is now an accepted part of scientific knowledge
    (E) was based entirely on indirect observation

30. The neutrino theory developed as a result of which of the following laws?

    (A) magnetism
    (B) conservation
    (C) inertia
    (D) motion
    (E) observation

Questions 31–35

One of the most important experiments in photosynthesis was performed by the English scientist Joseph Priestley. Priestley believed that mint could restore oxygen to an atmosphere from which this gas had been removed. To test this he placed a burning candle in a closed jar. Quickly the flame went out. A mouse was then placed in the jar; it, too, quickly died. From this Priestley concluded that a burning candle and a living mouse both extracted the same substance

from the air. Priestley observed by chance that a sprig of mint had the effect of restoring the injured air to a normal state. A mouse now placed in the jar thrived as though it were breathing atmospheric air.

The experiment made by Priestley was soon followed by others. Other plants besides mint were tested and were found to have the same effect on the atmosphere as mint. It was later found that it was only the green parts of plants that possessed the ability to produce oxygen. Moreover, it was found that the formation of oxygen occurred only in the presence of sunlight. It was further shown that in the process of adding oxygen to the air, plants simultaneously extracted another gaseous material, a substance we now know as carbon dioxide. In addition to the exchange of gases with the surrounding air there was the growth of the plant itself. From the above it was confirmed that plants consumed carbon dioxide in the production of organic material and oxygen. The plant gained considerable weight during the process. It was later established that the overall gain in weight, together with the weight of oxygen given off, equaled the weight of all the raw materials consumed by the plant. These raw materials consisted partly of the carbon dioxide removed from the air but largely of water, incorporated by the plant through a number of complex chemical processes.

31. If in Priestley's experiment the sprig of mint had been replaced by blades of grass, the results would most likely have been

    (A) inconclusive
    (B) similar
    (C) different
    (D) unchanged
    (E) irrelevant

32. "Priestley believed that mint could restore oxygen to an atmosphere from which the gas had been removed," can best be described as a statement of a(n)

    (A) observation
    (B) conclusion
    (C) hypothesis
    (D) analysis
    (E) hypothecation

33. According to this passage, which of the following would contain the greatest concentration of oxygen?

    (A) desert land
    (B) cave
    (C) wheat field
    (D) ice field
    (E) animal cage

34. We may infer from reading this passage that plants produce oxygen

    (A) independently of sunlight
    (B) only in the presence of sunlight
    (C) at any time of day
    (D) in their brown stems
    (E) all of the above

35. Which of the following statements is most essential for the conclusion that ''plants consume carbon dioxide in photosynthesis''?

    (A) Plants extracted another gaseous material.
    (B) Only the green parts of plants produce oxygen.
    (C) Mint restored the injured air.
    (D) The plant gained considerable weight.
    (E) Hydrolysis synthesizes anhydrous water.

Questions 36–40

The deliberate violation of constituted law (civil disobedience) is never morally justified if the law being violated is not the prime target or focal point of the protest. While our government maintains the principle of the Constitution by providing methods for and protection of those engaged in individual or group dissent, the violation of law simply as a technique of demonstration constitutes rebellion.

Civil disobedience is by definition a violation of the law. The theory of civil disobedience recognizes that its actions, regardless of their justification, must be punished. However, disobedience of laws not the subject of dissent, but merely used to dramatize dissent, is regarded as morally as well as legally unacceptable. It is only with respect to those laws that offend the fundamental values of human life that moral defense of civil disobedience can be rationally supported.

The assumption that a law is a valid target of civil disobedience is filled with moral and legal responsibility that cannot be taken lightly. To be morally justified in such a stance, one must be prepared to submit to legal prosecution for violation of the law and accept the punishment if his or her attack is unsuccessful. One should even demand that the law be enforced and then be willing to acquiesce in the ultimate judgment of the courts. As members of an organized society, each benefits from our government and our Constitution. This implies a duty to accept the verdict of its institution if we challenge the law and our challenge is not vindicated.

For a just society to exist, the principle of tolerance must be accepted, both by the government in regard to properly expressed individual dissent and by the individual toward legally established majority verdicts. No individual has a monopoly on freedom and all must tolerate opposition. Dissenters must accept dissent from their dissent, giving it all the respect they claim for themselves. To disregard this principle is to make civil disobedience not only legally wrong but morally unjustifiable.

36. The author feels that violation of a legally constituted law that violates human dignity is always

    (A) legally and morally wrong
    (B) legally right
    (C) legally wrong
    (D) morally right
    (E) morally wrong

37. The author also feels that violation of a law for the purpose of dissent against some other immoral law is always

    (A) legally and morally wrong
    (B) legally right
    (C) legally wrong
    (D) morally right
    (E) morally wrong

38. According to the author, a person who sees the value of civil disobedience will regard his or her arrest as the

    (A) ultimate injustice
    (B) proper conduct of the government
    (C) proof that his or her disobedience was justified
    (D) goal toward which he or she must strive
    (E) attempt of the establishment to suppress his or her rights

39. It can be inferred that a person guilty of civil disobedience and sentenced to prison should

    (A) continue to fight for what he or she believes
    (B) accept his or her punishment willingly
    (C) recognize that he or she was wrong
    (D) realize that dissent cannot be tolerated
    (E) understand the legalities of his or her trial

40. The author's attitude toward civil disobedience is one of

    (A) indifference
    (B) admiration
    (C) hostility
    (D) respect
    (E) contempt

MATHEMATICS

60 Minutes—40 Questions

Directions: Each of the questions or statements below is followed by five suggested answers. Choose the one that is best in each case.

1. 53% of the 1000 students at Jackson High are girls. How many boys are there in the school?

   (A) 470
   (B) 53
   (C) 47
   (D) 530
   (E) 540

2. Round 825.6347 to the nearest hundredth.

   (A) 800
   (B) 825.63
   (C) 825.64
   (D) 825.635
   (E) 825.645

3. If $820 + R + S - 610 = 342$, and if $R = 2S$, then $S =$

   (A) 44
   (B) 48
   (C) 132
   (D) 184
   (E) 192

4. A pill contains 0.2 grams of a medicine. How many pills can be made from 1 kilogram (1000 grams) of the medicine?

   (A) 20
   (B) 200
   (C) 500
   (D) 5000
   (E) 10,000

5. The rectangle below has a length twice as long as its width. If its width is x, its perimeter is

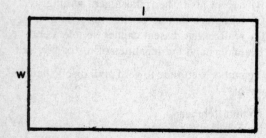

   (A) 6
   (B) $2x^2$
   (C) $6x$
   (D) $4x$
   (E) $8x$

6. If Joshua can mow a lawn in t minutes, what part of the job can he do in 15 minutes?

   (A) $t - 15$
   (B) $\frac{t}{15}$
   (C) $15t$
   (D) $15 - t$
   (E) $\frac{15}{t}$

7. The coordinates of point P on the graph are

   (A) $(2, -3)$
   (B) $(-3, 2)$
   (C) $(-2, 3)$
   (D) $(3, -2)$
   (E) $(-2, -3)$

8. Which one of these quantities is the smallest?

   (A) $\frac{4}{5}$
   (B) $\frac{7}{9}$
   (C) .76
   (D) $\frac{5}{7}$
   (E) $\frac{9}{11}$

9. If a discount of 20% off the marked price of a jacket saves a man $15, how much did he pay for the jacket?

   (A) $35
   (B) $60
   (C) $75
   (D) $150
   (E) $300

10. If $r = 5x$, how many tenths of r does $\frac{1}{2}$ of x equal?

    (A) 1
    (B) 2
    (C) 3
    (D) 4
    (E) 5

11.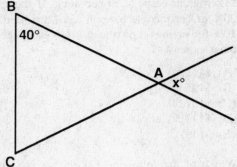

B
40°
A
x°
C

In the figure above, if $\overline{AB} = \overline{AC}$, then $x =$

(A) 40°
(B) 80°
(C) 100°
(D) 60°
(E) 90°

12. In the series 3, 7, 12, 18, 25 —, the 9th term is

(A) 50
(B) 63
(C) 75
(D) 86
(E) 88

13. A photograph is 8 inches wide and 10 inches long. If it is enlarged so that the new length is 25 inches the new width will be

(A) $18\frac{1}{2}$ inches
(B) 20 inches
(C) 24 inches
(D) $31\frac{1}{4}$ inches
(E) 34 inches

14. .10101 ÷ 10 is equivalent to

(A) 1.0101
(B) .0010101
(C) .1001
(D) .0100
(E) .010101

15. A certain type of board is sold only in lengths from 6 ft to 24 ft in multiples of 2 ft. A builder needs a large quantity of this type of board in $5\frac{1}{2}$ foot lengths. For minimum waste, the lengths to be ordered should be

(A) 6 ft
(B) 12 ft
(C) 24 ft
(D) 22 ft
(E) 18 ft

16. If *t* tons of snow fall in 1 second, how many tons fall in *m* minutes?

(A) 60 *mt*
(B) *mt* + 60
(C) *mt*
(D) $\frac{60m}{t}$
(E) $\frac{mt}{60}$

Items 17–19 refer to the graph below.

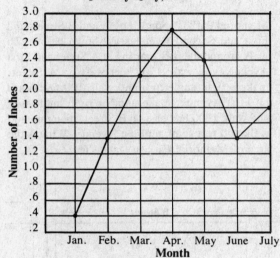

RAINFALL IN DAMP CITY
January–July, 1980

17. The total rainfall for the months January, February, and March was, in inches,

(A) 2.2
(B) 3.4
(C) 4.0
(D) 4.8
(E) 7.6

18. The average monthly rainfall, in inches, for April, May and June was

(A) 2.0
(B) 2.1
(C) 2.2
(D) 2.3
(E) 2.4

19. Which statement about the information given in the graph is *false*?

(A) The rainfall in April was twice the rainfall in February.
(B) June had greater rainfall than February.

(C) The month with the least rainfall was January.

(D) March had .4 inches greater rainfall than July.

(E) May had more rain than March.

20. Two ships leave from the same port at 11:30 A.M. If one sails due east at 20 miles per hour and the other due south at 15 miles per hour, how many miles apart are the ships at 2:30 P.M.?

(A) 25
(B) 50
(C) 75
(D) 80
(E) 35

21. Memorial Park is bounded by A and B Streets and First and Second Avenues as shown below. To walk around the park starting at A Street and First Avenue, you walk 1200 feet west on A Street, make a right angle turn and walk 100 feet north on First Avenue, make another right angle turn and walk 1200 feet east on B Street, then turn and walk 100 feet south on First Avenue. What is the area of Memorial Park in square feet?

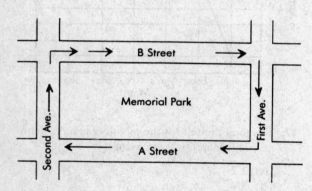

(A) 50,000
(B) 75,000
(C) 80,000
(D) 100,000
(E) 120,000

22. Riding a bike to school takes 25 minutes. Coming home only takes 20 minutes. If the trip to school is 3 miles long, what is the average miles per hour for the whole trip?

(A) 6
(B) 8
(C) 9
(D) 12
(E) 14

23. Ms. Marcus earns $250 per week. If she spends 20% of her income for rent, 25% for food, and 10% for savings, how much is left each week for other expenses?

(A) $112.50
(B) $125
(C) $137.50
(D) $132.50
(E) $140

24. Which of the following has the same value as $\dfrac{P}{Q}$?

(A) $\dfrac{P-2}{Q-2}$

(B) $\dfrac{1+P}{1+Q}$

(C) $\dfrac{P^2}{Q^2}$

(D) $\dfrac{3P}{3Q}$

(E) $\dfrac{P+3}{Q+3}$

25. If $a = b$ and $\dfrac{1}{c} = b$, then $c =$

(A) a
(B) $-a$
(C) b
(D) $\dfrac{1}{a}$
(E) $-b$

26. When the fractions $\frac{2}{3}$, $\frac{5}{7}$, $\frac{8}{11}$, and $\frac{9}{13}$ are arranged in ascending order of size, the result is

(A) $\frac{8}{11}, \frac{5}{7}, \frac{9}{13}, \frac{2}{3}$

(B) $\frac{5}{7}, \frac{8}{11}, \frac{2}{3}, \frac{9}{13}$

(C) $\frac{2}{3}, \frac{8}{11}, \frac{5}{7}, \frac{-9}{13}$

(D) $\frac{2}{3}, \frac{9}{13}, \frac{5}{7}, \frac{8}{11}$

(E) $\frac{9}{13}, \frac{2}{3}, \frac{8}{11}, \frac{5}{7}$

27. An estate was divided among three heirs, A, B, and C, in the ratio 2:3:4. If the total estate was $22,500, what was the smallest inheritance?

(A) $1000
(B) $1250
(C) $2500
(D) $4000
(E) $5000

28. If each of the dimensions of a rectangle is increased 100%, the area is increased

(A) 100%
(B) 200%
(C) 300%
(D) 400%
(E) 500%

29. A plumber needs eight sections of pipe, each 3'2" long. If pipe is sold only by the 10' section, how many sections must he buy?

(A) 1
(B) 2
(C) 3
(D) 4
(E) 5

30. The one of the following to which 1.86×10^5 is equivalent is

(A) 18,600

(B) 186,000
(C) 18,600,000
(D) $186 \times 500,000$
(E) 1,860,000

31.

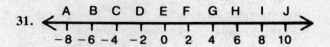

The sum of which points on the number line above would be equal to zero?

(A) B, D, E, I
(B) C, D, G, H
(C) A, C, F, I
(D) D, E, F, G
(E) B, C, H, I

Items 32 and 33 refer to the following graph.

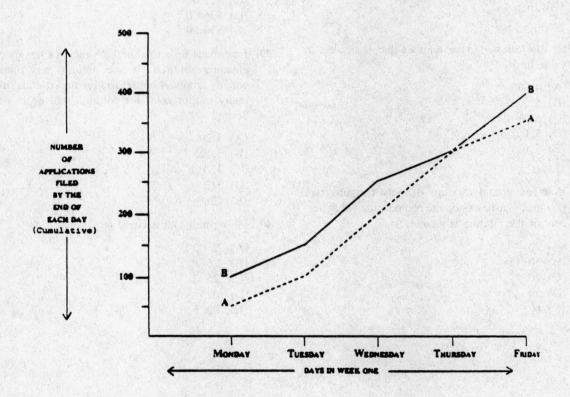

In the graph above, the lines labeled "A" and "B" represent the cumulative progress in the work of two file clerks, each of whom was given 500 consecutively numbered applications to file in the proper cabinets over a five-day work week

32. The day during which the largest number of applications was filed by both clerks was

    (A) Monday
    (B) Tuesday
    (C) Wednesday
    (D) Thursday
    (E) Friday

33. At the end of the second day, the percentage of applications still to be filed was

    (A) 25%
    (B) 50%
    (C) 66%
    (D) 75%
    (E) 85%

34. If $2x - 7 = 3$, then $3x + 1 =$

    (A) 4
    (B) 5
    (C) 7
    (D) 12
    (E) 16

35. Of the following, the number that is nearest in value to 5 is

    (A) 4.985
    (B) 5.005
    (C) 5.01
    (D) 5.1
    (E) 5.105

36. If a five-pound mixture of nuts contains two pounds of cashews and the rest peanuts, what percent of the mixture is peanuts?

    (A) 20
    (B) 30
    (C) 40
    (D) 50
    (E) 60

37. If the area of this figure, which consists of 7 equal squares is 63, find the perimeter of this figure.

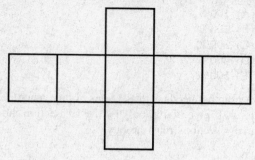

    (A) 48
    (B) 64
    (C) 84
    (D) 60
    (E) 63

38. Joan earns $4.00 per hour. On a day that she works from 9:30 A.M. to 3:00 P.M., how much will she earn?

    (A) $14.00
    (B) $18.00
    (C) $22.00
    (D) $26.00
    (E) $30.00

39. Jane made up a total of 1.28 liters of her special cleaning solution. If she divides the solution equally among 4 bottles to give to 4 friends, how many milliliters of the solution will be in each bottle?

    (A) 3.20
    (B) 5.12
    (C) 320
    (D) 512
    (E) 1280

40. $\frac{1}{4}\%$ written as a decimal is

    (A) 25
    (B) 2.5
    (C) .25
    (D) .025
    (E) .0025

WRITING: SECTION 1

30 Minutes—45 Questions

Part A

25 Questions: Suggested time—10 Minutes

Directions: The sentences below may contain errors in punctuation, capitalization, usage, word choice, and idiom. Parts of each sentence are underlined and lettered. Decide which underlined part contains the error and choose the corresponding letter as your answer choice. If the sentence is correct as it stands, choose E. No sentence contains more than one error.

1. Mrs. Lopez forgave the boy when she saw how
   A
   much he regretted his lapse in judgment. No error
   B   C   D   E

2. English people in the Renaissance were

   accustomed to consulting wizards and astrologers
   A   B
   for help in curing disease, identifying thieves, and
                     C
   to locate lost property. No error
   D   E

3. Although they're have been scores of vampire
                 A
   movies made both in this country and abroad , my
                                              B
   favorite is still a 1931 film starring Bela Lugosi.
                    C   D
   No error
   E

4. Because of the poor lighting, they mistakenly sup-
          A   B
   posed the intruder to be I. No error
            C   D   E

5. The possibility of collecting punitive damages
                      A
   are the consumer's major defense against wrong-
   B   C
   doing by insurers. No error
   D   E

6. *The Front Page,* a play by Ben Hecht and Charles

   MacArthur and written in 1928, was the basis for
                A   B   C
   Howard Hawks' film *His Girl Friday.* No error
   D   E

7. Thanks in large part to an excellent score and
          A   B
   imaginary staging , the musical had a successful
   C   D
   run. No error
        E

8. Research revealed that the migrating birds had no

   need of the sun or of landmarks but could orient
   A   B   C   D
   themselves by the earth's magnetic field. No
   error
   E

9. The woman gazed glum out the window at the
                 A   B
   smoke drifting over the devastated city.
                  C   D
   No error
   E

10. Admirers of American ballet have made the claim
    A
    that its stars can dance as well or better than the
        B   C   D
    best of the Russian artists. No error
                                 E

11. Because he had failed to attend the required
    A   B   C
    number of classes, he was unable in passing the
                                      D
    course. No error
            E

12. While some of the authors' criticisms may be
                       A   B
    valid, she conveniently ignores certain facts.
              C   D
    No error
    E

13. Lake Superior, with far fewer people living
                   A   B
    along its shores than Michigan's or Erie's, is
                                     C
    considerably less polluted than its sister lakes.
                D
    No error
    E

14. The investigation revealed that a large quantity
                                                    A
of chemicals has been removed from the store-
              B   C
room before the fire broke out. No error
                        D   E

15. Neither Los Angeles or Phoenix has an
                    A   B   C
abundant water supply. No error
    D   E

16. The spread of literacy in China has long
                                        A
been hampered by the vast differences of reg-
A   B   C
ional dialects, as well as by the lack of a simple
                D
standardized writing system. No error
                                  E

17. Some educators argue that young children who
have been exposed to too much television—
                        A
even educational programs—suffer from
B   C
unusually short attention spans. No error
D   E

18. Of the two accounts of the investigation I
have read, the one in last week's magazine was
A   B   C
the most informative. No error
    D   E

19. There was a time when the arctic was unknown
                          A
territory; now, scientists are manning
        B
research stations there and gathering data on
        C   D
the frozen region. No error
                    E

20. If the strip mining operation would have been
                                A

carried out, toxic wastes might have leached
        B   C   D
into the water supply. No error
                        E

21. Further acquaintance with the memoirs of
    A   B
Elizabeth Barrett Browning and Robert Browning enable us to appreciate the degree of influ-
    C
ence that two people of talent can have on each
                                          D
other. No error
        E

22. Penicillin, once a certain cure for
most types of venereal disease; is now inef-
A   B
fective in many cases because the bacteria involved have acquired a resistance to it.
        C   D
No error
E

23. The oldest surviving lyrics in a modern European
                A
language are the twelfth-century troubadour
        B   C   D
songs from southern France. No error
                              E

24. It is often easier to write a paper __ by revising
        A   B
several successive drafts than to try to organize
        C   D
everything perfectly in one's head once.

No error
E

25. The identity of the "Dark Lady" to which
                                        A
Shakespeare addressed many of his sonnets
            B
has never been definitely determined. No error
    C   D   E

Part B

20 Questions; Suggested time—20 Minutes

Directions: The sentences below may contain errors in grammar, sentence construction, word choice, and punctuation. Part or all of each sentence is underlined. Select the lettered answer that contains the best version of the underlined sentence. Answer A always repeats the original underlined section exactly. If the sentence is correct as it stands, select A.

26. By means of using a new live-virus vaccine, Swiss scientists hope to reduce the incidence of rabies among foxes in Europe.

    (A) By means of using a new live-virus vaccine,
    (B) By means of a new live-virus vaccine being used,
    (C) Using a new live-virus vaccine,
    (D) By means of using a new live-virus vaccine.
    (E) By means of using a new live-virus vaccine;

27. For six months the two astronauts lived in a trailer-sized craft, circling the earth at an altitude of 200 miles.

    (A) lived in a trailer-sized craft, circling
    (B) lived in a trailer-sized craft to circle
    (C) live in a trailer-sized craft, and it circled
    (D) live in a craft the size of a trailer, to be circling
    (E) lived in a craft sized like a trailer, which it circled

28. For one to accept constructive criticism without getting resentful is a sign that one is mature.

    (A) For one to accept constructive criticism without getting resentful is a sign that one is mature.
    (B) It is a sign that one is mature when one accepts constructive criticism without getting resentful.
    (C) Accepting constructive criticism without one getting resentful is a sign of maturity.
    (D) A mature sign is to accept constructive criticism without resentment.
    (E) Accepting constructive criticism without resentment is a sign of maturity.

29. Rising slowly into the air, the crowd waved as the balloon departed.

    (A) Rising slowly into the air, the crowd waved as the balloon departed.

    (B) Rising slowly into the air, as the balloon departed, the crowd waved.
    (C) The crowd waved to the balloon as it raised slowly into the air and departed.
    (D) The balloon rose slowly into the air as it departed, the crowd waved.
    (E) Rising slowly into the air, the balloon departed as the crowd waved.

30. Geronimo, a chief of the Apache tribe, lived to the age of eighty years old.

    (A) to the age of eighty years old
    (B) until eighty
    (C) until the age of eighty years old
    (D) to be eighty years old
    (E) up to eighty years old

31. The new officer is not only knowledgeable but also a congenial person.

    (A) is not only knowledgeable but also a congenial person
    (B) is not only knowledgeable but congenial as well
    (C) is not only a knowledgeable person but also a congenial person
    (D) not only is knowledgeable but also a congenial person
    (E) not only is knowledgeable but congenial

32. A coalition of citizens' groups condemned the continued use of a chemical fertilizer that had been proved carcinogenic.

    (A) the continued use of a chemical fertilizer that had been
    (B) the continued using of a chemical fertilizer as being
    (C) the continuation of using a chemical fertilizer
    (D) continuing the use of a chemical fertilizer
    (E) continuing using a chemical fertilizer that had been

33. Experts studying the pigments in cave paintings in the Pyrenees say that each prehistoric group of

artists maybe had its own hallmark paint recipes, just like the studios of Renaissance Italy.

(A) maybe had its own hallmark paint recipes, just like
(B) had, it may be, its own hallmark paint recipes, just as like
(C) may have had its own hallmark paint recipes, just as did
(D) may have had its own hallmark paint recipes, as likewise did
(E) might have had its own hallmark paint recipes, like as

34. Having neglected to inform the post office of her new address, Cheryl's mail was delayed a week.

(A) Cheryl's mail was delayed a week
(B) there was a week delay in the delivery of Cheryl's mail
(C) for a week Cheryl failed to receive her mail
(D) Cheryl experienced a week's delay in mail delivery
(E) the mail was delayed in being delivered to Cheryl for a week

35. One reason chemotherapy is such a hazardous treatment to undergo is because doses large enough to overcome a cancerous tumor often also destroys a patient's bone marrow.

(A) because doses large enough to overcome a cancerous tumor often also destroys
(B) because doses so large as to overcome a cancerous tumor often also destroy
(C) that doses so large as to overcome a cancerous tumor also often destroys
(D) that large enough doses to overcome a cancerous tumor often also destroys
(E) that doses large enough to overcome a cancerous tumor often also destroy

36. The doctor was surprised neither by his dishevelment of appearance nor by his erratic manner of behaving.

(A) neither by his dishevelment of appearance nor by his erratic manner of behaving
(B) neither by his dishevelment of appearance or by his erratic manner of behaving
(C) not by his dishevelment of appearance or erratic manner of behaving
(D) neither by his disheveled appearance nor by his erratic behavior
(E) nor by his disheveled appearance or erratic behaving

37. Married people tend to live longer than unmarried people; a recent study found that the death rate for divorced and widowed people in their 20's and 30's was up to ten times more than married people of the same age.

(A) up to ten times more than
(B) up to ten times higher than that for
(C) up more than ten times to that of
(D) up to ten times as high as
(E) increased up to ten times more than for

38. A recent report predicted dire consequences for the U.S. economy if engineering schools fail to attract the rising numbers of women and minorities joining the workforce.

(A) fail to attract the rising numbers
(B) fail in attracting the rising number
(C) should fail to attract the rising amount
(D) were failures in attracting the rising numbers
(E) were to fail to attract the the rising amount

39. The government admitted the presence of the troops, but claimed that they are serving solely as advisors.

(A) claimed that they are serving solely as
(B) claimed their service is solely to be
(C) claiming that they serve solely as
(D) claiming their service to be solely as
(E) was claiming that they serve solely for

40. When one applies for a loan, you may be required to supply a copy of your federal tax return.

(A) When one applies for a loan, you may be required to
(B) In applying for a loan, you may be required to
(C) When you apply for a loan, it may be required for you to
(D) In applying for a loan, you may be required that you
(E) When one applies for a loan, one may be required that you supply

41. I have no interest nor time to listen to their ceaseless complaints.

(A) no interest nor time
(B) no interest in listening to nor time
(C) no interest in nor time
(D) no interest or time
(E) no interest nor time either

42. As they drifted silently downstream, <u>the paddles were hardly used</u>.

    (A) the paddles were hardly used
    (B) the paddles were used hard
    (C) the paddles weren't hardly used
    (D) they used the paddles hardly at all
    (E) they hardly used the paddles

43. Yawning <u>with boredom and being exhausted</u>, she curled up in the back seat and fell asleep.

    (A) with boredom and being exhausted
    (B) with boring and being exhausted
    (C) with boredom and exhaust
    (D) with boredom and exhaustion
    (E) with being bored and being exhausted

44. By the time the call was made, the criminals <u>already escaped</u>.

    (A) already escaped

    (B) already were escaped
    (C) had already escaped
    (D) all ready escaped
    (E) escaped already

45. Findings from a recent study <u>suggest that there are several different kinds of memory, only one</u> of which worsens in old age.

    (A) suggest that there are several different kinds of memory, only one of which
    (B) suggest that there are several different kinds of memory, only one of them
    (C) suggests that there are several different kinds of memory, only one which
    (D) suggest that there are several different kinds of memory, one of which only
    (E) suggests that there are several different kinds of memory, of which one only

WRITING: SECTION 2

Essay

Time—30 Minutes

Directions: You will have thirty minutes to plan and write an essay on the topic given below. Read the topic carefully, and organize your ideas before you start writing. Remember to use specific examples and details where appropriate.

City life is criticized as being dangerous, expensive, and noisy, while suburban and country life is described by some as dull, culturally empty, and narrow. Explain some of the advantages and disadvantages of living where you do now. Be specific.

The space below is for any notes you may wish to make. Begin your essay on a separate sheet of paper.

ANSWER KEY FOR PRACTICE TEST 3

Reading		Mathematics		Writing	
1. E	21. E	1. A	21. E	1. E	24. D
2. C	22. D	2. B	22. B	2. D	25. A
3. A	23. B	3. A	23. A	3. A	26. C
4. B	24. D	4. D	24. D	4. D	27. A
5. C	25. C	5. C	25. D	5. B	28. E
6. D	26. B	6. E	26. D	6. A	29. E
7. A	27. D	7. B	27. E	7. C	30. D
8. D	28. A	8. D	28. C	8. E	31. B
9. B	29. D	9. B	29. C	9. B	32. A
10. E	30. B	10. A	30. B	10. C	33. C
11. D	31. D	11. C	31. A	11. D	34. D
12. C	32. C	12. B	32. C	12. A	35. E
13. C	33. C	13. B	33. D	13. E	36. D
14. A	34. B	14. E	34. E	14. A	37. B
15. C	35. A	15. D	35. B	15. B	38. A
16. D	36. C	16. A	36. E	16. C	39. A
17. B	37. A	17. C	37. A	17. E	40. B
18. C	38. B	18. C	38. C	18. D	41. C
19. E	39. B	19. B	39. C	19. A	42. E
20. A	40. D	20. C	40. E	20. A	43. D
				21. C	44. C
				22. B	45. A
				23. E	

EXPLANATORY ANSWERS FOR PRACTICE TEST 3

Reading

1. (E) The comparison of government's size to that of an octopus is based on the reach of each one. Octopuses have long tentacles that can reach into many places; likewise, the economic influence of government reaches everywhere. (B) and (C) are contrary to the passage. Whether or not the author believes (D) is not stated.

2. (C) Barring producers from the market clearly restrains competition, a situation Smith would not have favored. (A), (D), and (E) do not affect the free working of the marketplace. (B) conceivably limits competition, but presumably less than withdrawal of both the companies from the market would limit competition.

3. (A) Choice (A) restates the substance of the paragraph.

4. (B) The last sentence makes this clear. There are no predictions at all like (A) or (E). (D) does seem to be the trend, but suppose it was in eighth place, not mentioned for 1945? (C) is specifically contradicted by the last sentence: "except for accidents."

5. (C) Longevity is not mentioned at all until the 1945 list, so that we cannot infer any earlier breakdown such as (A) or (B). The last sentence proves (D) incorrect. Causes of death listed and causes of increased longevity are *not* discussed (E).

6. (D) In paragraph two, we learn that in 1945 cancer "had come up from eighth place," where it had been in 1910. Where it was in 1900 *may* have been known, which makes (E) incorrect, but it is not *mentioned* in the passage (D).

7. (A) This metaphor is evaluated positively by Jacobs and negatively by Morrison.

8. (D) Morrison says that it is a mistake to disregard biographical information.

9. (B) This is stated in Jacobs' argument.

10. (E) This is pointed out by Fran in the second paragraph.

11. (D) Joffrey maintains that people familiar with an art form are also familiar with the creators.

12. (C) The author points out a psychological example of unsupported inference; it would be inconsistent for him or her not to deplore such behavior in other branches of science. The other choices are unsupported by the passage.

13. (C) Note that the author does not explicitly disagree that we are running out of arable land or that solar energy is a good energy source, so that (A) and (D) are incorrect. Similarly, (B) is incorrect. (E) is not a good answer because the author is arguing against the "many" ecologists urging less growth. Since the author points out that the oceans have millions of years' worth of energy, he or she is virtually certain to agree that research on how to extract this energy is important. (C), therefore, is correct.

14. (A) The final sentence does not ask a real question. It begins, "When will someone tell me," when several of the things the author mentions can only have been told to him or her, so that the question is stamped as rhetorical. The sentence is quite consistent with the rest of the paragraph, for it expresses the author's own viewpoint on the subject of growth.

15. (C) In the second paragraph the author states that we have no confidence that the region will be free of earthquakes in the future.

16. (D) Based on the same line of reasoning in the preceding answer explanation, the past is not a definite predictor of the future.

17. (B) The second paragraph is totally concerned with earthquake activity in different parts of the world.

18. (C) At the end of the first paragraph, the author says that shocks could be produced "as large as magnitude 8.3 out of a possible 10.0."

19. (E) Proposition I is never mentioned.

20. (A) The only statement fully supported by the paragraph is that the current Supreme Court consists of nine justices. This number of justices was established in 1869, but the paragraph does not tell how many justices there were before that date. Choices (C) and (D) are in direct contradiction of the paragraph.

21. (E) A close examination of the passage indicates that the author uses all three to describe the vastness of space.

22. (D) As a kingdom contains many people, the author states that space must contain many heavens and many earths.

23. (B) The philosopher states that heaven and earth are large and small at the same time. It is reasonable to infer that he or she is referring to two different perspectives.

24. (D) The third sentence of the passage states that bad guys are aggressive and ambitious and implies that nice guys lack these qualities. The passage does not suggest that many people are neither good nor bad (A). No value judgment is offered about the goodness of being a bad guy (B). (C) is possibly true only in that sports success may correlate, in the author's view, with success in other aspects of life in the author's distinction between nice and bad guys. The author does not suggest that nice guys never marry (E).

25. (C) It is likely that if the human rights campaign winds up with a lot of sympathizers, as the passage states, that it is approved of by many people. (A) is probably correct only if it is further assumed that the speaker has the best interests of the U.S. at heart. (B) goes too far: the author may believe that some political leaders are now sympathetic to the human rights campaign, but never states that they will fall from power if their sympathy persists. (D) is wrong because it does not contain the proviso that the human rights campaign is continued, an essential part of the author's argument. (E) is farfetched.

26. (B) Statements (A) and (C) are much too general to be indicative of the article's purpose. Answer (D) is not correct because the dangers of neutrinos are not discussed. Answer (E), although mentioned, was not the purpose of the article. The selection as a whole describes the search for neutrinos, so choice (B) is the correct answer.

27. (D) The existence of neutrinos is based purely on theory. Neutrinos have not yet been found or observed. Paragraph two discusses this in detail. Answers (A), (B), (C), and (E) are all incorrect responses. The right answer is (D).

28. (A) The neutrino is described as a particle having a vanishingly small mass; because of this, it can be detected only inferentially. Answer (A) is the correct response. Since a neutrino has never been observed, a comparison in size to anything else would be inaccurate, making choices (B), (C), and (E) wrong. (D) is also wrong because neutrinos have not been observed.

29. (D) Answer (A) is an incorrect response, as there is no information in the passage to support this conclusion. (B) is wrong because scientists are still working to prove the existence of neutrinos. Choices (C) and (E) are also incorrect answers since there has been

no validated observation of the neutrino. The correct answer is choice (D), which is supported by the author's statement that the neutrino theory is an integral part of physics.

30. (B) The correct choice is (B). According to the final paragraph, "Certain quantities that physicists insist should be the same after an interaction as before . . . could only be conserved if another particle of zero charge and negligible mass were emitted." As the neutrino cannot be observed, choice (E) is incorrect, and no plausible mention of magnetism, inertia, or motion is made.

31. (D) Paragraph two clearly states that "Other plants besides mint were tested and were found to have the same effect on the atmosphere."

32. (C) Notice that Priestley held this *belief* and used it as the *basis* for an experiment. By definition, then, his belief was a "hypothesis," a supposition or guess that is subjected to scientific testing. It couldn't be a "conclusion" (B) because he had not at that point performed the test that would provide a conclusion. It couldn't be an "analysis" (D) because he had not yet subjected the guess to any analytic process. Choice (E), "hypothecation," is not as good an answer as (C). This roughly synonymous word: 1) is not used in scientific terminology for this kind of guess, 2) stresses the process rather than the result of making a hypothesis, and 3) has irrelevant legal meanings. Hence, *hypothesis* emerges as the term by which Priestley's belief can *best* be described.

33. (C) Of the five choices, the "wheat field" (C) would have many many more plants than either "desert land" (A), a "cave" (B), an "ice field" (D), or an "animal cage" (E), and hence would have the "greater concentration of oxygen."

34. (B) The fourth sentence of paragraph two states outright that "the formation of oxygen occurred only in . . . sunlight" (B). This rules out independence from sunlight (A) and "any time of day," since night is without sun (C). Since the passage definitely says "only the green parts" produced oxygen, (D) is impossible. With three of the five choices ruled out, (E) also becomes incorrect.

35. (A) The author says, in paragraph two, that "in the process of adding oxygen to the air, plants simultaneously extracted another gaseous material, a substance we now know as carbon dioxide." (B), (C), and (D) are not mentioned directly in this connection, and (E) is not even discussed in this passage.

36. (C) If civil disobedience is a violation of the law, it is illegal. The fact that the law that is being violated goes against human dignity provides a moral justification for violating that law but does not make violating it legally right. Answer (C) is the best response.

37. (A) The final paragraph of the selection supports choice (A) as the correct answer.

38. (B) The dissenter should, as paragraph three specifies, be prepared to submit to legal prosecution, accept his or her punishment, demand the law be enforced, and accept the judgment of the courts. The principle of tolerance must be accepted by the government and the individual. Answer choice (B) is the correct answer based on these facts. Responses (A), (C), (D), and (E) are all wrong because they do not illustrate the acceptance of the principle of tolerance by both parties.

39. (B) Paragraph three clearly points out the responsibilities of dissenters. One of these responsibilities is the acceptance of punishment as outlined in choice (B), which is the correct response.

40. (D) As the author states that the principle of tolerance must be accepted by both parties, his or her attitude toward civil disobedience is not one of hostility or contempt. Answers (C) and (E), then, are wrong. Choice (A) is also incorrect, as is choice (B), since the author does not totally admire civil disobedience. (D) is the best answer.

Mathematics

1. (A) 47% of 1000 are boys.

$$(.47)(1000) = 470 \text{ boys}$$

2. (B) To round 825.6347 to the nearest hundredth, consider 4, the digit in the thousandths place. Since it is less than 5, drop all digits to the right of the hundredths place.

$$825.6347 = 825.63 \text{ to the nearest hundredth}$$

3. (A)
$$820 + R + S - 610 = 342$$
$$R + S + 210 = 342$$
$$R + S = 132$$
If $R = 2S$, then $2S + S = 132$
$$3S = 132$$
$$S = 44$$

4. (D) 1 kilogram = 1000 grams
$$1000/.2 = 5000 \text{ pills}$$

5. (C) If the width is x, the length, which is twice as long, is $2x$. The perimeter is equal to the sum of the four sides: $2x + 2x + x + x = 6x$

6. (E) His rate is $\dfrac{1}{t}$ of the lawn per minute. Hence, in 15 minutes, he will do

$$15 \cdot \frac{1}{t} = \frac{15}{t} \text{ of the lawn}$$

7. (B) Point P has coordinates $x = -3$ and $y = 2$.

8. (D) $\frac{4}{5} = .8$

$$\frac{7}{9} = 9\overline{)7.00} \quad .78$$

$$\frac{5}{7} = 7\overline{)5.00} \quad .71$$

$$\frac{9}{11} = 11\overline{)9.00} \quad .82$$

Thus, $\frac{5}{7}$ is the smallest quantity.

9. (B) Let $x =$ amount of marked price. Then
$$\frac{1}{5}x = 15$$
$$x = 75$$
$$75 - x = \$60$$

10. (A) $r = 5x$
Divide both sides by 10

$$\frac{r}{10} = \frac{5}{10}x$$

$$\text{or } \frac{1}{10}r = \frac{1}{2}x$$

Hence, 1 is the solution.

11. (C) Angle $C = 40°$ (Congruent angles.)
Angle $BAC = 100°$ (Sum of the angles in a triangle is 180°.)
Angle $x = 100°$ (Vertical angles are congruent.)

12. (B) 3, 7, 12, 18, 25,
Differences are 4, 5, 6, 7, 8, ... etc.
Thus, series progresses as follows: 3, 7, 12, 18, 25, 33, 42, 52, 63

13. (B) The old dimensions and the new dimensions are in proportion. Let $w =$ new width.

$$\frac{\text{new width}}{\text{old width}} = \frac{\text{new length}}{\text{old length}}$$
$$\frac{w}{8} = \frac{25}{10}$$
$$10w = 200$$
$$w = 20$$

14. (E) Simply move the decimal point one place to the left and insert a zero in the newly created decimal place.

$$.10101 \div 10 = .010101$$

15. (D) There will be no waste if the lengths are multiples of $5\frac{1}{2}$ feet. This occurs between 6 and 24 only for 22 feet.

16. (A) $\dfrac{t}{1} = \dfrac{x}{60m}$

$x = 60\ mt$

17. (C)

January:	.4
February:	1.4
March:	2.2
Total:	4.0

18. (C)

April:	2.8
May:	2.4
June:	1.4
Total:	6.6
Average:	$6.6 \div 3 = 2.2$

19. (B) The rainfall in June was 1.4 inches, the same as the rainfall in February.

20. (C) In 3 hours, one ship went 60 miles, the other 45 miles. This is a 3-4-5 triangle as $45 = 3(15)$, $60 = 4(15)$. The hypotenuse will be $5(15)$, or 75.

21. (E) Memorial Park is a rectangle measuring 1200 feet by 100 feet. The area of a rectangle with the formula:

$A = L \times W$, or substituting,
$A = 1200 \times 100 = 120,000$

22. (B) The whole trip is six miles. The total time for the trip is 45 minutes, or $\frac{3}{4}$ of an hour. 6 divided by $\frac{3}{4}$ is equal to 8.

23. (A) 55% of her salary is spent. 45% is left. There is only one answer among the choices less than $\frac{1}{2}$ of her salary.

24. (D) $\frac{3P}{3Q}$ is obviously reducible to $\frac{P}{Q}$. The others cannot be reduced because we may not add or subtract the same numbers to numerator and denominator, or take the square roots of them.

25. (D) $a = b = \dfrac{1}{c}$

$a = \dfrac{1}{c}$

$ac = 1$

$c = \dfrac{1}{a}$

26. (D) Converting to decimals, $\frac{2}{3} = .666 \ldots$, $\frac{5}{7} = .7142 \ldots$, $\frac{8}{11} = .7272 \ldots$, and $\frac{9}{13} = .6923 \ldots$, so the order is $\frac{2}{3}, \frac{9}{13}, \frac{5}{7}, \frac{8}{11}$.

27. (E) Let $2x$, $3x$, and $4x$ represent the shares of the inheritance. The total estate was $22,500.

$2x + 3x + 4x = 22500$

$\dfrac{9x}{9} = \dfrac{22500}{9}$

$x = 2500$

$2x = 2 \cdot 2500 = 5000$
$3x = 3 \cdot 2500 = 7500$
$4x = 4 \cdot 2500 = 10,000$

The smallest inheritance was $2x$, or $5000.

28. (C) If each of the dimensions is doubled, the area of the new rectangle is four times the size of the original one. The increase is three times, or 300%.

29. (C) Eight sections, each $3'2''$ long, is equivalent to $8 \times 38'' = 304''$.

$304'' = 25\frac{1}{3}$ feet, therefore three ten-foot sections are needed.

30. (B) $1.86 \times 10^5 = 1.86 \times 100,000 = 186,000$.

31. (A) $-6 + -2 + 0 + 8 = 0$

32. (C) For both A and B, the greatest increase in the cumulative totals occurred from the end of Tuesday until the end of Wednesday. Therefore, the largest number of applications was filed on Wednesday. Notice that both A and B have filed zero applications (*the origin*) at the *beginning* of Monday.

33. (D) By the end of Tuesday, A had filed 100 applications and B had filed 150, for a total of 250. This left 750 of the original 1000 applications.

$$\dfrac{750}{1000} = .75 = 75\%$$

34. (E)

$$\begin{array}{rcl} 2x - 7 &=& 3 \\ +7 && +7 \\ \hline 2x &=& 10 \\ x &=& 5 \end{array}$$

If $x = 5$, $3x + 1 = 3 \cdot 5 + 1 = 16$

35. (B) Find the difference between each choice and 5:

5.000	5.005	5.01	5.1	5.105
-4.985	-5.000	-5.00	-5.0	-5.000
.015	.005	.01	.1	.105
		$= .010$	$= .100$	

The smallest difference is .005; therefore, 5.005 is closer than the other choices to 5.

36. (E) There are three pounds of peanuts.

$$\frac{3}{5} = .60 = 60\%$$

37. (A)
Area of each square = 9
Side of square = 3
Perimeter = 16 sides
$16(3) = 48$

38. (C) From 9:30 A.M. to 3 P.M. is $5\frac{1}{2}$ hours.

$$\$4 \cdot 5\frac{1}{2} = \$22$$

39. (C) 1.28 liters ÷ 4 = .32 liters

.32 liters = .32 ÷ .001 ml

= 320 ml

40. (E) $\frac{1}{4} = .25$

$\frac{1}{4}\% = .25\% = .0025$

Writing

1. (E) This sentence is correct.

2. (D) Parallel structure requires the form *locating*.

3. (A) The writer has confused *there*, an introductory expletive, with one of its homonyms, *they're*, the contraction for *they are*. Correct: "Although *there have been* scores. . . ."

4. (D) The complement of the infinitive *to be* should be in the objective case *(me)*.

5. (B) The subject is not *damages* but *possibility*, so the verb is not the plural *are* but the singular *is*.

6. (A) The phrase *and written* should simply be *written*.

7. (C) *Imaginary* means existing in the imagination. The right word here is *imaginative*, meaning creative or original.

8. (E) This sentence is correct.

9. (B) As a verb, *gazed* should be modified not by an adjective *(glum)* but by an adverb *(glumly)*.

10. (C) The phrase *as well as* is needed for a complete comparison: *its stars can dance as well as the best*.

11. (D) Idiomatic usage requires that *(un)able* be followed by *to:* unable *to pass* the course.

12. (A) As it is currently placed, the apostrophe in (A) indicates a plural possessive. But since the nonunderlined part of the sentence makes it clear that only a single author *(she)* is meant, the apostrophe should be moved before the *s (author's)* to indicate a singular possessive.

13. (E) The sentence is complicated but correct.

14. (B) If the removal occurred before the fire, and the fire *broke out* (in the past tense), then the chemicals *had been removed* (in the past perfect). The rule is: If two related events are described in the same sentence or passage, the one that occurred earlier must be put in the past perfect tense, the later one, in the past tense.

15. (B) *Either* is paired with *or, neither* with *nor:* "*Neither* Los Angeles *nor* Phoenix. . . ."

16. (C) The common idiom requires *differences in* or *among*.

17. (E) This sentence is correct as presented.

18. (D) Comparing only two accounts, the writer should describe one as the *more* informative. He or she should save the superlative form, *most*, for one of three or more accounts.

19. (A) As a proper noun, the first letter in "Arctic" should be capitalized.

20. (A) This sentence deals with a condition that is not a fact but a supposition, a possibility, an *IF*. In standard English, the *If* clause should be in the subjunctive mood, and the possible-result clause in the conditional mood, with modal auxiliary forms *(might, could, would)*. But the writer has cast both clauses in the conditional. You yourself would write, "If the strip mining operation *had been carried out*, toxic wastes *might have leached* into the water supply."

21. (C) The verb should be singular *(enables)* to agree with the singular subject *acquaintance*.

22. (B) The punctuation here should be a comma. Nonrestrictive clauses, such as the one modifying the noun *penicillin*, should be set off from the rest of the sentence by commas. A semicolon is used to separate independent clauses—that is, clauses that each contain at least a subject and a verb and can each stand alone as a separate sentence.

23. (E) This sentence is correct.

24. (D) In order to maintain the parallelism of this sentence, the verb form at (D) should be parallel in form to *by revising*. Therefore, (D) should be *by trying*.

25. (A) Use the personal pronoun *whom* to refer to people.

26. (C) *By means of using* is redundant. *Using* conveys the same idea more simply and effectively.

27. (A) The original sentence is correct as written. The other choices contain incorrect verb forms (B, D), incorrect verb tenses (C), and unnecessary pronouns (C, E).

28. (E) How is it that (E) says in ten words what (A) needs sixteen words to say? First, the opening phrase *For one to* is superfluous; the writer might as well start with *accepting*. Then, using *one* twice is unnecessary; if the writer is willing to use impersonal pronouns, he or she might as well be abstract. Thus, instead of *one to accept, one is mature*, we can use *accepting, maturity;* instead of *without getting resentful*, simply *without resentment*.

29. (E) Was *the crowd* really ascending into the wild blue yonder? If not, why are the words *the crowd* placed right after the introductory gerund *Rising slowly into the air* (A)? When a participial phrase opens a sentence, you expect that the very next word(s) will be 1) the very word(s) the gerund modifies and 2) the subject of the main verb. Only (E) meets these requirements. (B) still means that the crowd rose heavenward, this time with the implication that the crowd was *in* the balloon. (C) errs in using the transitive *raised* instead of the intransitive *rose*, and it avoids entirely the problem of properly relating the modifier and its subject. (D) creates a run-on sentence; to be correct it would have to have a period after *air* and a capital *A* in *as*.

30. (D) The constructions *the age of* and *years old* fulfill the same function, so the use of the two together in choices (A) and (C) is redundant. Choices (B), (C), and (E) are also unidiomatic. (D) is best.

31. (B) The writer knew enough about parallel structure to balance *not only* with *but also*. However, he or she didn't balance the terms they introduce. The first is an adjective: *knowledgeable*. The second is a noun phrase: *a congenial person*. The simplest correction is to make them both adjectives.

32. (A) The original sentence is correct.

33. (C) The use of *maybe* in the original is too colloquial, and the original illogically compares paint recipes to studios. Choices (B), (D), and (E) are unidiomatic, and (E) also illogically changes the tense of the clause describing the prehistoric artists to the present. (C) presents the correct tense and correctly compares having paint recipes in prehistoric times to having paint recipes in the Renaissance. In this structure, *did* substitutes for and carries the same sense as *had*.

34. (D) The original (A) means, literally, that Cheryl's mail neglected to inform the post office. An introductory participial phrase must be followed by the subject of the sentence, as in (D).

35. (E) Choice (E) is best. *One reason . . . is because* in (A) and (B) is redundant. The phrase *so*

large as to overcome is not idiomatic; *doses,* a plural noun, should be matched by *destroy,* the plural form of the verb.

36. (D) The original (A) is wrong on two counts. The phrases *dishevelment of appearance* and *erratic manner of behaving* are needlessly wordy. And they are not strictly parallel, one using a gerund (*behaving*) after *of,* the other, a regular noun (*appearance*) in that position. *Dishevelment of appearance* is easily reduced to *disheveled appearance,* and *erratic manner of* simply to *erratic,* since *behaving* already implies *manner.* The final touch is conversion of the gerund *behaving* to the regular noun *behavior* to correspond with *appearance.* (C) and (E) also loosen the parallelism by omitting the second *by his,* necessary in such an emphatic correlative expression. Also, (B), (C), and (E) use incorrect structures of negation; the correct expression is *neither . . . not.*

37. (B) Choices (A), (D), (E) illogically compare *death rate* to *married people*. The demonstrative pronoun *that* must be added as a noun equivalent to *death rate* in order to present a structure that logically compares the death rate of one group to the death rate of another group. The use of *more* in (A), (C), and (E) is a diction error; one rate may be *higher* than another, but not *more* than another. In addition, (C), (D), and (E) are unidiomatic in their expressions of the comparison.

38. (A) The original sentence is correct. When an "if" clause describes a condition that is likely or possible, as is the case here, the main verb of the clause appears in the indicative mood. The subjunctive mood is used only if the condition described is impossible or contrary to fact. Sentence (A) correctly uses the indicative and also uses *numbers* rather than *amount* to refer to women and minorities, who can be counted. Use *amount* when referring to *uncountable* things.

39. (A) The original sentence is best. In (C), (D), and (E), the participial form of the verb is incorrect. (B) is awkward and unidiomatic.

40. (B) (B) is consistent in its use of pronouns—it does not shift from *one* to *you* or vice versa and it correctly uses the infinitive form of the verb after *required.* A "that" clause after *required* is not appropriate for this structure and is unidiomatic.

41. (C) The idiom is *interest in.* The words *no interest* will not be connected to *their ceaseless complaints* if the preposition *in* is omitted. Only (C) meets this requirement. (D) is also incorrect on another count. The correlative pairs are *either . . . or, neither . . . nor, no . . . nor.*

42. (E) Unless the subject of the main clause can also serve as the subject of any introductory modifier, the modifier is considered "dangling." *The paddles* is the subject of (A)'s main clause, but it cannot relate properly to the modifier: Are the paddles what drifted downstream? So you must undangle this freak. Assuming that the *they* who *drifted . . . downstream* is the same *they* that *hardly used the paddles*, you have a choice of (D) or (E). But (D) is bloated, while (E) is lean and neat.

43. (D) Here again, you see the need to line up related ideas in similar grammatical structure. Since her *being exhausted* is also a cause of her *yawning,* it should be parallel with her *boredom,* as in (D).

44. (C) If two related past events occurred at different times, the later one is expressed in the past tense, the earlier one in the past perfect. You ascertain that *the call was made* is in the past and that the criminals' escape was made before the call. Therefore you describe the earlier action with: the criminals *had already escaped.*

45. (A) The original sentence is correct. Sentences (C), (D), and (E) all link a singular verb, *suggests,* to a plural noun, *findings.* The placement of *only* in (D) and (E) changes the intended meaning of the sentence. (B) also illustrates a comma splice.